OTHER LOSSES

Publisher's Note

We caution the reader not to be *so* lost in the politics of horrors as to equate the brutal revenge described in this book with the much greater evil of a state-instigated campaign of hatred and systematic murder that was the singular legacy of Nazi Germany. There are those who would cynically use this work to fan hatreds in their attempt to flatten the differences in atrocities by equating, and thus nullifying, them.

We have lived in the shadow of World War II for so long that we've grown accustomed to seeing only the inhumanity of the enemy. Thus, we were able to live with the comforting idea that because our cause was noble, our actions, too, were largely beyond reproach.

There is still no doubt in the mind of any but a tiny group of historical revisionists that the fight against Nazi Germany was, as Studs Terkel calls it, "the Good War." However, in this dark, brooding, and painstakingly well-researched book, you will discover that at the end of World War II, when Germany was conclusively defeated, a policy of hatred deliberately and indifferently caused the death by disease, exposure, and starvation of massive numbers of disarmed German soldiers and some civilians.

Certainly, few books in recent memory have instigated as much controversy among scholars and other interested readers. And yet, James Bacque keeps ferreting out more information that makes his arguments more convincing all the time. (This edition contains a new epilogue and a new appendix not previously published in the original Canadian edition of this book.) Furthermore, even Eisenhower apologists cannot deny the graphic descriptions of both American and German eyewitnesses, as well as the newly discovered document quoting Konrad Adenauer.

In a free society, the truth must be exposed, regardless of the consequences—*especially* if we don't like to hear it.

OTHER LOSSES

The Shocking Truth Behind the Mass Deaths of Disarmed German Soldiers and Civilians Under General Eisenhower's Command

JAMES BACQUE

Prima Publishing

First published in 1989 by Stoddart Publishing Co. Limited, Canada

Reprinted with permission from Macdonald & Co., England

Prima Publishing

Distributed to the trade by St. Martin's Press, 175 Fifth Avenue, New York, NY 10010; telephone (212) 674-5151.

Library of Congress Cataloging-in-Publication Data

Bacque, James, 1929-

Other losses : the shocking truth behind the mass deaths of disarmed German soldiers and civilians under General Eisenhower's command / by James Bacque.

p. cm.

Reprint. Originally published, Toronto, Canada : Stoddart, 1989.

Includes bibliographical references and index.

ISBN 1-55958-099-2

1. World War, 1939-1945—Prisoners and prisons, American. 2. World War, 1939-1945—Prisoners and prisons, French. 3. Prisoners of war—Germany—History—20th century. 4. Prisoners of war—France—History—20th century. 5. World War. 1939-1945—Atrocities. I. Title.

D805,G3B218 1991 91-2101

940.54 ' 7273—dc20 CIP

91 92 93 94 RRD 10 9 8 7 6 5 4 3 2 1

Printed in the United States of America

The worst sin
towards our fellow creatures
is not to hate them
but to be indifferent to them;
that's the essence of inhumanity.

George Bernard Shaw, *The Devil's Disciple*

To

L'Abbé Franz Stock
and
Victor Gollancz

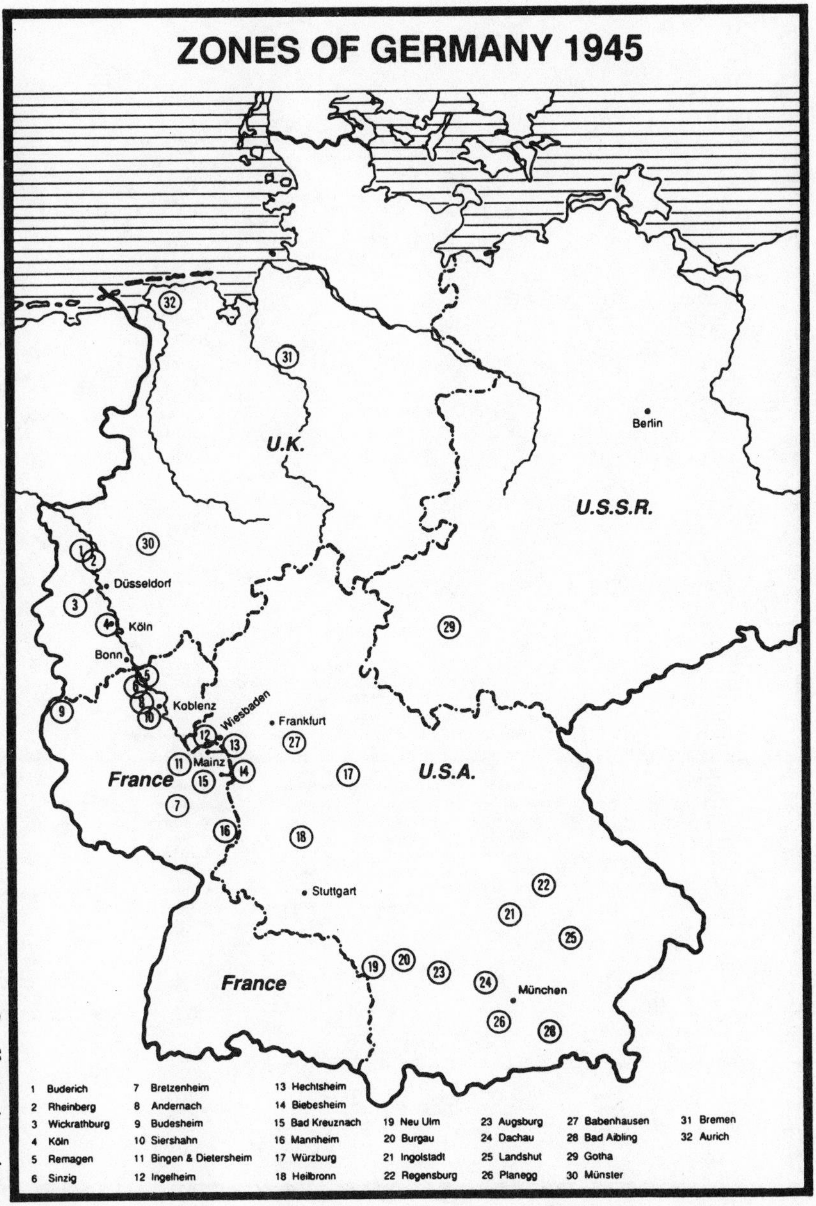

Ouellette Associates

The U.S. had about 200 camps in Germany. At least five were taken over by the French army when the French zone was set up in the summer of 1945.

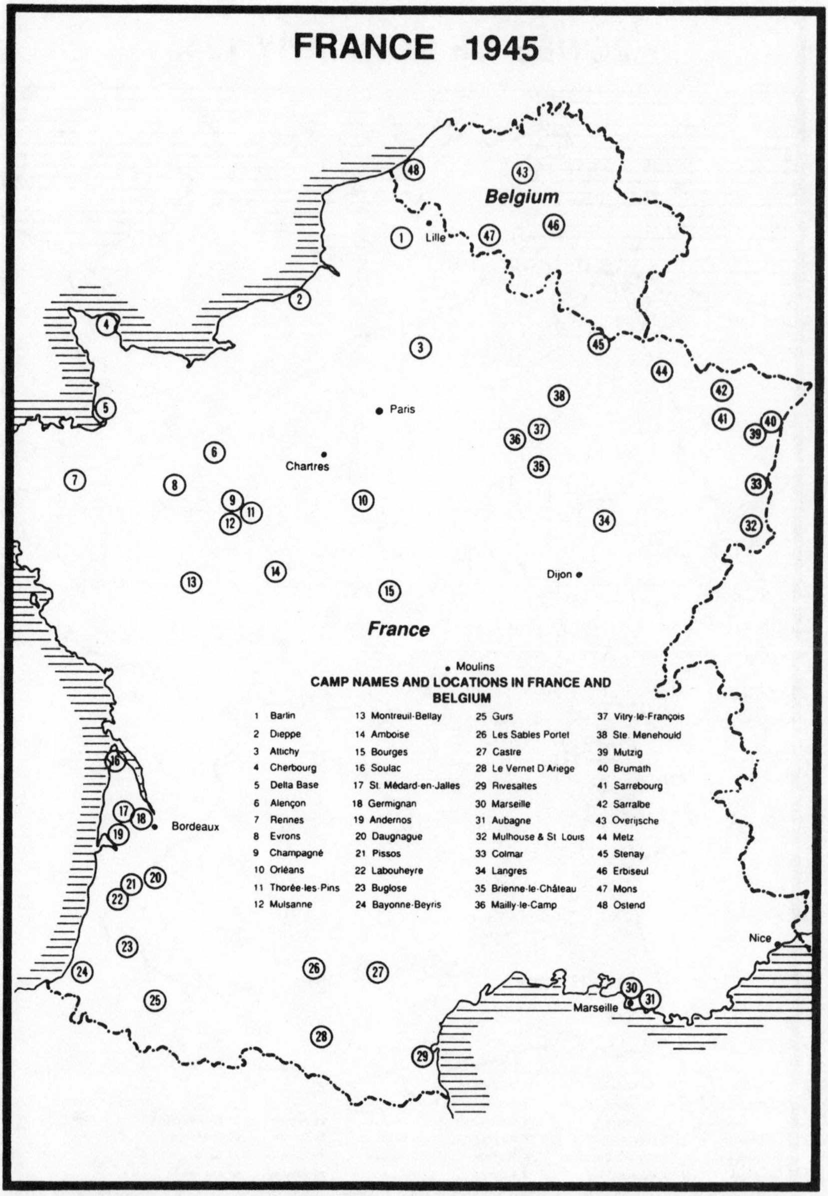

Ouellette Associates

The French had more than 1,600 camps scattered across France and their zone of Germany. Many had been taken over from the U.S. Army after the war.

Contents

* *Important:* New material for the U.S. edition—not previously published in the UK or Canada.

Principal Events Relating to This Book

1939

September 1: Germany attacks Poland.

September 3: Britain and France declare war on Germany

September 10: Canada declares war on Germany

September 17: Russia invades Poland

Winter 1939–1940

Massacre of Polish army officers by Russians at Katyn.

1940

June 21: Defeat, surrender and partition of France. About 1,500,000 French soldiers held as POWs in Germany.

1941

June: Germany attacks Russia.

December: Japan attacks USA. Hitler declares war on USA.

1942

August: Dieppe raid by Canadians. Canadians accuse Germans of chaining prisoners taken at Dieppe; Germans accuse Canadians of similar atrocity.

November: Allies land in North Africa.

1943

January: Churchill and Roosevelt meet at Casablanca and call for the unconditional surrender of Germany.

May: Axis forces surrender at Tunis. Biggest prisoner round-up of war to date. Eisenhower complains to Marshall, "It's a pity we could not have killed more."

November–December: Teheran Conference, Stalin and Roosevelt toast to the deaths of 50,000 German officers to be shot after the war; Elliott Roosevelt toasts to many more being shot, and says the U.S. Army will support this. Churchill storms out of the room.

1944

February: Eisenhower appoints General Everett S. Hughes as his special assistant.

June 6, D-Day: Americans, British and Canadians invade Normandy.

September: Quebec Conference; the Morgenthau Plan to destroy German industry is initialed by both Roosevelt and Churchill. The Allies reach the Rhineland. A newspaper furor breaks out over the Morgenthau Plan.

October: Stalin agrees to the Morgenthau Plan with Churchill in Moscow.

November 4: Hughes advises Eisenhower to keep secret all orders dealing with prisoner rations.

1945

February: Yalta Conference; Roosevelt, Churchill and Stalin discuss dismemberment of Germany and reparations.

March 10: Eisenhower initials and signs an order creating the lethal DEF status for prisoners, which breaks the Geneva Convention. He gives a speech in Paris saying that the U.S. obeys the Geneva Convention.

April: The CCS approve the DEF status for some prisoners in U.S. hands, but the British refuse to go along. Littlejohn reduces prisoner rations.

May 8: Germany surrenders. The U.S. removes Switzerland as the Protecting Power for German prisoners, contravening the Geneva Convention. Eisenhower tells Churchill he has reduced prisoner rations and may reduce them further. Patton releases captives rapidly. Eisenhower orders his generals to stop releasing prisoners. POW rations are reduced again.

June: General Lee strongly disputes incorrect prisoner totals being given out by Eisenhower's HQ (June 2). Littlejohn complains that he cannot feed the prisoners, now about 4,000,000. Many prisoners are secretly transferred to the lethal DEF status without food or shelter. German civilians are prevented from feeding prisoners. Civilians themselves begin to starve. The ICRC attempts to send food into Germany, but the trains are sent back by the U.S. Army. Prime Minister King of Canada complains about the removal of Geneva Convention protection from German prisoners. The British Foreign Office silences him.

July: Many U.S. prisoners are transferred to the French army in dying condition. Captain Julien says one American camp looks like Buchenwald.

August: An order signed by Eisenhower consigns all remaining POWs to lethal DEF status. The death rate immediately shoots up. General Littlejohn complains in writing to Eisenhower that 1,550,000 people supposed to be getting U.S. Army rations are receiving nothing. The ICRC is forced to return food to donors because it is not allowed to send it to Germany.

September: Jean-Pierre Pradervand of the ICRC tells de Gaulle that one-third of prisoners in French hands recently received from the U.S. Army will soon die unless help quickly arrives. French papers break the Pradervand story. Eisenhower and Gen. Smith deny U.S. guilt. The *New York Times* reports bad conditions in French camps, nothing about U.S. camps recently visited by star reporter Drew Middleton.

October 10: Littlejohn writes a report to Eisenhower pointing out food surplus in U.S. Army and suggests sending food to U.S.

1945–6 The U.S. winds down prisoner holdings to almost zero by the end of 1946. The French continue holding hundreds of thousands through 1946, gradually reducing their holdings to nothing by about 1949.

1947–1950s Most records of U.S. prison camps are destroyed. Germans determine that over 1,700,000 soldiers, alive at war's end, have never returned home. All Allies deny responsibility; the U.S., Britain and France accuse Russia of atrocities in camps.

1960s–1972 The West German Foreign Office under Willy Brandt subsidizes books which deny atrocities in U.S. camps. U.S. senators accuse Russians of atrocities, but say nothing of U.S. camps.

1980s The ICRC refuses to release essential documents to researchers working on U.S. and French camps, and claims no knowledge of Pradervand, who was their chief delegate in France. The ICRC admits two other researchers into the archives to look for material on Nazi death camps. The Ministry of Defence in the UK refuses to release the important Phillimore report to author, although requested to do so by a British cabinet officer. Willy Brandt refuses to discuss his role in censoring and subsidizing books that hide U.S. atrocities.

Acronyms and Short Forms

Ad Sec Advance Section (of the U.S. Army) nearest the battlefront.

Belsen (Bergen-Belsen) Nazi concentration camp uncovered by the British.

Boche Slang term for Germans.

Buchenwald Nazi concentration camp uncovered by Americans.

CCS Combined Chiefs of Staff of Britain and the USA. Canada was represented by the British.

CIGS Chief of the Imperial General Staff, UK.

Com. Z. Communications Zone, U.S. Army, rear area.

CRALOG Acronym for Council of Relief Agencies Licensed to Operate in Germany (U.S.).

Dachau Nazi concentration camp.

D-Day Day of the landing of Allies in Normandy, June 6, 1944.

DEF Disarmed Enemy Forces. Certain German prisoners in the hands of the U.S. Army in northwest Europe. They were not treated according to the Geneva Convention.

DP Displaced Person.

ETO European Theater of Operations, U.S. Army.

ETOUSA European Theater of Operations, U.S. Army.

Holding Power The power detaining prisoners of war.

ICRC International Committee of the Red Cross, based in Switzerland which represented Red Cross ideals and carried out the Red Cross mandate under the Geneva Convention.

JCS Joint Chiefs of Staff of the United States.

JCS 1067 and 1067/6 Directives issued to Eisenhower regarding the conduct of the army towards Germans after conquest.

Länder States or provinces in Germany.

Midnight Shift Author's term for means by which POW statistics were secretly changed to hide transfer to worse conditions.

Military Governor (also OMGUS, Office of Military Governor, United States) Government of Germany run by the U.S. in its zone after surrender. Eisenhower held this post until mid-November 1945, when he was succeeded by General Clay.

Missing Million Prisoners eliminated from the rolls of the U.S. Army in June 1945.

MP Military police (U.S.).

MTOUSA Mediterranean Theater of Operations, U.S. Army.

OKW Oberkommando Wehrmacht. German Army headquarters.

POW Prisoners of war, supposed to be protected by Geneva Convention. Some documents use the abbreviation PW.

Protecting Power Under the Geneva Convention, the power (state) of which prisoners of war were citizens.

PWE (U.S.) Prisoner of war enclosure.

PWTE (U.S.) Prisoner of war temporary enclosure.

SCOFOR Allied force stationed near Bremen.

SEP Surrendered enemy personnel. Term used by British and Canadians for those German prisoners whom they did not intend to treat strictly according to Geneva Convention.

SHAEF Supreme Headquarters, Allied Expeditionary Force. Command organization of all Allied armies in northwest Europe (excluding Italy) to July 14, 1945. After that, the U.S. Army was organized only as USFET, British as 21st Army Group (later British Army of the Rhine, or BAOR).

S.S. (Schutzstaffel) Protective staff, or elite guard units of Nazi Party.

Tommies Slang term for British soldiers.

TPM and PM Theater provost marshal. Division of army in charge of legal aspects of personnel, prisoners, etc.

TSFET Theater Service Forces, European Theater (U.S. Army, Europe).

21st Army Group (later British Army of the Rhine) Under Montgomery, chiefly British and Canadian.

UNRRA United Nations Relief and Rehabilitation Administration.

U.S. Army Rations A rations were normal garrison rations; *B* were a limited type of *A* for use in transit; *C* and *K* were field ration versions of *A* that required no cooking, and *10 in 1* were like *C*, but packaged for a squad of 10 men for one day.

USFET United States Forces, European Theater.

VE Day Victory in Europe Day, May 8, 1945.

WASt Acronym for official German tracing agency, Berlin.

Zone (of the) Interior U.S. Army argot for United States.

Chief Characters

Barnes, Lt. Colonel Valentine: deputy provost marshal, Ad Sec Com Z.

Beasley, Colonel Charles H.: U.S. Medical Corps, ETO.

Buisson, General: head of the French Army Prisoner of War Service.

Churchill, Winston S.: prime minister of Great Britain during World War II.

Clay, General Lucius: successor to Eisenhower as military governor of Germany in November 1945.

Devers, General Jacob L.: commander, U.S. 6th Army Group, 1945.

Doenitz, Karl: grand admiral, commander of German navy, Führer of Germany after Hitler's death.

Eden, Anthony: foreign secretary, Great Britain.

Eisenhower, Dwight D.: commanding general of SHAEF. He reported to General George C. Marshall of the (U.S.) Joint Chiefs of Staff in Washington.

Fisher, Colonel Ernest F.: lieutenant with U.S. 101st Airborne in 1945, later a senior historian with U.S. Army.

de Gaulle, Charles: leader of the Free French, later president of France.

Hitler, Adolf: Führer (leader) of Germany during World War II.

Huber, Max: president of ICRC, Geneva.

Hughes, General Everett S.: U.S. Army. Friend of Eisenhower.

Hull, Cordell: secretary of state under Roosevelt.

Juin, Alphonse: general of the French army.

King, William Lyon Mackenzie: prime minister of Canada.

Lee, Lt. General J. C. H.: commander, Com Z, Europe.

Littlejohn, General Robert: Eisenhower's quartermaster general at SHAEF.

Luttichau, Charles von: Former member of German armed forces who after the war became a U.S. citizen and wrote history for the U.S. Army.

Marshall, General George C.: army chief of staff during World War II. Commander of Eisenhower.

Montgomery, Field Marshal Bernard Law: commander of the British and Canadian armies in 21st Army Group under SHAEF.

Morgenthau, Henry C.: secretary of the U.S. Treasury during World War II.

Patton, General George C.: commander of U.S. 3rd Army.

Pradervand, Jean-Pierre: head of the ICRC delegation in France, 1945–6.

Reckord, Major General Milton A.: theater provost marshal, ETO.

Roosevelt, Franklin D.: president of the United States during World War II.

Smith, General Walter Bedell: Eisenhower's chief of staff at SHAEF and, after July 1945, USFET.

Stalin, Josef: premier of the Soviet Union during World War II.

Stimson, Henry L.: secretary of war under Roosevelt.

Tedder, Air Marshal Arthur W.: Eisenhower's deputy supreme commander in SHAEF.

Truman, Harry: president of the United States following Roosevelt.

White, Harry Dexter: assistant to Morgenthau in the U.S. Treasury Department.

Foreword

OVER MOST OF THE WESTERN FRONT in late April 1945, the thunder of artillery had been replaced by the shuffling of millions of pairs of boots as columns of disarmed German soldiers marched wearily towards Allied barbed wire enclosures. Scattered enemy detachments fired a few volleys before fading into the countryside and eventual capture by Allied soldiers.

The mass surrenders in the west contrasted markedly with the final weeks on the eastern front where surviving Wehrmacht units still fought the advancing Red Army to enable as many of their comrades as possible to evade capture by the Russians.

This was the final strategy of the German High Command then under Grand Admiral Doenitz who had been designated Commander-in-Chief by Adolf Hitler following Reich Marshal Goering's surrender to the west.

From the German point of view this strategy delivered millions of German soldiers to what they believed would be the more merciful hands of the Western Allies under supreme military commander General Dwight Eisenhower. However, given General Eisenhower's fierce and obsessive hatred not only of the Nazi regime, but indeed of all things German, this belief was at best a desperate gamble. More than five million German soldiers in the American and French zones were crowded into barbed wire cages, many of them literally shoulder to shoulder. The ground beneath them soon became a quagmire of filth and disease. Open to the weather, lacking even primitive sanitary facilities, underfed, the prisoners soon began dying of starvation and disease. Starting in April 1945, the United States Army and the French army casually annihilated about one million men, most of them in American camps. Not since the horrors of the Confederate-administered prison at Andersonville during the American Civil War had such cruelties taken place under American military control. For more than four decades this unprecedented tragedy lay hidden in Allied archives.

How at last did this enormous war crime come to light? The

first clues were uncovered in 1986 by the author James Bacque and his assistant. Researching a book about Raoul Laporterie, a French Resistance hero who had saved about 1,600 refugees from the Nazis, they interviewed a former German soldier who had become a friend of Laporterie in 1946. Laporterie had taken this man, Hans Goertz, and one other, out of a French prison camp in 1946 to give them work as tailors in his chain of stores. Goertz declared that "Laporterie saved my life, because 25 percent of the men in that camp died in one month." What had they died of? "Starvation, dysentery, disease."

Checking as far as possible the records of the camps where Goertz had been confined, Bacque found that it had been one of a group of three in a system of 1,600, all equally bad, according to ICRC reports in the French army archives at Vincennes, Paris. Soon they came upon the first hard evidence of mass deaths in U.S.-controlled camps. This evidence was found in army reports under the bland heading "Other Losses." The terrible significance of this term was soon explained to Bacque by Colonel Philip S. Lauben, a former chief of the German Affairs Branch of SHAEF.

In the spring of 1987, Mr Bacque and I met in Washington. Over the following months we worked together in the National Archives and in the George C. Marshall Foundation in Lexington, Virginia, piecing together the evidence we uncovered. The plans made at the highest levels of the U.S. and British governments in 1944 expressed a determination to destroy Germany as a world power once and for all by reducing her to a peasant economy, although this would mean the starvation of millions of civilians. Up until now, historians have agreed that the Allied leaders soon canceled their destructive plans because of public resistance.

Eisenhower's hatred, passed through the lens of a compliant military bureaucracy, produced the horror of death camps unequaled by anything in American military history. In the face of the catastrophic consequences of this hatred, the casual indifference expressed by the SHAEF officers is the most painful aspect of the U.S. Army's involvement.

Nothing was further from the intent of the great majority of

Americans in 1945 than to kill off so many unarmed Germans after the war. Some idea of the magnitude of this horror can be gained when it is realized that these deaths exceed by far all those incurred by the German army in the west between June 1941 and April 1945. In the narrative that follows, the veil is drawn from this tragedy.

DR. ERNEST F. FISHER JR., COLONEL
ARMY OF THE UNITED STATES (RETIRED)
ARLINGTON, VIRGINIA, 1988

Introduction

For a long time my assistant* and I could scarcely believe what we were finding. We stood on chairs in the attic of a French *mairie* (town hall) tugging down dusty file-boxes that ought to have contained death lists from the camps where German prisoners of war were held, but did not. That they were empty might prove only a postwar labor shortage in one commune, we thought. The uneasy eyes of a French priest who contradicted himself twice about the number of German prisoners he had buried in his camp might have been caused by the distressing subject of the French camps, not by guilt, we supposed. The complaint in a letter by a Red Cross official in 1945 that the army wouldn't give him gasoline to deliver food to starving prisoners seemed to be important news, but scrawled beside it was "*C'est fait,*" meaning he did get the gas, we imagined. Then we found a later letter from the stranded Red Cross official complaining that despite promises he still could not get the gas. French guards who had been in the same camp as the priest said the deaths were even greater than the priest had admitted. More and more pieces emerged until we were in a strange state — convinced by great evidence that leaders of our society had committed an appalling crime against humanity which we did not want to believe. Every day, we had to choose between the horrible truth and the pretty myths we had been taught about our history.

By the time we had finished the first stage of the French research, which proved beyond doubt a catastrophe in those camps, we had found many small proofs of the American tragedy. We decided we had to look in Washington, though it seemed futile to expect the United States Army to have stored evidence of its own atrocities. In the United States National archives on Pennsylvania Avenue, we found the documents with the heading "Weekly Prisoner of War and Disarmed Enemy Forces Report." In each report was the heading "Other Losses" giving statistics that paralleled the French statistics.

This was convincing, but only to us. Other Losses could only

* She has asked to remain anonymous

mean, but did not say, deaths. Below it, the numbers fitted everything else we knew. Here was the proof, in a code. But who could decode it?

Searching, I came to the door of Colonel Philip S. Lauben, whose name appeared on the SHAEF (Supreme Headquarters, Allied Expeditionary Force) circulation list of the secret documents. He had been chief of the German Affairs Branch of SHAEF in charge of prisoner transfers and repatriation for many critical months, so I knew he would know.

In his living room, I unrolled the xeroxes of the documents, trying to keep calm. What he would say in the next few minutes would nullify all the work we had done for over a year, or prove that we had made a major historical discovery. Lauben and I went over the headings one by one till we got to Other Losses. Lauben said, "It means deaths and escapes."

"How many escapes?" I asked.

"Very, very minor," he said. As I found later, the escapes were less than one-tenth of one percent.

With this unassailable evidence secure, it was gradually possible to assemble the other information around it in the coherent form of this book.

Because of the widespread cover-up, and because some prisoner documents were deceptive when made, the number of dead will probably always be in dispute. Many records were destroyed in the 1950s or hidden in euphemisms. Many lies have been layered deep over the truth.

It is beyond doubt that enormous numbers of men of all ages, plus some women and children, died of exposure, unsanitary conditions, disease and starvation in the American and French camps in Germany and France starting in April 1945, just before the end of the war in Europe. The victims undoubtedly number over 800,000, almost certainly over 900,000 and quite likely over a million. Their deaths were knowingly caused by army officers who had sufficient resources to keep the prisoners alive. Relief organizations that attempted to help the prisoners in the American camps were refused permission by the army. All of this was hidden at the time, then lied about when the Red Cross, *Le Monde* and *Le Figaro* attempted to tell the truth publicly. Records have been destroyed, altered or kept secret. This is still going on.

Canada and the United Kingdom, who were the allies of France and the USA, also took in millions of prisoners under the same command, SHAEF, so we looked for evidence of events in their camps. The fate of the Germans in the British and Canadian camps is not so clear, but there is no sign of a similar atrocity. Some skimpy evidence from the armies themselves, from the International Committee of the Red Cross (ICRC) and from the prisoners, indicates that almost all of them continued in fair health, except for about 400,000 transferred to the British by the U.S. in 1945. Many of these people were dying when transferred. The British government, when asked in 1988 by the Canadian army for the important Phillimore monograph on German prisoners in British hands, refused to release it, on the ground that it was "still in use." Virtually nothing about the treatment of millions of German prisoners in Canadian and British hands in Europe survives in the archives in Ottawa or London. The International Committee of the Red Cross in Geneva, which recently opened its archives to two writers seeking material on Nazi prison camps, refused to allow me to search in the same archives for reports on British and Canadian prisoner of war camps. The ICRC also repeatedly refused me permission to see letters on the subject, although my requests were transmitted to them by the Canadian Army and by the Canadian Red Cross.

Both the British and the Canadians were aware of what was being prepared in the American camps. The British witnessed the atrocities in at least one camp. Only the Canadian government protested, once.

The value of a humane, free press, and legislature, is one of the motifs of the book.

To three people above all, I owe especial thanks. To Colonel Ernest F. Fisher, this book owes a great deal more than an eloquent preface. A former lieutenant in the 101st Airborne, later a colonel in the Army, Ernest Fisher is also a distinguished army historian, author of the study *Cassino to the Alps,* written while he was a senior historian with the United States Army Center For Military History. Ernest Fisher had the knowledge to guide me, which he generously did. Together he and his wife Elsa spent many hours surveying documents in the U.S. National Archives. He was the one who found the crucial document entitled "Medical History of the ETO." We sat together studying that and many other documents in Washington, Suitland, Maryland, and Lexington, Virginia. A brave, wise, modest man, Ernest Fisher is an adornment to his country, a meticulous scholar, and faithful friend.

For Elisabeth, who has never limited me and always supported me: Here be dragons, but joy is to come.

Doubtless many scholars will find faults in this book, which are only mine. I welcome their criticism and their further research, which may help to restore to us the truth after a long night of lies.

JAMES BACQUE
TORONTO, 1989

1

DECIDING GERMANY'S FATE

MARSHAL JOSEF STALIN SAID AT THE dinner table that he wanted to round up fifty thousand German officers after the war and shoot them. Winston Churchill was violently angry. "I would rather be taken out in the garden here and now to be shot myself than sully my own and my country's honor by such infamy," he said vehemently. Franklin Roosevelt, seeing the animosity rise between these two former enemies, fatuously suggested a compromise of 49,000 prisoners to be shot. Stalin, the host for this critical meeting with his two powerful allies, diplomatically took a poll of the nine men at the table. The president's son, Elliott Roosevelt, a brigadier-general in the United States Army, responded with a toast to the deaths of "not only those fifty thousand . . . but many hundreds of thousands more Nazis as well." Churchill, astounded, heard him add, "and I am sure the United States Army will support it." Delighted, Stalin embraced young Roosevelt, proposing that they drink to the deaths of the Germans.

Churchill got up. "Do you know what you're saying?" he

hurled at Elliott Roosevelt. "How dare you say such a thing."

He stormed out of the banquet hall into a dark empty room adjoining. The house, which in 1943 held the Russian Embassy in Teheran, was strange to him, he was far from his own troops, he had just turned his back in fury on the best American friend the British ever had, but he had no regret for what he had done. After a moment, he felt an arm round his shoulder. Stalin was standing there with Molotov. The dictator was charming. It was all a joke, he explained. We weren't serious. Come back.

Churchill went back into the room. But he did not believe then or later that "there was no serious intent lurking behind" their words.[1]

There was no room for doubt in the mind of either Roosevelt or Churchill that Stalin meant what he said, because Churchill had already informed Roosevelt of the conclusion of an international tribunal at Katyn in Poland that in 1940 the Russians had massacred many thousands of Polish army officers after they had surrendered.*

Until this conference at Teheran in late 1943, almost no attention had been given to what the British and Americans hoped to achieve by their immense struggles. Some platitudes had been announced as a result of earlier meetings between Churchill and Roosevelt, but they amounted to no more than restatements of the good intentions of western democracies. The only clear aim of the Allies was to win the war. Then suddenly Roosevelt had announced at his meeting with Churchill at Casablanca in January 1943, after almost no consultation, that the terms to be offered to Germany and Japan were simply "unconditional surrender." The disaster in the camps lay coiled under this term like a snake, because unconditional surrender meant the abolition of the German government and that meant the loss of treaty rights including the protection of prisoners under the Geneva Convention. Stalin disliked the term, so the foreign ministers, meeting in Moscow in November 1943, set up the European Advisory Commission to study the problem of the postwar treatment of Germany including the idea of

* Russia attacked Poland in alliance with Hitler in 1939.

dismembering the country.*[2] In 1943 this still seemed far from urgent, for the Germans occupied Europe from the north end of Norway to the middle of the Mediterranean, from the Spanish border deep into Russia.

The dilemma faced by the planners had been part of European history for almost a century. Germany was so aggressive that all the other powers lived in fear of their lives. How could they protect themselves against the Germans? Even the prospect of a beaten Germany scared the Allied planners, because they could foresee Germany rising from the ashes for the second time in the century to begin a Third World War. How could this be prevented? Churchill and the British thought of weakening Germany just enough to make her a useful satellite against Russia.[3] The Americans were divided, some for a mild peace, some vengeful. Roosevelt at various times was both.

The first American cabinet official to take seriously the work of the commission was the secretary of the Treasury, Henry C. Morgenthau. On a trip to Europe in the summer of 1944, Morgenthau discovered that the Allies under Supreme Commander Dwight Eisenhower had some first-rate plans for getting into Germany, but no idea of what to do once they got there. Foreign Secretary Anthony Eden read to him from the minutes of the Teheran Conference the discussion of the proposed dismemberment of Germany, but no one there had figured out how to carry this out. Morgenthau could not understand the lackadaisical British. He knew that Eden understood what had been decided, because he had been there, but still his man Sir William Strang, who represented England on the European Advisory Commission, was not following his instructions.[4] Morgenthau was satisfied only with the Supreme Commander of the Allied Expeditionary Force, General Dwight Eisenhower, who, Morgenthau said, wanted to "treat them rough," when he got to Germany.[5]

But the European Advisory Commission was making no plans for this, Morgenthau reported to Roosevelt in the White House. "No-one is studying how to treat Germany roughly

* This was the origin of the division of Germany into four Allied zones, Russian, British, American and French.

along the lines you wanted," he told the president. "Give me thirty minutes with Churchill and I can correct this," Roosevelt replied. "We have got to be tough with Germany and I mean the German people, not just the Nazis. We either have to castrate the German people, or you have got to treat them in such a manner that they can't just go on reproducing people who want to continue the way they have in the past."[6]

Henry Morgenthau, who was "Franklin's conscience," according to the president's wife, Eleanor Roosevelt, set to work quickly to produce plans for treating Germany roughly. A few days later, Roosevelt invited Morgenthau to Quebec City to tell Churchill about his plan.

Morgenthau was in a peculiar situation when he got off the train in the rain at Quebec on September 13, 1944, to join the great men in their deliberations. He was there to help plan policy for Germany, which was properly the business of the State Department. But the secretary of state, Cordell Hull, was not present at Quebec. Hull had also missed the conference at Teheran. Not even the minutes of the Teheran Conference had been shown him, although he had asked to see them.[7] Some of this was nominally because Roosevelt liked to handle foreign affairs himself — yet he had asked Henry Morgenthau to come with his plan. Morgenthau suspected that this was because Roosevelt had failed to convince Churchill to treat Germany roughly. Roosevelt, confused about what he wanted to do with Germany after the war, turned to his "conscience" — Morgenthau — for a decision.

Time was growing short. The city of Aachen in the west of Germany was just ahead of General Eisenhower's lead tanks. The Canadian and British armies were roaring northeast through the Low Countries when Morgenthau and Lord Cherwell, Churchill's senior advisor, met to discuss what the Allies ought to do once they were across the German border.

The definite idea in Morgenthau's briefcase was that Germany would be "pastoralized," through the destruction of her industry and mining. The most advanced of the industrialized nations of the world would be turned into a huge farm. German industry had grown up partly in order to pay for imports of food for a population that did not have enough land to feed itself. Hitler had proposed to remedy this by taking over lands in the east for "the German plow." The area of Germany would now be shrunk because of Russian and Polish acquisitions while the German population in the west of the country would rise with the influx of German refugees from these lands. There would be massive starvation if the industrial base were destroyed. According to Cordell Hull, "the Morgenthau Plan would wipe out everything in Germany except land, and the Germans would have to live on the land. This meant that only 60 percent of the German population could support themselves on German land, and the other 40 percent would die." Hull is speaking here of the deaths of about 20 million German civilians.[8]

Morgenthau and his brilliant assistant, Harry Dexter White, had little time to prepare their case before Churchill pounced on it. At dinner that same evening in the Citadel at Quebec City, Churchill wanted to discuss Germany right away. Roosevelt turned to Morgenthau asking him to explain the plan. Churchill immediately saw what Hull had seen. According to White, Churchill said the plan was "unnatural, unchristian and unnecessary."[9] Testily, he asked if he had been brought all this way to discuss a scheme that would "mean England's being chained to a dead body." Admiral Land of the United States Navy was all for it. He thumped the conference table with his fist, vigorously supporting Morgenthau. The discussion was abandoned for the evening.

Walking that night in the invigorating air of Quebec, Morgenthau and Churchill's advisor Lord Cherwell figured out a plan to get around Churchill's resistance. At the next meeting, which included Cherwell, Morgenthau, Roosevelt, Churchill, British foreign secretary Anthony Eden and his assistant Cadogan, when the question of Germany arose again, Churchill asked for the minutes of the previous discussion. Cherwell and Morgenthau, who had agreed to pretend that the minutes were not ready, asked Churchill to summarize. Proud of his extempore speaking and his memory for detail, Churchill improvised the minutes, in the process taking a much harsher line against

Germany than before. This was what Cherwell had anticipated. Morgenthau pointed out eagerly that if German industry were destroyed, new markets for British manufactures would open up. Competition for resources would be reduced. All of this would be true for the Americans and the French as well.

Morgenthau disputed that the Germans would starve. Later, in his book *Germany Is Our Problem*, published in 1945 with Roosevelt's approval, Morgenthau wrote that prewar Germany produced 98.2 percent of its own breadstuffs, all of its potatoes and sugar, 92.3 percent of its vegetables, 96.7 percent of its meat and poultry, and all of its milk. Only about 14 percent of this on average would be lost under the proposed re-arrangement of Germany's borders.[10]

The economic argument convinced Churchill, who now swung over to Morgenthau and Cherwell. Anthony Eden was shocked. "You can't do this," he exclaimed. "After all, you and I have publicly said quite the opposite."

After a long argument, Churchill silenced Eden: "Now I hope Anthony you are not going to do anything about this with the War Cabinet if you see a chance to present it . . . After all, the future of my people is at stake, and when I have to choose between my people and the German people, I am going to choose my people."[11]

Morgenthau was "terrifically happy" about the conference because "we got just what we started out to get." That was the initials WSC and FDR on the bottom of a secret memo[12] that reads:

> At a conference between the President and the Prime Minister upon the best measures to prevent renewed rearmament by Germany, it was felt that an essential feature was the future disposition of the Ruhr and the Saar.
>
> The ease with which the metallurgical, chemical and electric industries in Germany can be converted from peace to war has already been impressed upon us by bitter experience. It must also be remembered that the Germans have devastated a large portion of the industries of Russia and of other neighboring Allies, and it is only in accor-

dance with justice that these injured countries should be entitled to remove the machinery to repair the losses they have suffered. The industries referred to in the Ruhr and in the Saar would therefore be necessarily put out of action and closed down. It was felt that the two districts should be put under some body under the world organization which would supervise the dismantling of these industries and make sure that they were not started up again by some subterfuge.

This programme for eliminating the war-making industries in the Ruhr and in the Saar is looking forward to converting Germany into a country primarily agricultural and pastoral in character.

The Prime Minister and the President were in agreement upon this programme.
OK
FDR
WSC
September 16, 1944.

Soon after it was initialed, this memo was bitterly debated by the United States cabinet. Cordell Hull said: "This whole development at Quebec I believe angered me as much as anything that had happened during my career as Secretary of State. If the Morgenthau Plan leaked out, as it inevitably would, it might well mean a bitter-end German resistance that would cause the loss of thousands of American lives."[13]

The power of the press and public opinion were immediately apparent as the leaks began. Enemies of the plan knew they had a good chance to defeat it simply by appealing through the press over the heads of Morgenthau and Roosevelt straight to the electorate. The public reaction was almost entirely against vengeance, as Hull had thought.[14] Drew Pearson in the *Washington Post*, Arthur Krock in the *New York Times* and many others all revealed aspects of the plan, along with fizzy details of the controversy raging inside the halls of power.

The St. Paul, Minnesota, *Pioneer Press* eloquently destroyed the idea in seven paragraphs beginning, "President Roosevelt has a penchant for being devious and delusive in his pronouncements, in an effort to cover up mistakes." The president had tried to fool the press and public about the leaked Morgenthau Plan by issuing a letter on another subject that showed the Morgenthau Plan was not official policy. The paper continued, "The world knows that Herr Goebbels [Hitler's minister of propaganda] saw that the plan reached the ear of every German. This, he explained, is what you can expect in defeat. This is what the United States plans to do with Germany . . . It was about this time that General Eisenhower was sending leaflets over Germany promising no reprisals against innocent people . . . The most effective counter propaganda came through Goebbels from Washington." The paper concluded, "Because he exercises the authority to conceal the facts, his statement cannot be disproved . . . [but] he has been forced to repudiate [the plan]." In California, the *San Francisco Chronicle* commented sardonically, "This is now settled as far as such conflicts are ever settled in this Administration, which continually permits interference by one agency with the proper business of another."[15]

Roosevelt soon dissociated himself completely from the blame. With a grin, he told Henry L. Stimson, his secretary of war, that he thought "Henry has pulled a boner,"[16] as if the initials on the memo with Churchill's were HCM and not FDR.

Roosevelt tried to avoid the arguments because he was growing frail in the last six months of his life. He was also frighteningly forgetful. Morgenthau used to repeat important points to him at least once, to make sure he understood. He admitted that he did not understand the catastrophic consequences of what he had signed with his friend Churchill at Quebec. Stimson read to him the three sentences including the phrase "converting Germany into a country primarily agricultural and pastoral in character." Roosevelt was "staggered," according to Stimson. "He said he had no idea how he could have initialed this."[17] That was on October 3, less than three weeks after he had endorsed it.

The bizarre difficulties of planning a foreign nation's future were illuminated by a strange statement of Roosevelt's. He was looking back fondly to his happy years exploring the high woods of Dutchess County on the banks of the Hudson when he suggested that "there's no reason Germany couldn't go back to 1810 . . . They would be perfectly comfortable but they wouldn't have any luxuries."[18] He explained that he was thinking of "how the people lived in homespun wool" in Dutchess County early in the nineteenth century. If the Germans were short of food, the president said, they could be fed from army soup kitchens. He was sometimes even slap-happy in his notions, as when he remarked that dealing with the coal problem would be simple. "I'll appoint a committee of three German businessmen to run the coal mines. If they don't get out the coal, we'll shoot them."[19]

Stalin agreed with the Morgenthau Plan as outlined to him by Churchill in the middle of October in Moscow. As Churchill said, "Russia's intention to take away German machinery was in harmony with Great Britain's interest in filling the gap left by Germany. This was only justice."[20] Churchill had a much harder time convincing the war cabinet that the Morgenthau Plan was wise. Morgenthau's friend Lord Cherwell, a principal advocate of the plan in Britain, enraged Anthony Eden with the assertion that Eden's concerns about starvation in Europe were quite wrong. Churchill himself had to step in to smooth the feathers on Eden's ruffled back. The British remained undecided on major questions of the treatment of Germany, such as reparations and dismemberment, up to the Yalta Conference in February 1945.

In Washington, the struggle for Roosevelt's approval went on through the winter without a decision that endured more than a few weeks, because Roosevelt now tended to agree with the last person he'd seen. Sometimes he was wistful, sometimes he said that he was in a tough mood and determined to be tough as well with Germany.[21] By the time the three Allied leaders were to meet again, at Yalta, the matter was crucial. Significant parts of Germany were in Allied hands, the first of the big captures of the decaying German army were being made on both fronts. Many hundreds of thousands of Germans were already in Allied prison camps in the west. The British, Canadians and Americans were all signatories of the Geneva Convention, so they were publicly committed to treat their prisoners according to the humane provisions which they had written. These provisions were enforced by the threat of retaliation against the hostages held by each side, about 2,000,000 Western Allied held in Germany, about 700,000 Germans held by the Western Allies. The painful consequences of this threat were clear after the Canadian raid on Dieppe in 1942. Canadians and Germans traded accusations of brutality against each other, as they chained prisoners in retaliation for prisoners being chained.

It had been decided that the Allied armies would run Germany at first, but there was no clear policy to guide them. Eisenhower said vaguely that he would "treat them rough." What would "rough" and "tough" mean to the German prisoners once the Allied hostages were released? What would "rough" and "tough" mean to the whole nation once the army had surrendered unconditionally?

These were matters that only the three Allied leaders could decide. They came from Washington, London and Moscow to meet at Yalta in the Crimea in February 1945.

2

WITHOUT SHELTER

"My heart is saddened by the tales of the masses of German women and children flying along the roads everywhere in 40-mile long columns to the West before the advancing [Russian] armies. I am clearly convinced they deserve it; but that does not remove it from one's gaze. The misery of the whole world appalls me."[1]

—WINSTON CHURCHILL

WINSTON CHURCHILL, SEEING THE GERMANS suffer the fate he had feared for his own countrymen, was not in a vengeful mood as the last Big Three conference of the war opened at Yalta in February 1945. Roosevelt stared grimly from his car at the destruction caused by the retreating Germans. As soon as he saw Stalin, he said that the destruction made him feel "more bloodthirsty than ever toward the Germans." Stalin replied that he hadn't seen anything; the destruction in the Ukraine was much worse. Then Roosevelt responded, "[I hope you will] again propose a toast to the execution of 50,000 officers of the German army."[2]

When the subject of Germany's future came up in the second session the next day, Stalin asked if the Allies could agree on some plan for the dismemberment of Germany to be specified to any German anti-Nazi groups seeking peace. Churchill said he saw no need for this, without adding that he opposed the country's division. Stalin raised the subject again near the end of the conference, accusing Churchill of opposing dismemberment because he wanted to do business with a strong Germany. Churchill, who had already told Roosevelt that he feared having no strong nation "between the white cliffs of Dover and the white snows of Russia,"[3] retorted that there was no point in bleeding Germany white, because she would collapse, as she had before, under the weight of reparations. Dismemberment or the Morgenthau Plan, now temporarily in abeyance, would make reparations even more burdensome. Roosevelt suggested a compromise: the three foreign secretaries should produce a plan for Germany's dismemberment within thirty days. Churchill deferred to Roosevelt. Once again, major decisions about the future of Germany were about to be postponed, but Stalin this time would not allow the issue of reparations to disappear into a committee. Hissing his words as he squeezed his chair so hard his knuckles turned white, he insisted that Russia had a right to recompense for the vast devastation caused by Germany. Not a single usable house could be seen on the long flight from Moscow to the Polish frontier. Reluctantly, Churchill and Roosevelt agreed to take the figure of $20 billion as "a basis for discussion." Of any agreed amount, Russia would get half. Yet Stalin's attitude to the prisoners of war, who would supply a vast pool of slave labor for reparations after the war, was very casual. When asked later by Harry Hopkins, special assistant to Roosevelt, what he was doing with the prisoners Russia had taken, he said vaguely that he thought they were being made to work.[4]

The refugees noted by Churchill soon included millions of soldiers of the Wehrmacht, seeking to escape the Russians as they fled to a haven in the west. An arrogant and heartless army if there ever was one, the Wehrmacht of 1940–41 had by now been destroyed on the eastern front: about half of its soldiers now were teenagers or men over 35, many running away to the Western Allies who they thought would treat them better than the Russians.

While the war lasted, Eisenhower and his staff were responsible for the care and feeding of all prisoners according to the Geneva Convention. What he actually did with these men was largely determined by what Hitler did with about two million French, American, British and Canadian soldiers in his prison camps. Besides the western soldiers, many more millions of Russians had fallen into his hands. Many of the Russians were now presumed dead because of the harsh conditions imposed by the Germans.[5] The Geneva Convention provided the rules for the treatment of prisoners; the only enforcement was the threat of retaliation against prisoners.

Eisenhower complained after the Allied victory in North Africa in May 1943 that he had never been told in staff college what to do with prisoners when transport was scarce.[6] He sought help from his old friend, General Everett S. Hughes, who had been with him at staff college at Fort Leavenworth, Kansas.

Hughes was named Eisenhower's special assistant, with an office at the headquarters of the Communications Zone (Com Z) in Paris after its liberation in August 1944.[7] Here he kept an eye on manpower replacements, prisoner of war rations, and General J. C. H. Lee, who was in charge of logistics for the European Theater of Operations (ETO). "Nobody knew quite what he did but he did a lot," said Buel F. Weare, an officer on the staff of Eisenhower's quartermaster. "He was one of the inner circle boys."[8]

Hughes was a tall impressive man, saturnine and quiet in manner. Eisenhower trusted Hughes completely, because he thought that Hughes was a man of the highest ability and great integrity. Hughes understood Eisenhower's method of managing by winks and nods.[9] Hughes was welcome in the bosom of the Eisenhower family where he was called "Uncle Everett."[10]

Eisenhower helped Hughes to rise in the army in several ways. For instance, in February 1944, Eisenhower signaled to

General McNarney in Washington that he now wanted General Hughes back beside him at SHAEF* in Europe: "I can use General Hughes very advantageously in this Theater. Request you issue orders transferring him at once."[11] Hughes was immediately transferred to Europe to help Eisenhower. There he became in Eisenhower's words "my eyes and ears."[12]

Eisenhower depended on Hughes because he was loyal, efficient and above all discreet. The discretion was vital to Eisenhower because he never liked "to take direct action requiring his personal participation where indirect methods could accomplish the same results."[13] This characteristic, later described by his vice-president, Richard M. Nixon, was fully developed when Eisenhower was running SHAEF in Europe in 1944. General George S. Patton commented on it in a letter to Beatrice Patton.[14] Describing how difficult it was to get a decision from Eisenhower, who did not like people to know what was in his mind on controversial subjects, Patton said, "[It's] hell to wage war by inadvertence [and] to conquer by deceit." As Eisenhower's grandson David wrote, Eisenhower developed the "habit of confronting even the proposals he favored with skepticism or a sharp no." General Lucius Clay explained, "He found he discovered a lot of weak people that way."[15]

This method required the services of subtle subordinates who knew how to rule by indirection. "Even when he was in a position to issue clear and direct orders he apparently preferred to work by more tortuous methods. He moved by stealth."[16] Sometimes his orders were so unclear that he had to issue clarifications the next day. This frustration sometimes made him terribly angry. As Hughes noted on July 21, 1944, "The man is crazy. He won't issue orders that stick. He will pound on the desk and shout."[17]

Hughes had great influence but little direct authority. His subtle methods disguised the origin of policy. For instance, although rations were reduced in May by Eisenhower's com-

* Supreme Headquarters, Allied Expeditionary Force. SHAEF covered U.S., French, Canadian and British forces through all of northwest Europe under Eisenhower.

mand,* the order itself has not survived. The junior officers were showing some reluctance in the initial stages; if they had asked for written orders, Hughes could not have complied without getting Eisenhower's signature. This policy was so thoroughly established that in October 1945, when a special feeding of prisoners was ordered for publicity purposes, the officer in charge demanded written orders from Eisenhower before he would comply.** Policy was thus carried out by denial of essential food and other supplies without written orders. Everything was done by doing nothing.

Eisenhower had made very clear the limits on Hughes's authority in his letter of February 24, 1944, when he appointed Hughes. Eisenhower wrote, "Emphasis will be placed on the consultive aspect of your duties rather than on the inspection aspect. After discussing them with responsible commanders, bring to me any problems which, in your opinion, require my decision as Theater Commander."[18]

"It was through logistics perhaps more than any other way, that Eisenhower controlled Montgomery," his authoritative biographer Stephen Ambrose pointed out. "Montgomery could take an extremely broad view of Eisenhower's orders and in essence follow his own inclinations. But he could not conjure up supplies out of thin air. He had to fight within a framework that was tightly constricted by the amount of material Eisenhower chose to give him."[19] Eisenhower's chief of staff, Bedell Smith, wrote that "with the needs and assigned missions of the various forces familiar to him, he alone could have the knowledge to allocate supplies and divisions for the separate operations."

Eisenhower had a very high opinion of Hughes's judgment as well as his discretion. In the summer of 1944, he acceded to Hughes's suggestion that he rewrite an important order, even though this meant issuing an embarrassing clarification only one day after the original. Hughes was one of the very few officers who reported directly to Eisenhower, which enabled them both to deal discreetly with controversial subjects. Eisen-

* See Chapter 5.
** See Chapter 8.

hower authorized Hughes "to consult and confer with the officers and enlisted men of all units, organizations and Headquarters of the United States Army in ETOUSA [European Theater of Operations, U.S. Army]." He was to advise others from his great experience, and to advise Eisenhower himself on manpower, supplies and organization. Under this extraordinary, broad-ranging mandate, Hughes could go anywhere and talk to anyone he wanted. Whoever he questioned had to reply or risk displeasing Eisenhower.[20] Many and sensitive were the subjects that Hughes handled discreetly: "the issuance of liquor"; Kay Summersby, Eisenhower's driver and sometime secretary, who accompanied him on long trips; Patton's indiscretions, and rations for POWs. All these he wrote about in his diary for the period, the 1945 part in a French notebook which he had been given by General George S. Patton.

Hughes and Eisenhower discussed prisoner rations during a walk on August 4, 1944 near Widewing, the SHAEF headquarters in England. "I had a long talk in the woods with Ike, Kay, Tedder.* I told Ike about replacements, POW etc to explain my beef against Lee's use of manpower. In his attitude he's an International Rotarian. Ike wants me to continue in the job — says he doesn't trust Lee." This was significant because of the power over supplies wielded by the scrupulous General J. C. H. Lee (nicknamed Jesus Christ Himself), who was in charge of logistics for the European Theater of Operations (ETO). Through Special Assistant Hughes, Eisenhower had the private view he wanted on logistics and many other areas.

Hughes took an extraordinary interest in the rations of POWs, which he was constantly reducing below the levels set by the subordinate supply officers who based their requisitions for supply on the Geneva Convention provision that the prisoners must be fed and housed to the same standard as U.S. base troops. This was why on May 31, 1943, Hughes noted in his diary, "I have difficulty in getting German POW rations . . . cut down."[21]

In the autumn of 1944, Hughes had a long luncheon with

* British Air Marshal Arthur W. Tedder was Eisenhower's Deputy Supreme Commander.

Eisenhower, during which they again discussed rations for prisoners of war. This was becoming a headache for Eisenhower, as he told Army Chief of Staff George C. Marshall on September 18. "Incidentally, the care of our mass of prisoners* constitutes quite a problem."[22] This problem was not new to either Marshall or Eisenhower. In May 1943, Eisenhower had complained to Marshall about the difficulty of dealing with the several hundred thousand German prisoners captured by the Allies at Tunisia. "It is a pity we could not have killed more," he said in the postscript of a letter which has been suppressed from various official editions of the Eisenhower Papers.[23]

Hughes advised Eisenhower "not to issue any orders about feeding POWs and issue of liquor."[24] Hughes passed the message about the need for secrecy down the line to a subordinate officer in Europe on Friday, November 24. "You shouldn't put yours or your staff's views about POW rations on paper," he ordered. Further, the officer should not say aloud such things as, "Of course we must not do anything that will get the TC [Theater Commander, Eisenhower] in bad." A week later, Hughes wrote in his diary, "Conference on POW rations in John's office." (A hand probably not Hughes's has written in "Littlejohn" for "John," meaning Robert Littlejohn, who as quartermaster of the ETO was in charge of Eisenhower's supplies.) "Finally, I think put across the idea that POWs must be fed less and not what the French don't have." He reported this conference directly to Eisenhower on the following Monday. "Told him about [the] directive to reduce POW rations which wound up with advice to be careful — finally got to Littlejohn."[25]

Hughes enjoyed Littlejohn, a big bear of a man who traveled around France in his own train. Wherever it stopped for breakfast, the morning paper was delivered to him. Hughes worked carefully on him, appealing to Littlejohn's sense of loyalty. On January 18, he noted wearily that instead of roaring along in Littlejohn's luxurious train, he was forced to go "home by car"

* The total of prisoners on his hands as of October 1 was 205,337, or approximately six percent of the size of the U.S. Army in Europe under his command.

without seeing his friends Brad, Hodges and Simpson. "Seven hours with Codman in a Buick," he lamented.* "Stopped at PWE [prisoner of war enclosure] near Stenay. Find Germans eating full B rations. I wonder if I can kick that problem." Another problem he was trying to "kick" was that Lee had apparently been wasting men in the rear areas on such low priority jobs as guarding and maintaining POW camps.

Lee, Hughes noted, traveled by plane or by car, usually followed by his train. The plane he frequently sent to North Africa to bring back oranges for his breakfast. Among Hughes's odd jottings, which include the amazing number of registered whores in Reims (3,000), the size of Eisenhower's furlough party going to Cannes (12), the request from Eisenhower for silk stockings for Kay, and the number of cases of Scotch he had been able to wangle (15), he frequently mentions the efforts he is making to reduce the rations of the prisoners.[26]

The critical role that Hughes was playing for Eisenhower during these difficulties was emphasized by Eisenhower himself on February 25, 1944, in a cable to General Somervell who had asked for Hughes to be returned to Washington: "I do not repeat not desire to spare his services. It would be embarrassing to me to lose him at this juncture. I am sorry I can not help you out in the matter."[27]

The handling of the prisoners at the front in U.S. hands was so disorganized in late 1944 that General Bruce Clarke in Patton's fast-moving Third Army, unable to spare any guards, simply disarmed the captives, crushed their weapons under the treads of his tanks, then turned them loose to walk back through France without guards.[28] Many of the surrendered men were beaten up by French civilians. Colonel R. J. Gill in the Theater Provost Marshal's office complained in February 1945 that only 7,004 POWs of a shipment originally numbering 17,417 were received by his unit.[29] Several times in March, American guards opening rail cars of prisoners arriving from Germany found them dead inside. At Mailly le Camp on March 16, 104 were found dead. A further 27 were found dead at Attichy.[30]

---

* His friends were Generals Bradley, Simpson and Hodges. Charles R. Codman was on Patton's staff.

Dealing with this irritated Eisenhower, because it meant apologizing to Germans. "I loathe having to apologize to the Germans," he wrote to Marshall in Washington about his investigation into the deaths of the Germans who had "accidentally suffocated" in boxcars while being shipped. "It looks as if this time I have no other recourse."[31] The fear of reprisal against Allied prisoners was nevertheless not enough to make the army improve its care of POWs. More Germans were soon dead in another incident for which Eisenhower did not apologize, probably because the war was almost over and reprisals seemed unlikely.

Major General Milton A. Reckord, Theater Provost Marshal, who was then in charge of guarding captives, warned Eisenhower that "[these] two recent incidents resulting in the death of German POWs . . . were caused by lack of personnel. This lack is so serious and has continued so long that it has become the paramount consideration in every operation of handling PWs."[32]

Reckord had already written to the War Department through the European Theater of Operations headquarters, warning them about the increased prisoner load, but in more than a month had received no reply. Part of the problem was that the British and Canadians had not accepted responsibility for all the POWs they were supposed to take over from the U.S. Reckord finished with a stern warning that the possibility of further deaths "concerns the highest levels in ETO, SHAEF and the War Department. Protests and even reprisals are possible that would affect the standing of the U.S. before world opinion. Since high levels would be affected by failure, . . . it seems that the same high levels should know if the personnel . . . is not supplied through normal channels."

Eisenhower hated Germans, he told his wife Mamie in a letter in September 1944. Why? "Because the German is a beast." In front of the British ambassador to Washington, in August, he said that all the 3,500 or so officers of the German General Staff should be "exterminated." He would include for liquidation all leaders of the Nazi party from mayors on up, plus all members of the Gestapo.[33] This would total about 100,000 people. He and his lunch guests agreed that nature could be left to run its course if the Russians were given a free hand in postwar Germany. Eisenhower told them that Germany should be divided into zones, one to each nation which had been overrun, so that justice could be done.[34]

As the British and Canadians fought their way into Holland, starvation began to threaten Dutch civilians trapped behind German lines. Eisenhower asked the Germans for help in feeding the Dutch. He told Marshall, "I am done trifling with them and while I have held my hand in the fear of intensifying the Dutch suffering, if the German doesn't play the game absolutely, I intend really to punish him when I can turn my attention in that direction."[35] His feelings against the Germans grew stronger the more desperately they fought, the more he saw of the horrors of the concentration camps, until he felt ashamed that he bore a German name.[36]

Fear that chaos would follow war in Europe, resulting in revolutions that would either nullify the sacrifices of American lives or else demand further sacrifices, had made the far-sighted Roosevelt commission his old friend Sam Rosenman to look into the world food situation. Roosevelt was especially afraid of chaos in France. If the country were starving, the communists would find it easier to ignite the final revolution which they believed would destroy capitalism. Some authorities were already talking about the danger of a "World Food Shortage" creating civil unrest all over Europe. In February 1945, Brigadier General T. J. Davis warned Eisenhower that the "heavy supply commitment resulting from giving [the German prisoners] status as PWs could not be met."[37] Rosenman reported to the president in April that "shortage . . . in supplies rather than in shipping[38] will be the limiting factor within the immediate future." He added mysteriously, "Supplies will not be called forward or distributed by SHAEF unless it becomes necessary as a matter of military necessity to do so."[39] Two mysteries are contained here. One is the implication, previously dismissed, that there was in truth enough food for all civilians apart from Germans; the other is the phrasing "military necessity" in referring to civilians in postwar Germany. Rosenman is obviously thinking, as were the president and Eisenhower, of the possibility of famine causing unrest among German civilians, which would have to be suppressed by the army. The danger was visible in the rations allotted: for German civilians, the maximum food from all sources "will be approximately 1,500 calories per head per day." The minimum to maintain life for adults lying down, doing no work but self-care, varies from 1,800 to 2,250 calories per day, according to various experts.[40]

The notion of a World Food Shortage was first spread by General Hughes in North Africa in 1943. He wrote in April 1945: "The world shortage of food is being talked about. I talked it [*sic*] long ago. Started in NA [North Africa]."[41] At that time, and later, the shortage was not of food. In the area now known as West Germany, the population was 4 percent less in May 1945 than it was in the same area in 1939, although the German population there was rising every day with the influx of refugees from the east.[42] There was a lot more wheat available in the combined area of western Germany, France, Britain, Canada and the USA than there had been in the same physical area in 1939. This was because increased wheat production in North America and the UK more than replaced the production lost in western Germany and France. The wheat surplus in Canada at the end of both the crop years 1943 – 44 and 1944 – 45 was over 440 million bushels. In the USA, it was the same. There was also a large surplus of corn (maize). The potato crop was down in the overall area by a relatively small amount, caused mainly by a 30 percent drop in the western part of Germany in 1945.[43] Nevertheless, in France, wheat production in 1944 was 500,000 tons more than consumption.[44] As Churchill noted to Roosevelt in March 1945, there was no overall shortage of wheat, although sugar, meat and some fats were scarce for many people in Europe.[45] On the world scale,* food production measured in calories per capita for the 1945 — 46 crop year was 90 percent of the 1935 — 39 average production, according to the U.S. Office of Foreign Agricultural Relations in October 1945.[46]

In March, as Germany was being cracked like a nut between the Russians and the western Allies, a message signed and

* For a fuller discussion of food, see chapters 6 and 8.

initialed by Eisenhower proposed a startling departure from the Geneva Convention — the creation of a new class of prisoners who would not be fed by the army after the surrender of Germany. The message, dated March 10, reads: "Although it is intended to place the responsibility for feeding and maintaining all Allied prisoners of war [meaning Germans in Allied hands] and displaced persons upon the German authorities, it is anticipated that in the state of chaos that is likely to exist, this will prove beyond their capacity and that the Allies will be faced with the necessity of providing very large quantities of food pending their repatriation. The additional maintenance commitment entailed by declaring the German Armed Forces priosners [*sic*] of war which would necessitate the provision of rations on a scale equal to that of base troops would prove far beyond the capacity of the Allies even if all German sources were tapped. Moreover it would be undesirable to place the German Armed Forces upon a scale of rations far in excess of that available to the civil population." Prisoners taken after VE Day would be called "disarmed enemy forces" (DEF) "pending discharge administered and maintained by the German Army under supervision of Allied Forces." The message ended with, "Your approval is requested. Existing plans have been prepared upon this basis."[47]

3

NO PUBLIC DECLARATION

ON APRIL 26 1945, A MESSAGE[1] from the Combined Chiefs of Staff clattered onto the machines at SHAEF in Reims in response to Eisenhower's message of March 10 creating the status of DEF (disarmed enemy forces). The CCS approved the DEF status *for prisoners of war in American hands only*. The British members of the CCS refused to adopt the American plan for their own prisoners. The major conditions set forth for Eisenhower were as follows:

> . . . B) Germans are responsible for feeding and maintaining disarmed German troops.
> C) Procedure adopted will not apply to war criminals nor to other categories of wanted German personnel nor to other persons found amongst the German Armed Forces and retained on security grounds. You will continue to imprison all such persons as suspected war criminals or on grounds of military security and not as prisoners of war. They will be fed, housed and otherwise administered by Allied Forces. German authorities will exercise no control over them whatsoever.

> D) There should be no public declaration regarding status of German Armed Forces or of disarmed troops.

Under this provision, the contravention of the Geneva Convention was kept secret.

Section Two of the message reads: "Following statement is added by British Chiefs of Staff: . . . If UNITED KINGDOM decides it requires additional prisoners of war . . . such personnel will not be included by you in category of disarmed troops." The final section adds: "It is assumed that you will have no occasion to declare additional Germans to be prisoners of war after defeat . . . to meet the labor requirements of SHAEF outside Germany."

This refusal to agree on the DEF policy with the Americans is a startling departure from the cooperation that the Allies had given each other up to now. The British were obliged to accept prisoners from the Americans in order to share the load more equitably. To refuse prisoners in advance would have been grossly insulting if the Americans had not concurred in advance that the British were justified in doing so. The Americans knew as well as the British that any Germans subjected to the DEF status would certainly not be fit to work. Most likely, they would be dying.

The dissenting British also decided they would not even use the American term DEF for any prisoners whom they knew they could not treat according to the letter of the Geneva Convention. They used the term "surrendered enemy personnel" (SEP) to distinguish their post-surrender POWs from the others.

The British refusal to accept the American DEFs had been accepted without comment by the American Chiefs, but not by the U.S. officers at SHAEF. A message signed "Eisenhower" complained that "the British with their smaller load,[2] are able to maintain higher standards, which, by comparison, prejudice the American position."[3] Nothing at this date prevented the Americans from treating their captives as well as the British treated theirs, for U.S. supplies, now supplemented by captured stocks, were more than adequate for the job.[4]

No dissent existed about certain prized prisoners such as war criminals, spies and high-tech scientists whom the British and Americans were determined should live. They were actually called "wanted" to distinguish them from the others, who were not wanted. Both the British and the Americans specified that these wanted prisoners should not be included in the DEF category, but should be fed, housed and otherwise administered by Allied forces.[5] This order not only helped to isolate the suspects in one place for later trial, but also preserved them from the conditions to be imposed by the DEF status. Attention was sure to focus on the famous criminals, so they could not be kept among the DEF prisoners. That the conditions in the DEF camps were certain to be unacceptable to the Allied public in Europe and North America* was demonstrated with the Chiefs' order to Eisenhower that "there should be no public declaration regarding status of German armed forces or of disarmed troops." It was scarcely necessary to give this last order, for Eisenhower was already lying to the public about the plans for the prisoners. At a press conference in Paris he said: "If the Germans were reasoning like normal human beings they would realize the whole history of the United States and Great Britain is to be generous toward a defeated enemy. We observe all the laws of the Geneva Convention."[6]

This Convention, which the U.S. Government and the United States Army repeatedly said they observed,[7] provided three important rights for the prisoners: that they would be fed and sheltered to the same standard as base or depot troops of the Capturing Power (USA), that they could send and receive mail, and that they had the right to be visited by delegates of the International Committee of the Red Cross (ICRC), who would then report in secret to the Protecting Power (the German government) and to the U.S. authorities. In the case of abuses, the Protecting Power could threaten exposure or retaliation.[8]

Responsibility for the treatment of the German prisoners in American hands belonged to the commanders of the U.S. Army

* Among other denunciations of U.S. occupation policies was a speech by Senator Henrick Shipstead in 1946 denouncing "America's eternal monument of shame, the Morgenthau Plan for the destruction of the German people." (Congressional Record, Senate, May 15, 1946, p 5039.)

in Europe, subject only to political control by the government. All decisions about prisoner treatment were in fact made solely by the U.S. Army in Europe, except for three basic ones, all of which broke the Convention: the decision to prevent the delegates of the ICRC from visiting the U.S. camps (the ban also applied to British and Canadian camps); the joint U.S.-UK decision to transfer prisoners for reparations labor to the French,* provided the French obeyed the Convention, and the decision to send certain prisoners to Russia against their will. The most important decision, which also broke the Convention, was the creation of DEF status, devised by Eisenhower and approved by the CCS.

The "chaos" which Eisenhower had said would prevent the Germans from feeding themselves was of course going to be created in part by the Allies themselves, because they would dismantle the central German institutions, including welfare agencies. They would also hamper or abolish production of a list of over 500 items, as the Morgenthau Plan had stipulated.[9] Yet the message said that the army would place responsibility upon "German authorities." There were no "authorities" to do the maintaining, once the army, the government, the welfare agencies including the German Red Cross and important elements of trade were abolished.

As American soldiers were rounding up the beaten Germans in the rubble-heaps of the Ruhr, suited bureaucrats in Washington were arguing over what to tell Eisenhower to do with those Germans. Representatives of the State Department, the Treasury and the War Department met day after day of that bright warm spring, deciding the details of Germany's fate that had been left open by the Big Three. The directive they were writing, JCS 1067, specified to Eisenhower the policy he must adopt toward every institution in Germany. He was to abolish the central government, the Nazi party, the Wehrmacht, to close schools, universities, radio stations, newspapers, to prevent his soldiers even from speaking to Germans, except to give orders. Much of the Morgenthau Plan was incorporated in this direc-

* The French first asked for 1,750,000 but received only about 730,000 (possibly 886,000), mainly from the U.S. Army.

tive, in both spirit and letter. This was largely the work of the three Treasury representatives on the committee, Harry Dexter White, Frank Coe and Harry Glasser.

By April, the Allies knew that in the smoking ruins of Germany the danger was not a sudden surge of militarism, but diseased despair leading to a communist takeover. This threat worried both Roosevelt and Eisenhower. But to create "a Carthaginian peace,"* according to Military Governor Lucius Clay[10] was precisely the aim of JCS 1067.[11] Howard Trivers, a State Department official watching the three Treasury men working on JCS 1067, observed later on:

> During the committee discussions these Treasury representatives consistently and persistently argued for the dismemberment of Germany and the transformation of industrial Germany into a bucolic pasture. They were representing faithfully the views of Henry Morgenthau, the Secretary of the Treasury. Later, I wondered whether they also had been acting under Soviet instructions, if they really were members of a communist cells [*sic*]. At that time Stalin was proclaiming that his enemies were the Nazis, not the German people, and that the German nation and state would continue after the hostilities in its unity. The Soviets had organized a Free Germany Committee consisting of Communists and POWs and an Association of German Officers [captured officers] who were espousing the same view about the future. It would have been typical Soviet policy and practice to instruct American Communists to support vocally the dismemberment and pastoralization of Germany and to seek to determine American policy along these lines. In this way, contrary to the Americans, the Soviets could present themselves to the Germans as the champions of the German national cause, the ultimate aim, of course, veiled at first, being a United Germany under Communism."[12]

Ultimately, White was revealed as a subversive who had

* The peace settlement imposed by the Romans on Carthage was total destruction. They salted the earth so nothing could be produced.

disobeyed Senate instructions on gold policy in an attempt to destroy the economy of Chiang Kai-shek's China.[13]

Morgenthau was in Warm Springs, Georgia the night before Roosevelt died on April 12. The president's last words to him on policy were, "Henry, I am with you 100%."[14] Thus this plan which imposed a Carthaginian peace on Germany remained an important element of U.S. policy towards the Germans at the time of Roosevelt's death. Together with all other Roosevelt policies, it was adopted and continued by the new president, Harry S. Truman, who made no serious changes in U.S. policy or in the cabinet for several months after Roosevelt died.

On April 21, 1945, another SHAEF message signed "Eisenhower" told Marshall that the new prisoner enclosures "will provide no shelter or other comforts . . . ." It added that the enclosures would be improved by the prisoners themselves, "utilizing local materials." These "enclosures" were open fields surrounded by barbed wire, called "prisoner of war temporary enclosures" (PWTE). They were not temporary, but they were certainly enclosed, by barbed wire, searchlights, guard towers and machine guns. Far from permitting the prisoners to provide shelter "utilizing local materials," an army engineer's order[15] issued on May 1 specifically forbade the provision of housing in the cages. If the message to Marshall had meant what it said about the prisoners maintaining themselves with local materials, the engineer's order would never have been issued, because it directly countermanded what had just been sent to Marshall. The order was allowed to stand.[16]

Tents, food, barbed wire, medical supplies and so on were scarce in the camps not because the army lacked supplies, but because requests for supplies were denied. As Hughes said on March 19, after he visited the huge supply dumps at Naples and Marseille: "[Marseille is] Naples all over again. More stocks than we can ever use. Stretch as far as eye can see." He continues two days later: "Littlejohn says he is under pressure from US and ETO because he has cut POW rations. I advise him to take it up with Ike without delay. Ike may not support him."[17] One week later, when Littlejohn still had not settled the matter with the War Department, Hughes's comment was, "I suppose that all are afraid of Geneva Convention."

Because the ICRC delegates were still visiting camps to make reports under the Geneva Convention, the possibility of retaliation against Allied prisoners in German hands was at this time a very live issue at SHAEF. Eisenhower himself wrote a message telling the Combined Chiefs of Staff on February 18 that the Germans were moving Allied prisoners south and west away from the Russians, exposing them to unusual hardship and hazard. "I suggest that proposals be made to the German government by the United States and United Kingdom governments through the protecting power,* along the following lines . . . [that the German forces] should leave the prisoners of war with adequate supplies [and] . . . a nominal roll or sufficient description of those released should be left with the camp leader and a duplicate rendered to the protecting power." All of this indicates a practiced familiarity with the routine of a prison camp and the role of the various powers under the Geneva Convention. He ends with, "This is a matter of extreme urgency."[18]

Contrary to Hughes's assumption of March 21, Littlejohn soon received approval from Washington to reduce rations. Hughes's diary does not say whether Eisenhower intervened directly to defend Littlejohn's action, but Eisenhower, who called Littlejohn "the best Quartermaster I know," did not oppose him, according to the cable log. Littlejohn was again reducing rations by April 23. This was in line with the U.S. Chiefs' usual policy of deferring "all questions in the European Theater to General Ike," as Eisenhower's good friend Harry C. Butcher noted in his diary.[19]

"There was certainly not sufficient rations to properly accommodate this tremendous amount of Prisoners of War," wrote Deputy Provost Marshal Lt. Colonel Valentine M. Barnes, author of a history of the Provost Marshal, Advance Section, where most of the prisoners were kept. Because the Provost

* At this date, Switzerland was acting as protecting power in lieu of the German government.

Marshal's office was responsible for the prisoners, Barnes must have known when he wrote his history that there were in fact plenty of tents and food in U.S. Army depots in April, but he does not mention why they did not reach the camps.[20] On April 22, the army had in stock in Europe 50 days supply of nutritionally balanced rations that gave 4,000 calories per person per day for five million people, although the army was feeding at that time only about 2,600,000 in the "military" category. Enough supplies of the unbalanced rations were on hand for a further 50 days.[21] This 100-day stockpile remained at the same level all summer. The Ruhr, according to General Smith, "was quite plentifully supplied when it was closed in . . . . There was plenty of ammunition . . . . Food was plentiful in some places. In others, the larder was bare."[22]

Barnes earnestly outlines the efforts of his men "who drove many miles both day and night" in April to bring water "in barrels" to hundreds of thousands of prisoners.[23] While his men drove around with barrels of water, essential German and American supplies were going unused. There were plenty of spare tents to cover the prisoners, as well as German food, medicine and tents. "German supplies were uncovered in huge quantities . . . [but] the discovery of useful captured materials did not in itself assure their availability for either military units or Civil Affairs."[24] The supply officers in the field could not get what they needed for the prisoners, because the commanding generals refused to issue it.[25] Theater Provost Marshal Reckord's warning seems to have sunk without a trace except in the archives. Guards, water, food, tents, space, barbed wire — everything necessary for the prisoners was kept fatally scarce. Camp Rheinberg on the Rhine, six miles in circumference, had no food at all when it was opened on April 17.[26] As in the other big "Rhine meadow" camps, opened in mid-April, there were at first no guard towers, no tents, no buildings, no cooking facilities, no water, no latrines. There was not even enough barbed wire. The official allotment of space was 175 square feet per man, but at Rheinberg and elsewhere, for a while, the space was anywhere from a fifth to a half of that.[27] In some camps, the men were so crowded they could not even lie down. The situation at one camp was reported as follows: "The highest 'On Hand' figure at Continental Central Prisoner of War Enclosure #18 was 32,902 prisoners of war. Attention is invited to the fact that the Holding Capacity of Continental Central Prisoner of War Enclosure #18 does not exceed between 6 to 8,000 Prisoners of War."[28]

All of this happened while the number of prisoners was well inside the range of captures predicted. Marshall was told by a SHAEF message signed "Eisenhower" on April 21 that the captures had "exceeded all expectations," but the forecast at the beginning of April[29] that the army would have 2,050,000 prisoners by the end of the month was better than 99 percent accurate.[30] On April 30, the army had on hand in Europe 2,062,865 prisoners.[31] It is clear that there had been plenty of warning about the huge influx that came in April.[32]

Disastrous overcrowding, disease, exposure and malnutrition were the rule in the U.S. camps in Germany beginning in April despite the considerable risk that the Germans would retaliate against the millions of Allied hostages in Germany. It was about now that the guards at some German concentration camps speeded the rate of killings, to get rid of as many people as they could before the Allies reached them. If they found out about the DEF plan, the Germans would use it in propaganda to prolong the desperate resistance which Eisenhower had deplored.

The conditions in the American camps along the Rhine in early April were observed by two U.S. Army colonels, James B. Mason and Charles H. Beasley:

> April 20 was a blustery day with alternate rain, sleet and snow and with bone-chilling winds sweeping down the Rhine valley from the north over the flats where the inclosure was located. Huddled close together for warmth, behind the barbed wire was a most awesome sight — nearly 100,000 haggard, apathetic, dirty, gaunt, blank-staring men clad in dirty field grey uniforms, and standing ankle-deep in mud. Here and there were dirty white blurs which, upon a closer look were seen to be men with bandaged

> heads or arms or standing in shirt sleeves! The German Division Commander reported that the men had not eaten for at least two days, and the provision of water was a major problem — yet only 200 yards away was the river Rhine running bank-full.[33]

The view from inside the camps was worse.

> In April 1945, hundreds of thousands of German soldiers as well as the sick from hospitals, amputees, women auxiliaries, and civilians were caught . . . . One inmate at Rheinberg was over 80 years old, another was aged nine . . . . Nagging hunger and agonizing thirst were their companions, and they died of dysentery. A cruel heaven pelted them week after week with streams of rain . . . . amputees slithered like amphibians through the mud, soaking and freezing. Naked to the skies day after day and night after night, they lay desperate in the sand of Rheinberg or slept exhaustedly into eternity in their collapsing holes.[34]

4

THE CRUELTY OF THE VICTOR

The spirit of Goethe, a holy spirit, keeps me alive.
— ANONYMOUS PRISONER

AT NIGHT, SEARCHLIGHTS THREW BLINDING light over the men lying in the shadowy holes. They watched uneasily the dark shapes standing high above them on the paths lit by the searchlights. Men shuffled along the slippery banks between the holes all night, lining up for water. Charles von Luttichau lay in his hole curled up next to one of his brother officers wondering if he could get himself released before he was shipped to France. Men cried out in their nightmare sleep. He resolved to try again with the guards the next day. "I am half-American," he thought, rehearsing his English. "My mother is American. I gave myself up to you. I don't belong in here. I am half-American."*

He had not been captured in battle but was convalescing at home when he decided to surrender voluntarily to U.S. troops

* Von Luttichau, who survived three months at Kripp, later moved to Washington. He has written military history for the U.S. Army.

about to occupy his house because otherwise he might be accused of plotting further underground resistance.

"We were kept in crowded barbed wire cages in the open with scarcely any food," he has said of his camp at Kripp near Remagen on the Rhine.

> The latrines were just logs flung over ditches next to the barbed wire fences. To sleep, all we could do was to dig out a hole in the ground with our hands, then cling together in the hole. We were crowded very close together. Because of illness, the men had to defecate on the ground. Soon, many of us were too weak to take off our trousers first. So our clothing was infected, and so was the mud where we had to walk and sit and lie down. There was no water at all at first, except the rain, then after a couple of weeks we could get a little water from a standpipe. But most of us had nothing to carry it in, so we could get only a few mouthfuls after hours of lining up, sometimes even through the night. We had to walk along between the holes on the soft earth thrown up by the digging, so it was easy to fall into a hole, but hard to climb out. The rain was almost constant along that part of the Rhine that spring. More than half the days we had rain. More than half the days we had no food at all. On the rest, we got a little K ration. I could see from the package that they were giving us one tenth of the rations that they issued to their own men. So in the end we got perhaps five percent of a normal U.S. Army ration. I complained to the American camp commander that he was breaking the Geneva Convention, but he just said, "Forget the Convention. You haven't any rights."[1]
>
> Within a few days, some of the men who had gone healthy into the camp were dead. I saw our men dragging many dead bodies to the gate of the camp, where they were thrown loose on top of each other onto trucks, which took them away.[2]

One 17-year-old boy who could see his village in the distance used to stand weeping near the barbed wire fence. One morning the prisoners found him shot at the foot of the fence. His body was strung up and left hanging on the wire by the guards as a warning. The prisoners were forced to walk by the body. Many cried out "*Moerder, moerder* [murderer, murderer]!"[3] In retaliation, the camp commander withheld the prisoners' meager rations for three days. "For us who were already starving and could hardly move because of weakness, it was frightful; for many it meant death."[4] This was not the only time when the commander withheld rations to punish prisoners.

Private Heinz T.* had just turned 18 in hospital when the Americans walked into his ward on April 18. All the patients were taken out to the camp at Bad Kreuznach. Heinz was wearing only a pair of shorts, along with shoes and a shirt, when he was herded into Bad Kreuznach with several hundred thousand others. The camp spread over a long field between a narrow country road and a line of low hills to the west. Here he was kept for weeks with no roof, almost no food, little water, no mail or sign of anyone else's knowledge of their situation. Because many of the men had been fleeing the eastern front, they were not in their original units, so few of the men knew any of the others.

"The Americans were really shitty to us," said Heinz T. At the beginning, when there were still trees in the camp, some men managed to cut off some limbs to build a fire. The guards ordered them to put it out. In many of the cages, they were forbidden to dig holes in the ground for shelter. "All we had to eat was grass," he remembers. Some of them climbed up a walnut tree when it came into leaf, to get the leaves to smoke, or to eat. Several times a small plane flew slowly overhead, turning constantly. The men realized they were being photographed for an American magazine or newspaper.

His feet swelled up so he took his shoes off. When the swelling had abated a little, he tried to get the shoes back on, but they still wouldn't fit, so he tucked them under his head at night. Inside one of them he put a small bag of the coffee which

* The prisoner's name has been withheld at his request.

had been given to the prisoners by the Americans. He thought, "I'll take this coffee home with me when I go. They'll be so glad." One morning he woke up to find both coffee and shoes gone. He wept.[5]

He was far from the youngest in the camp. Children as young as six years of age, pregnant women, men over 60, were among the prisoners in these camps. Because no records were made in the DEF camps, and most of the POW records were destroyed in the 1950s[6] no one knows how many civilians were imprisoned, but French reports show that among about 100,000 people the Americans turned over to them supposedly for labor, there were 32,640 women, children and old men.[7] Lt. Colonel Valentine Barnes, making his report on Bad Kreuznach, noted on April 22 that "a female infant was born to a female prisoner of war in enclosure A-3."[8]

George Weiss, a tank repairman, said his camp on the Rhine was so crowded that "we couldn't even lie down properly. All night we had to sit up jammed against each other. But the lack of water was the worst thing of all. For three and a half days we had no water at all. We would drink our own urine. It tasted terrible, but what could we do? Some men got down on the ground and licked the ground to get some moisture. I was so weak I was already on my knees, when finally we got a little water to drink. I think I would have died without that water. But the Rhine was just outside the wire. The guards sold us water through the wire, and cigarettes. One cigarette cost 900 marks. I saw thousands dying. They took the bodies away on trucks."[9]

At that date, the captives at Bad Kreuznach were being packed in at more than three times the planned rate.[10] Because the soil and the clothing were all dangerously infected and the people were already weak, to be constantly crowded near barbed wire was extremely dangerous. High rates of death by septicemia (blood poisoning) were reported in these camps.[11]

After about a month at Bad Kreuznach, where Heinz T. had the impression that not many men died despite the conditions, he was given to the French along with 2,000,000 others, according to the rumor. The rumor was not totally inaccurate: the

French had originally asked the Americans for as many as 1,700,000, but were negotiating now for 1,300,000 captives to help repair war damage in France. Looking around the famished men bloated with edema from their hunger, in ragged clothes, dirty, with gaunt faces and shuffling gait, Heinz thought, "A strange sort of present to give the French." Then he was loaded on a train to go to Rennes in Brittany.

One of the boys in the town of Rheinberg, ten-year-old Herbert Thelen, was allowed to take food to his father in the camp, three kilometers west of the town. He passed the food through the barbed wire in the outer fence to his father sitting inside upon the perimeter road. Thelen never saw anyone else at the camp on the same sort of errand.[12] One of the captives wrapped a note around a rock which he flung out towards the road leading into Rheinberg. It was found by a Rheinberger who saved it. The note, on brown wrapping paper now turning dark, reads: "Dear Reader. Please please send us two comrades a package of cooked potatoes with salt. We are terribly hungry. We are waiting by the guard tower in the perimeter road. Please write on the package the name Sgt. Jakob Lohr, Camp E."[13]

A 50-year-old sergeant with a Ph.D. kept a diary in ink on toilet paper at Rheinberg.* He writes:

> *Camp Rheinberg, May 17, 1945*
>
> I usually lie on the ground. During the heat I crawl into an earth-hole. I wear a coat and boots, with my forage-cap pulled down over my ears; my field bag, in which I have a silver spoon and fork, serves as my pillow. During a thunderstorm one wall of my earth-hole falls in on me. My coat and socks are wet through and through.
>
> During the night I wander restlessly through the camp. I see the moon rise, listen to nightingales singing in the

---

* The prisoner asked not to be named. Extracts from his diary appeared in Kurt W. Böhme, *Die deutschen Kriegsgefangenen in amerikanischer Hand, Die deutschen Kriegsgefangenen des Zweiten Weltkrieges,* Band 10,2, Bielefeld 1973 Anlage 13, page 309.

woods nearby. I recite poems by Goethe and in order not to fall asleep, I argue with myself about "Nietzsche's life and theory."

Fellow soldiers complain about being in prison. I advise them not to concentrate on the barbed wire but instead to look through the space in between.

I often sing "The thoughts are free, who can divine them . . ." I especially rejoice in the verse about prisoners.

In the evening, the people who like to sing, sing German folk songs. Singing unites people.

Protestant and Catholic prayers are held every evening but their dogmatic narrowness doesn't satisfy me.

I meditate on the topic "The technique of brain work." I imagine myself teaching students, maybe I could write a booklet entitled "the workshop of an intellectual worker."

At home I could use literary sources. Here in the camp I only possess my thoughts and depend on my memory but mere book knowledge is worthless.

New plan: to write my own book of prayers. What I consider of value might mean something for others as well.

I thank God that I am in this camp. Nowhere else would I have been so lost in my thoughts or seen humans in their total nakedness. Nor would I ever have believed the victors to be capable of such cruelties.

Rheinberg, May 19, 1945

Protestant evening prayers: dogmatic attitude — we have to be prepared to receive the Holy Spirit.

Two fingers of my left hand are inflamed. A young medical student puts a bandage around my thumb. If they don't get better, I will be sent to the military hospital. Discussion with the young student about demoralization in the soldiers.

My last will concerning my children: it will be their duty to preserve a strong and lively relationship to peasantry. All my ancestors have been peasants. My children should acquire land if possible and learn the tasks of a farmer to cultivate and live off the land. Those not qualified for studies at the university should become farmers.

Thoughts about my dear wife.

The Nazis, airmen, artillery-men and tank corps leave the camp, probably for labor duties. Long discussion among the fellows about which fate is to be preferred, to starve in camp or work outside with the prospect of occasionally getting more food. Some men [try to] escape from the camp. Some are caught, others get away. Few try. One told me, "We went on the 10th over the barbed wire. Everything rattled. The guard fired at us. One ran ahead, another turned back. Pursuit of the fugitives. A few put their hands up to surrender. They were shot without mercy. I threw myself on the ground and played dead. The guard kicked me but I didn't move. When he moved off, I squeezed under the wire back into the camp. The escape failed but I'm still alive."

I regret that I don't know more poems by heart.

Meditation: God is love, love is God; God is truth, truth is God; God is kindness, kindness is God; God is perfection, perfection is God. (Goethe)
God is of the East possessed
God is ruler of the West
Northland, southland, each direction

Rests beneath his calm protection.*

The spirit of Goethe, a holy spirit, keeps me alive.

If I ever survive this camp, I will collect poems under the title Comfort and Praise.

Today I got four potatoes. What riches!

I can imagine life as a monk because poverty, purity and obedience are easy to bear as long as I have enough free time to think. Thoughts are my passion.

Rheinberg, May 20, 1945 (Whitsuntide)

Protestant service in the morning, in the open of course. Dogmas. The soul should reign over the body. I begin to understand Professor Jaspers's point of view towards the church. According to him the church's duty is to prepare the masses for the absolute, the eternal. Maybe he is right that philosophy can only help a few people.

How long will we have to be without shelter, without blankets or tents? Every German soldier once had shelter from the weather. Even a dog has a doghouse to crawl into when it rains. Our only wish is finally after six weeks to get a roof over our heads. Even a savage is better housed. Diogenes, Diogenes, you at least had your barrel.

Rheinberg, May 21 1945

Prayers have to be understood from the human-psychological not from the theological point of view. The mind needs to be the dominating principle. It has started to rain again. Despair. At first I seek shelter under the minuscule trees. I am drenched. I squeeze my back up against a

* Translated by Edwin H. Zeydel, *Goethe the Lyrist* (Chapel Hill: University of North Carolina Press, 1955).

broken-down wall that at least cuts off the wind and rain from one side. The next day I get into a small cellar by climbing down a ladder. It is full of men. I doze for a couple of hours, feeling like a king. Then I must roam the field again like a common soldier.

Rheinberg, May 22 1945.

Light rain. Stayed in earth-hole. Wet.

The story of the cardboard: Our rations come into the camp in large cardboard cartons. Broken apart, these can serve as a kind of bed. The cardboard, about one meter 20 centimeters long and body-width, provides good insulation against the damp ground. Every day about 25 such "beds" are given out by the doctor to those who can prove they have no tent, blanket or coat. Properly speaking, I was not really entitled to one because I still had a coat. At about eight o'clock on the morning of the first day that I tried to get one, there were over 25 men in line before me. Next morning I got up about 6:30 before reveille. Lucky me! I had my cardboard. Profoundly happy, I clutched it under my arm and lugged it to my hole. From then on it was my prize possession. We are hand in glove together.

Wolfgang Iff said that in his sub-section of perhaps 10,000 people at Rheinberg, 30 to 40 bodies were dragged out every day.[14] A member of the burial commando, Iff was well placed to see what was going on. He got extra food so he could help drag the dead from his cage out to the gate of the camp, where they carried them in wheelbarrows to several big steel garages. There Iff and his team stripped the corpses of clothing, snapped off half the aluminum dog tag, spread the bodies in a layer of fifteen to twenty, threw ten shovelsful of quicklime over them, put on more layers till they were stacked a meter high, placed the personal possessions in a bag for the Americans, then left. Some of the corpses were dead of gangrene following frostbite suffered on the freezing nights of April. A dozen or more others, including a 14-year-old boy too weak to cling to the log flung across the ditch for a latrine, fell off and drowned. Some were dragged out; dirt was thrown over some of them where they lay. Sometimes, as many as 200 died each day. In other cages of similar size Iff saw about 60 to 70 per day going out. "Then the trucks moved this sad freight. What a macabre picture," Iff has said.[15] The prisoners were never told what happened to the corpses, but German construction crews in the fifties and gravediggers in the eighties have discovered at Rheinberg human remains with German Army World War II aluminum dog tags jumbled closely together in common graves with no sign of coffin or gravemarker.[16]

Watches and jewelry taken from dead bodies were supplied to the vast black market in Germany, according to former Attorney General of the United States Francis Biddle. He visited the black market in the Tiergarten section of Berlin, which he told his daughter was "terrific . . . . There were several thousand people bartering. Our mechanic sold his watch for $400 and five cartons of cigarettes for $100 a carton. Our guide yesterday told us he made $8,000 selling watches and smuggled it back through their Secret Service man who was at the Potsdam Conference and was going to buy a farm in Michigan with it. The watches apparently came off dead Germans."[17]

Part of the problem for a long time at Rheinberg was the crowding. One cage measuring roughly 300 meters by 300 meters was supposed to hold 10,000 people, but at the beginning, as many as 30,000 were forced in. This would leave about three square meters per person.

Prisoner Thelen whispered to his son through the barbed wire that 330 to 770 people per day were dying.[18] The camp then contained between 100,000 and 120,000 people.

The clergy of Rheinberg protested to the American camp commander along with the Archbishop of Cologne, who, it was rumored, had also written directly to Pope Pius XII. The Pope, who had remained aloof from the situation in Hitler's death camps, continued his policy.

How was it that the middle-rank officers and doctors seeing

these things happen show scarcely a flicker of interest or concern? Their impassive descriptions and statistics contrast amazingly with the reports, protests, diaries or art of the prisoners, with the pleas of the clergy, and the huge death counts entered under the category Other Losses.

It is possible to get an idea of how this state of mind came about as we read the daily situation reports of a discerning, articulate man who had been trained to save life. Colonel C. H. Beasley, who with Colonel Mason wrote the chilling report of a Rhine camp in April, describes Rheinberg on April 30 like this: "This camp is well organized and is running smoothly. In the past 48 hours there have been seven deaths . . . At Sinzig, [there were] five deaths allegedly due to exposure."[19]

The word "allegedly" is revealing. The reports came to Beasley from the camp commanders, who had no interest in accusing themselves of committing an atrocity. So why would Beasley use the word "allegedly"? He knew that the prisoners were not protected, as we see in his own description of them freezing in the sleet in their shirtsleeves in these same camps. So it is highly significant that he discredits the notion of death from exposure, *without specifying why*. He is not contradicting the report; he is refusing to join the accusation inherent in it. Beasley is calling the exposure "alleged" only because he doesn't want to lend any credence to the accusation. Strangely, a few lines on in his own report, he more or less confirms the charge of death by exposure, as he describes the "old and infirm unable to live under the conditions to which they are exposed. Seven hundred are in tents. At Sinzig there are also old, crippled and infirm."

Again it is significant that Beasley reports a seemingly large number (700 people) under shelter, without saying that there were 90,000 more with no shelter at all.

"Running smoothly" or "well under control" as used by Beasley usually mean only one thing: that DDT has been dusted on the prisoners in order to prevent an outbreak of typhus, which would threaten prisoners, guards and the whole of Germany.[20] Beasley seems to be avoiding, as far as he can, telling the truth about what he has seen, probably because he deplored it yet could not bring himself to write down accusations against the army.

In that report, Beasley says he has ordered 1,600 blankets for the 9th Field Hospital at Lintfort, "supporting the PWTE at Rheinberg." Taking this U.S. Army surgeon at his word, one imagines a hospital at Lintfort which was taking in sick people from Rheinberg in a humane effort to save life. But there clearly was no proper hospital in Lintfort at that time, for the camp commander on the tenth of May, after much persuasion, reluctantly permitted a small area within the camp to be set aside for a few tents for the sick. After numerous pleas, he permitted Mrs Greta Schweitzer, Mrs Herte Brandt and Father Borgmann to convert houses in Lintfort into a hospital, provided that it be staffed, funded and run entirely by the civilian Germans. Later, some medicines were delivered, possibly only DDT.

Beasley, reporting what he heard on the telephone, perhaps did not know that many of the so-called U.S. Army "hospitals" were just dying grounds where terminally sick patients were hidden from the others and left to die without treatment, conveniently close to their graves.[21]

The pressures on Beasley to excuse, euphemize, *cover up*, were immense. His brother officers in the Medical Corps, who were doing a large-scale special survey of death and disease in these same camps, reported that the deaths totaled only 11 percent of what they had actually found.[22]

Beasley could not be accurate even if he wanted to be. The need to make a daily report, the long distances between the camps magnified by shattered roads, made it impossible for Beasley or anyone to inspect the camps every day. His report for April 30 covers more than a quarter of a million prisoners in two pages.

All he had were phone calls from harassed camp commanders who themselves did not want to put a polished boot into the infected mud inside the cages. The very gates at Remagen were posted "Typhus Fever, Keep Out," on Beasley's telephoned orders.[23]

The death rate for two days for Rheinberg and Remagen cited by Beasley[24] is so far under the figures reported by the prisoners, the corrected ETO survey, the 12th Army Group and by USFET (United States Forces, European Theater)*, that they cannot be reconciled. Either Beasley is right, or all the others are. Perhaps Beasley is beginning to break down here, to give in to the coverup which he cannot correct on his own. He would be tempted to take refuge in indifference because he must report what he knows cannot be true. Beasley is not responsible for these conditions: he is trying to cope with them, but he is beginning to despair. Of the major cause of death, dysentery, he says, "There must be proper mass sanitation. The standard deemed necessary with present supplies is impossible even to approach."[25] But at this date, April 30, he still obeys his training: he notes that he has filled out a requisition for medical supplies, which he apparently expects to be delivered to the camps, although they are a palliative, not a cure for the real physical causes — starvation, overcrowding, exposure.

It appears that Beasley soon realized that he was treating the symptoms, the camps, rather than the disease, cruel indifference. Within a couple of weeks, Beasley is noting of his earlier hopeful blanket request for the 9th Field Hospital, "Cots, blankets, field ranges and mess equipment needed badly for hospitals servicing PWTEs. QM has been contacted and claims none of these items available." Beasley is changing: before, atrocity noted by others was "alleged"; now he suspects it himself. The word of the superior officer who "claims" nothing is available is openly doubted. It seems that Beasley is weary of the cynical indifference of "high levels."[26]

Beasley did not protest, perhaps because he could not believe the cause of what he saw happening. People who feel no ill will seldom see it in others.

---

* This was the official title of the army in Europe. It was commanded by Eisenhower. It was a component of SHAEF until SHAEF disbanded on July 14, 1945.

5

SUMMER OF STARVATION

GENERAL EISENHOWER AND PRIME MINISTER Churchill talked about reducing prisoner rations on May 15. Churchill asked for an agreement on the scale of rations for prisoners, because he would soon have to announce cuts in the British meat ration. He wanted to make sure that "as far as possible they should be fed on those supplies which we could best spare." Eisenhower replied that he had already "given the matter considerable attention." He had been told that a scale of 2,150 calories was required, but he had already reduced this to 2,000. The scale for prisoners, he said, had for some time been lower than for Allied troops. (For U.S. troops, it was 4,000 calories per day.) He was planning to examine the whole thing further to see "whether or not a further reduction was possible."[1] He was talking about reducing rations for prisoners of war who were already dying of starvation under the eyes of U.S. Army doctors.[2]

Rations were reduced soon after this.[3] Some of the prisoners of war continued to get some food from U.S. and captured German stocks, but at a lower scale. A million others, who had been receiving at least some food because of their nominal POW status, lost their rights and their food when they were secretly transferred to the DEF status. These people got far less than the 2,000 calories mentioned by Eisenhower, in many cases far less than half.[4] What Eisenhower did not tell Churchill was that the army was not feeding the DEFs at all, or was feeding them far less than 2,000 calories per day, while reducing the rations to the POWs. "Operational rations C, K and 10 in 1 will be used only as a last resort," said the orders. "Every means of improvisation will be exhausted prior to their use." The 2,000 calories were the maximum at that date, and only to be supplemented from U.S. food if German sources failed, which they had already done in the 7th Army area around Munich and elsewhere.[5] These orders applied only to captives who were officially recognized as being "on hand."

The reclassification to DEF did not require any shift of men to new camps, or new organization to get German civilian supplies to them. The men stayed where they were, with no more shelter, or less. All that happened was that by the clatter of a typewriter, their skimpy bit of U.S. Army food was stopped.

Patton's was the only army in the whole Theater to release significant numbers of captives during May 1945, saving many of them from starvation. Both General Omar Bradley and Lee ordered the release of prisoners on May 13,[6] but a SHAEF order signed "Eisenhower" countermanded them on May 15.[7] As a result, the meticulous General Lee grew so worried about the famished state of the men for whom he was responsible that he fired off a challenging cable from his headquarters in Paris to SHAEF HQ in Frankfurt:

> This Headquarters is having considerable difficulty in establishing adequate basis for requisitioning rations for prisoners of war currently held in Theater. Prisoners on hand are in excess of estimated captures and in excess of numbers for which rations had been previously requisitioned from the Zone of Interior [the United States]. Present food situation both in Theater and Zone of Interior is extremely critical. Additional food supplies required to maintain minimum ration level for prisoners of war cannot be obtained from Zone of Interior without firm and

DECLASSIFIED PER EXECUTIVE ORDER 12356, SECTION 3.3, 795008
by RSW NARA, Date 9/23/87

C O N F I D E N T I A L

HEADQUARTERS
[redacted] EUROPEAN THEATER OF OPERATIONS
UNITED STATES ARMY
Office of the Theater Provost Marshal
APO 887

IN
JUN 1945
CHIEF SURGEON
APO 887
55603

Daily PW Report for 2 June 1945

	(as of)	Total on Previous Report	Since Last Report	Accumulated Totals to Date
1.a. Cptd by US 12 AG	18 May	2,561,895	No Report	2,555,556*
b. US Cpts 6 AG	10 May	684,128	No Report	684,128
(1) MTOUSA responsibility to 1 Nov '44				39,528
(2) ETOUSA responsibility 6409 in French Custody				638,391
c. Total ETOUSA responsibility US cpts				3,193,747
d. Evac to ZI by US	1 June	142,797		142,797
e. Net trfs to British	27 May	100,409	1	100,410
f. Trfd to French	27 May	31,450	1,374	32,824
g. Trfd to Other Allies	27 May	27,381		27,381
h. Trfd to Civil Auth	27 May	13,371	144	13,515
i. Repatriations fr ETO	27 May	1,920		1,920
j. Deaths	29 May	4,421	79	4,500
k. In US Custody, ETO		2,878,537		2,870,400*
2.a. Cptd by Br 21 AG	10 May	516,148	No Report	516,148

3. Status of 50-50 Ownership Agreement Com Z.

	(as of)	Total on Previous Report	Since Last Report	Accumulated Totals to Date
a. Trfd to Br by US	27 May	109,796	1	109,797
b. Trfd to US by Br	27 May	9,387		9,387

c. Balance on completed transfers US = 100,410 Br = 100,410
d. Credit to British on Account of Transfers to French 10,000
e. To equalize, on adjustment made 31 Dec 1944 for 42,622 Due Br 42,622 Due US
f. To equalize, on cpts & trfs as of this rpt. Due Br 2,228,389 Due US

4.a. Breakdown of PWs on hand in Com Z (as of 1800 hrs 1 June 1945):

	IN CENTRAL ENCLOSURES		IN LABOR CAMPS	IN HOSPITALS	TOTALS
	On Hand	Available for Labor			
Seine	51		11,299	213	11,563
Channel	25,187	4,128	19,013	748	44,948
Delta	68,260	1,981	54,017	3,768	126,045
Normandy	318,990	57,324	92,004	11,956	422,950
Oise	120,787	7,648	151,196	2,618	274,601
U.K.	3,022	863	24,653	3,887	31,562
TOTALS	536,297	71,944	352,182	23,190	911,669
	IN TRANSIENT ENCLOSURES				
ADSEC	754,400			42,951	
CONAD	244,457				
TOTAL	998,857				1,041,808

With armies, in transit, unreported in hospitals, etc. 916,923

GRAND TOTAL 2,870,400

For the Theater Provost Marshal:

Robt. J. Gill
ROBT. J. GILL,
Colonel, CMP,
Chief, PW Division.

OUT
THEATER PROVOST MARSHAL
USA

*Adjustment in accordance with revised report by SHAEF
CAPITULATED TROOPS
12 AG 1,101,177**
6 AG 84,534
21 AG 95,806
**Includes undetermined number of PWs.
Breakdown not available to date.

[redacted]
C O N F I D E N T I A L

Final report, this form, to be superseded by weekly report in accordance with Sec I, Circular 77, Com z, 27 May 1945

Last of the daily POW *reports of the U.S. Army Theater Provost Marshal, June 2, 1945, shows a total of 2,870,400 captives classified as prisoners of war, including those held by the 6th Army.* (U.S. National Archives)

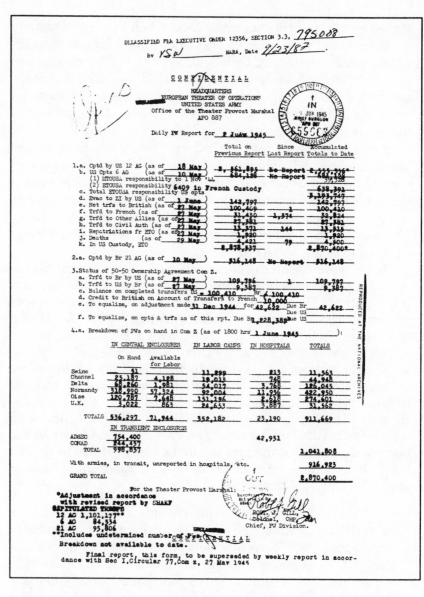

RESTRICTED

HEADQUARTERS
EUROPEAN THEATER OF OPERATIONS
UNITED STATES ARMY
Office of the Theater Provost Marshal
APO 887

61078

WEEKLY PW STATUS REPORT
Recapitulation as of 2 June 1945

1. US Capts (ETO) not including British, French nor 39,328 by MTOUSA in Southern France	3,193,747
2. Evacuated to ZI by US	142,797
3. Net transfers to British Ownership	100,480
4. Transferred to French Ownership	32,824
5. Transferred to other Allies, Special Nationals	29,511
6. Transferred to Civil Authorities	13,762
7. Repatriations	1,920
8. Deaths	4,790
9. Total due British under 50-50 Agreement	1,228,319

Weekly Report as of 2 June 1945

	Total on Previous Report	Since Last Report	Accumulated Totals From 2 June 1945
			Initial Report
1. Rec'd from Armies			
2. Rec'd from ZI			
3. Trfd to Fr. Ownership			
4. Trfd to Other Allies			
5. Trfd to Civil Auth.			
6. Deaths			
7. Trfd to Armies			
8. Trfd to Br. Ownership			
9. Discharges			
a. Miners			2,814
b. Agricultural			1,372
c. Transportation			744
d. Women			225
e. 50 yrs or over			443
f. Medical			
g. Civilian Police			1,001
h.			27,755*
i.			
		Total Discharges	34,354

10. PWs on hand in COM Z.

	IN CENTRAL ENCLOSURES	IN LABOR CAMPS	IN HOSPITALS	TOTALS
Seine	34	11,299	216	11,549
Channel	25,227	19,004	757	44,988
Delta	67,682	54,609	3,841	126,132
Normandy	329,055	92,165	11,754	432,974
Oise	124,599	152,370	2,616	279,585
U. K.	2,944	24,887	3,736	31,567
TOTALS	549,541	354,334	22,920	926,795

IN TRANSIENT ENCLOSURES

ADSEC	659,922	2,558	11,874	674,354 ✓
CONAD	225,325	9,526		234,851 ✓
TOTALS	885,247	12,084	11,874	909,205 ✓

11. Total PWs on hand in COM Z. 1,836,000

For the Theater Provost Marshal:

OUT
10 JUN 1945
THEATER PROVOST MARSHAL
HQ EUROPEAN T OF OPNS
US ARMY

*Breakdown by occupational category not available this date.

[redacted]

ROBT. J. GILL,
Colonel, CMP,
Chief, PW Division

RESTRICTED

First of weekly POW reports of U.S. Army Theater Provost Marshal, June 2, 1945, excludes over one million prisoners shown in the daily report for the same day. (U.S. National Archives)

Total Captured And On Hand in Europe as of June 2, 1945
(Discrepancies among U.S. Army reports)

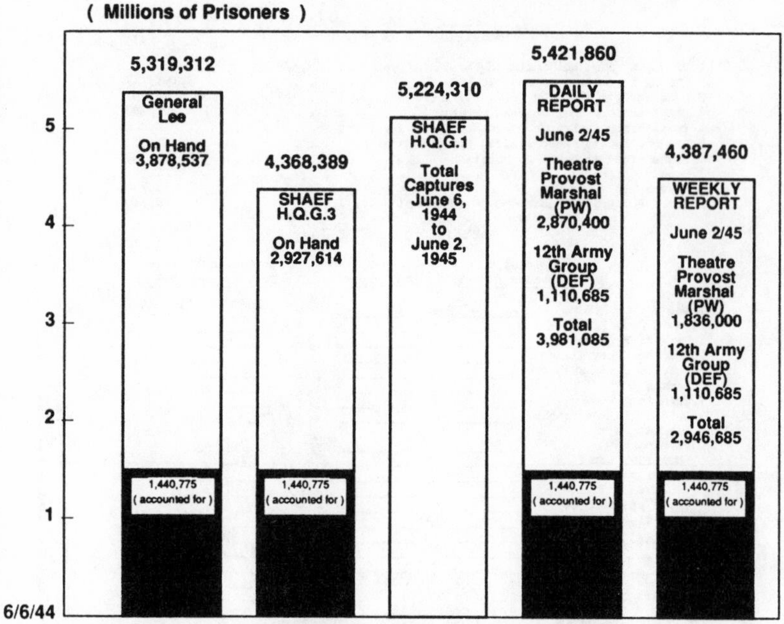

■ **Captured but no longer on hand in Europe (already accounted for) on June 2, 1945.**

[1] Evacuated/Transferred P.W.'s	353,728
[2] Transferred D.E.F.'s	456,408
[3] Other Losses D.E.F.'s	101,053
[4] Discharged P.W.'s & D.E.F.'s	529,586
TOTAL	1,440,775

sources:

1. Weekly POW Report, June 2, TPM. This was chosen instead of the total in the Daily Report because the higher Accounted For figure (at June 2) reduces the On Hand figure, thus leading to lower death estimates.
2. SHAEF G1 WO219/145 PRO.
3. 12 Army Group DEF Report June 2 1945 NARS Washington.
4. 12 Army Group DEF Report loc cit and SHAEF G3 Weekly PW and DEF report, Abileno.

> complete justification. Several requests have been made by this Headquarters for statement as to prisoners of war on hand . . . so that adequate basis could be established with War Department for placing requisitions for rations. In response to inquiries from this Headquarters . . . several varying statements of number of prisoners held in Theater have been published by SHAEF.

He then cites the latest SHAEF statement:[8]

> Cable . . . dated 31 May states 1,890,000 prisoners of war and 1,200,000 disarmed German forces on hand. Best available figures at this Headquarters show prisoners of war in Com Z 910,980, in Com Z transient enclosures 1,002,422 and in 12th Army Group 965,135, making a total of 2,878,537 and an additional 1,000,000 disarmed German forces GERMANY and AUSTRIA.[9]

The situation was astounding: Lee was saying there were *a million more men* in the U.S. Army camps in Europe than SHAEF would admit. Lee said there were 3,878,537 POWs and DEF; SHAEF G3 on the same day, June 2, issued its first table showing only 2,927,614 DEF and POWs "on hand." This went far towards defeating Lee's purpose of feeding the captives because it was this SHAEF G3 table that provided the basis for rationing the camps. We can actually see the captives disappear between two reports of the Theater Provost Marshal, issued on the same day. The last report of the daily series of the TPM says that there were 2,870,400 POWs on hand at June 2. The first report of the new weekly series, dated the same day, says that there were only 1,836,000 on hand. Lee was wrestling with the wind: SHAEF simply ignored his meticulous figurings. There was nothing more he could do. He had to base his issue of food on the number of prisoners on hand given him by SHAEF G3, even though he knew it was low by a million.[10] These missing million men are called henceforth "the Missing Million" to distinguish them from the other prisoners.

That was one way that rations were reduced. Another was through some strange doings in the army bookkeeping during

June and July, when men with POW status were secretly transferred to DEF status. Under the bizarre USFET bookkeeping practice of June – July, which was divided into weeklong periods ending at Saturday midnight, the closing balance for each week, which ought to be exactly the same as the opening balance for the following week starting one second later, differs by any number the bookkeeper found convenient. From June 2 through July 28, the transferred and discharged come to 588,533 more than the drop from those on hand at the beginning to those on hand at the end.* This "midnight shift" is deceitfully hidden from the casual observer, because the USFET tables do not give the opening balance each week, only the closing balance and the transactions producing it. So the innocent onlooker, assuming the opening balance is omitted as an unnecessary repetition, begins working with figures that can never come out right because hundreds of thousands of human beings are added or subtracted at the whim of the bookkeepers. Only when the figures are painstakingly checked category by category, week by week for many sets, does the deception slowly become apparent.

This supply of men did not come from the minds of the bookkeepers. They had no reason to invent fictitious captives, nor did they. Just as the DEF total rose although no new captures were made, so the prisoners of war on hand declined by far more than the discharges, which were the only shrinkage reported. During the period June 2 – July 28, the prisoners of war on hand shrank by 586,003 more than the discharges while those on hand in the DEF camps rose by 588,533.

This shift from the disastrous POW status to the catastrophic DEF status was made deliberately over many weeks, with careful attention to maintaining plausible balances in the weekly POW and DEF reports. The discrepancy between those "shifted" from POW status and those "received" in the DEF status is only 0.43 percent. So successful was this deception that it went undiscovered for seventeen years after the documents were opened to everyone in the world, including German scholars.

The effect of the policy conveyed by winks and nods —

* See Appendix 7.

without written orders — was first to mystify, then to frustrate, then to exhaust the middle-rank officers who had to cope with the deaths that resulted. This was neatly euphemized in the official *Army History of World War II* in the words: "ADSEC [Advance Section Communications Zone]was by this time [early May] fully aware that normal requisitioning methods would not promptly bring the required materiel and that captured stocks could not be expected from army sources without special pleading, and then only in token quantities."[11] Middle-rank officers in the field who were responsible for the POWs at first sent in their requisitions in the normal manner, but received in return far less than the minimum to maintain life. Colonel Smithers in the Quartermaster Section of Ad Sec wrote a personal plea to Quartermaster Robert Littlejohn on April 27: "Aside from the 750 tons received from Fifteenth Army, no subsistence has been received nor do I expect any. What desirable Class II and IV [rations] we have received has been entirely at the sufferance of the Armies, upon personal appeal and has been insignificant in relation to the demands which are being put upon us by the influx of prisoners of war. We have taken every means at our command to increase these amounts but with negligible results."[12] On May 23, Quartermaster Littlejohn told his good friend Bob Crawford, Assistant Chief of Staff, G4 (Supplies), "I do know I can not continue to feed 3,000,000 of these prisoners." He also reported that he could not supply the needed clothing and camp equipment such as tents, because the War Department had never furnished them. "In fact, a number of my requisitions have been disapproved." He does not say why he could not issue tents from the stocks on hand, which were plentiful.[13] He also asked his friend U.S. Army Major General Ray Barker at SHAEF to assign an assistant to study the problem.[14] On May 30, General Barker took up the cry, telling Eisenhower's Chief of Staff, Bedell Smith, that "the problem of feeding and maintenance of the very large numbers of Prisoners of War and disarmed German forces now in Allied hands has become acute."[15] That the evasion of responsibility by the shift of status was a forgettable fiction in the minds of the more realistic officers is seen here as Barker refers to the feeding of all the captives, not just prisoners of war. His recommendation, however, was not that they should be fed, but that they should be discharged. "Such disbandment must however, allow for the labor requirements of the United Nations for reconstruction work outside Germany."[16] Therefore, a cable was drafted to the Combined Chiefs of Staff urgently requesting a reply to an earlier cable to which there had been no response.

The next day, a cable signed "Eisenhower" remarked on the prisoner problem to Washington, pointing out that the British were not performing under the 50/50 prisoner-sharing agreement. The cable complained that they were liable for at least 935,000 Germans more than they had, and possibly many more. But it also contradicted itself in the next sentence, with the statement that "the U.S. has held for them an average of 150,000." The cable ends, "Urgently recommend . . . transfers to partially relieve a very serious situation."[17] On June 4, another cable signed with Eisenhower's name told Washington that "it is imperatively necessary to arrange for the early disposal" of large numbers of prisoners of war and disarmed enemy forces still held in Europe.[18] It is hard to understand what prompted this cable. No reason for it is evident in the massive cable traffic that survives in Abilene, London and Washington. Eisenhower himself had only a few days earlier prevented Bradley, Lee and Patton from releasing DEFs. Far from ordering Eisenhower to take or hold onto prisoners, the Combined Chiefs' message of April 26 had urged him not to take in any more prisoners even for labor after VE Day. Yet the army had taken in more than 2,000,000 DEF after that. There was no need to cable Washington for permission to discharge prisoners, for Patton had already discharged half a million men in twenty-seven days. If the whole U.S. Army had discharged prisoners at the same rate as Patton, all the Germans would have been gone by the end of June. But only about 500,000, or 10 percent, had been discharged by June 2. About 2,200,000 were discharged by September 8. The other 3,700,000 (of the total American take in all European theaters)[19] were still in the camps, or dead, or transferred to British or French custody.

Field Marshal Montgomery believed the Americans had

loaded themselves down with huge numbers of prisoners out of vainglory, not military necessity. When all Germany lay virtually defenseless before Bradley in April, he halted "the entire American effort of 12th Army Group to 'clean up' the Ruhr . . . allowing himself to be infected by the American pre-occupation with numbers of prisoners — bags — like some proud participant in a Scottish shoot."[20] Bradley wrote later: "My most pressing task [in early April] was to mop up the Ruhr. Fortunately, almost all the German forces inside the Ruhr pocket surrendered without a fight. The total bag by April 18 was double the Intelligence estimate: 317,000. This was a larger German force than the Russians had captured at Stalingrad, or than we had captured in Tunisia."[21]

For General Patton, taking prisoners was a sporting event, so he proudly counts in his book only those taken in war, not rounded up in peacetime, "although the numbers went into the millions."[22]

Eisenhower asked for more food on May 4[23]; then as it was arriving, he asked for permission to distribute it if he found it necessary, to avoid trouble in Germany that might be "prejudicial to military operations."[24] He referred to "the present critical shortage of food supplies not only in this Theater but also in the UNITED STATES, which has necessitated 10% reduction in rations of all officers, enlisted personnel and civilian employees."[25] The World Food Shortage was now supposed to be affecting not only the army but the whole of the United States, where in fact there were surpluses of wheat and corn higher than they had ever been, and production of potatoes higher than it had ever been.* The 100-day backlog of rations shown in the April report of the quartermaster in Europe was sufficient for for five million people at 4,000 calories per day.[26] The most important study of the situation, done in June by Lieutenant General A. E. Grasett for SHAEF, said that the "present food situation in Western Germany is critical. It is estimated however, that the 630,000 tons of imported wheat will meet the minimum food needs of German civilians prior to the next harvest."[27] There was no

* See Chapter 2, note 46.

doubt in Grasett's mind that the wheat was there to be requisitioned. In fact it was already arriving as previously planned, and continued to arrive that summer, as foreseen.

The supposed 10 percent reduction in the rations was a morsel of propaganda which fed the gullible, not the starving. No reduction in the army's allotment of 4,000 calories per day was noticed by Lieutenant Fisher, who recollected that "except for a few days at Bastogne, we had plenty of food all the time, as the G4 records show.[28] I never heard of a reduction in rations." Nor did Colonel Henry C. Settle, in replacement command of the 106th Division at Le Havre, who was in charge of 4,000 U.S. soldiers. "We had so much food we didn't know what to do with it," said Settle. "Our problem was cooking it."[29] The general records of the quartermaster confirm the individual experiences. There was a huge food surplus in the army[30] existing beside starvation in the camps. This surplus in the account for U.S. Army personnel actually grew during the period when Eisenhower said that rations for U.S. Army personnel were cut. The intake from U.S. and local (German) sources grew by 7 percent during this period.[31]

A few days after the flurry of cables telling Washington that food was short there was a meeting in the SHAEF Economics Branch to discuss the problem. High representatives of the army and the American Red Cross were looking for ways to get existing Red Cross food parcels to civilian Displaced Persons (DPs). Lieutenant Colonel Bailey at SHAEF said that SHAEF was not "in any desperate need of extra food stuffs," but that the situation in Europe in the winter was going to be difficult. There were 13,000,000 Red Cross food parcels in Europe, each of which could provide 500 calories per person per day for one month.[32] In addition the French had 1,600,000 not counted in the general pool.

Far from depriving itself of food to feed the starving masses of Europe, by early July the army was in fact taking food from Europeans, including Czechs and Germans, nominally to feed prisoners, but in fact for its own purposes. The procurement figures of the quartermaster general[33] show that although in June the army issued slightly more rations (5,000) per day than it requisitioned from U.S. and local sources for the POWs, during July it was running a huge daily surplus on the prisoner account. From "U.S. and local procurement," the army took in 2,500,000 more rations per day in July on the prisoner account than it issued to the prisoners. In August, this rose to 3,000,000 per day.[34] This phrase "local procurement" refers to the army's requisitioning of food from Germans, which was causing massive shortages. Refugees were starving as a result, according to the ICRC.[35] Lieutenant Colonel Bacque of the French army in the French-occupied zone of Germany received an outraged report from one of his units that a raiding party of Americans had seized 100 sheep from the local villagers.[36] The State Department complained to the War Department in June that at Domazlice and Hosfoun in Czechoslovakia, 100,000 tins of meat, many tons of dried peas, and sugar, cattle and 700 stud horses had been confiscated as booty.[37] The situation was summarized by an objective observer, M. Layeillon, a French diplomat who reported to Paris that "the [authorities among the] Allies have closed their eyes to the requisitions made for the provisioning of troops stationed in Germany . . . . These come to a very considerable total."[38]

General Littlejohn himself said it was urgent and essential to protect "indigenous stocks [of German food] which are being rapidly depleted, and a serious shortage is anticipated during the winter and early spring." In August Littlejohn repeated exactly what Lee had said in May: the army was reporting fewer prisoners than it had. After an extensive tour in his train through the army areas to find out what was going on, Littlejohn concluded, in a long memorandum[39] written for the commanding general of the Theater Service Forces on August 27, that the army's data were so "inaccurate" that the true number of people to be fed was higher than reported by 1,550,000 people. "[They] total 5,250,000 as compared with the official requisitioning basis of 3,700,000," he wrote. It was necessary to study holdings of POWs and the army's needs for labor in the Theater to replace U.S. personnel going home. Only thus could an "authoritative basis" be made for requisitioning rations from the United States. He "strongly recommends" that "accurate data as to the number of PWs, disarmed Germans, displaced persons and civilians who are a responsibility of the American forces be assembled and published so that proper action may be taken in the ration requisitions prepared by my office. This should include . . . a factual statement of those who are our responsibility." The 960,000 DPs in the U.S. zone "are being fed from indigenous stocks supplemented by issues from civil affairs stocks [which were themselves partly derived from 'local procurement']."[40] Littlejohn expresses concern about shortages *only* in Germany; he mentions no shortage anticipated or existing in the army, Zone of the Interior, or the world. The army had so much food that when a whole warehouse-full was dropped from the supply lists by accident in England, it was not noticed for three months.[41] Approximately 6 percent of the permanent surplus of army rations in Europe would have supplied enough food (an extra 1,300 calories per day) to keep alive for 100 days 800,000 people in the camps who were starving in the midst of plenty. The obstacle that stood in the way of getting food to the prisoners was still the inaccurate rationing figures — although this had already been noticed in Lee's rocket of June 2, which attempted to correct it. Littlejohn's memo — decisive, well-written and urgent — once again recommends clearing up the problem by clearing up the figures. In August as in June, this high-level effort had no effect on the rationing in the camps. The death rate among the newly-created DEFs continued to rise through September 8.

The squalor of the camps came from the moral squalor polluting the higher levels of the army. These officers were so cynical about the prisoners that while they were writing their anxious memos, presumably to absolve themselves of blame, if it ever came,[42] their underlings in at least six cases refused to let German civilians bring food to the people in the camps.[43] Lieutenant Fisher was told by several German women that they had been refused permission to take food to their husbands in the camps near Frankfurt in the summer of 1945. Ten-year-old Herbert Thelen at Rheinberg was the only civilian permitted to bring food to that camp. The prisoners starving in three U.S.

Army camps at Dietersheim taken over by the French Army in July 1945 had never been supplied from local sources — which were abundant at the time.[44] The most damaging ban, covering all the U.S. camps, was imposed by the War Department against the mailing of Red Cross parcels to the prisoners.[45] This ban was extended to cover even donations which the German prisoners in the USA wanted to make to help clothe and feed prisoners in the camps in Europe. The Germans in the U.S. were forbidden by the Secretary of the Treasury, Frederick M. Vinson, to specify that any gifts they made to the Red Cross would be delivered to the European prison camps.[46]

The refusal of mail was the refusal of life, just as it would have been to Allied prisoners in German hands during the war, when much of their food arrived via mail from the Red Cross. Surplus food parcels which the Red Cross had gathered in various countries were confiscated by SHAEF.[47] In any case, the army had imposed a limit on the amount of food that could be provided from German sources for the men in the DEF camps. "These men are authorized a maximum of 1,150 calories per day for non-workers and 1,850 calories for workers."[48] This was sentencing them to death in a fairly short time, especially considering the lack of shelter and clean water.

The shortage of goods in Germany was caused partly by the prevention of manufacture for export trade which could have been quickly re-established: Germany still had about 75 percent of her manufacturing capacity in operation on May 8. Some of the shortage was caused by the imprisonment or death of so many potential workers. Coal was lacking for processing the crops that were coming in; so was transport and field labor. In the British zone, which was by far the most devastated and populous, the German crops of wheat and rye were coming in at a surprisingly high rate, over 70 percent of normal, mainly because the British rapidly discharged prisoners to help with the harvest during Operation Barleycorn.[49]

On August 4, when the captives still on hand in the U.S. camps were only about 50 percent of the total captured, because of death, discharge or transfer, a one-sentence order signed "Eisenhower" condemned all prisoners to the worst possible conditions. "Effective immediately all members of the German forces held in U.S. custody in the American zone of occupation in GERMANY will be considered as disarmed enemy forces and not as having the status of prisoner of war."[50] No reason is given. For the POWs now being treated like DEFs, the death rate quadrupled within a few weeks, from 0.2 percent per week to 0.8 percent for the week ending September 8.[51]

Eisenhower had deplored the Germans' useless defense because of the waste of life. But Germans were dying far faster now that they had surrendered than they had during the war. At least 10 times as many Germans died in the French and American camps as were killed in all the combat on the western front in northwest Europe from June 1941 to April 1945.[52]

A vicious indifference spread downwards into all the guard personnel and even into the Medical Corps doctors assigned to the camps. While massive surpluses of food went unused, 4,000-calorie officers visited the camps asking for details about the dead. In their general report of the survey, the doctors specified with excruciating precision the causes of death, which could only have been obtained in many cases by autopsy of the famished, stinking, dangerous corpses.[53] Except in the death totals, these reports have the coherent detail of authenticity, undistracted by any note of sympathy, outrage or horror. The doctors were not responsible for the conditions, only for examining the effects in odious detail. They note the incidence of intimate symptoms in the living such as Vincent's angina, scabies, gingivitis, all culled from visits to camps holding 80,583 men during May. In camps along the Rhine, between May 1 and June 15, 1945, the Medical Corps officers recorded a horrendous death rate, 80 times as high as anything they had ever observed in their lives. They efficiently totted up the causes of death: so many from dysentery and diarrhea, so many from typhoid fever, tetanus, septicemia, all at rates unheard of since the middle ages. Medical terminology itself was strained by the catastrophe to which they were witnesses: people were reported dead of "emaciation" and "exhaustion." The three main killers were diarrhea and dysentery (treated as one category), cardiac disease and pneumonia. As the survey prepared by these doctors shows, other causes directly attributable to exposure, over-crowding and lack of sanitation were important killers as well.[54] The ETO doctors found that only 9.7 percent to 15 percent of the prisoners had died of causes clearly associated with lack of food, such as emaciation and dehydration, and "exhaustion." Others died of diseases caused by the foul exposed conditions which were undoubtedly exacerbated by starvation. As the report noted, "In evaluating these data, consideration must be given to the age groups of the prisoners. Their ages ranged from fourteen (14) to well over fifty (50). Many were captured in an exhausted state. Others were formerly hospital patients. Exposure, overcrowding of pens and lack of food and sanitary facilities all contributed to these excessive rates."[55] The surveying doctors were calm in their knowledge that "former patients" like young Heinz T. were taken from their hospital beds and sent sick and half-naked into barbed wire cages to sleep in the mud, while thousands of beds in the same hospitals went empty.[56]

In the figures for the so-called hospitals,[57] the ETO survey doctors noted rates for many diseases, but none for "exhaustion" or malnutrition. The widespread diseases were common respiratory conditions, diarrhea and dysentery, accounting for some 85 percent of the so-called admissions. These derived much more from filth and exposure than from starvation.

These data were taken from the POW camps, not from the DEF camps, it must be remembered, so it is plain that as early as May 1 the prisoners of war, who apparently were the best treated, were already exposed to conditions that killed them at the rate of over 30 percent per year.[58] No trace of any study of causes of death among the DEFs has been found, but it is clear from the evidence of survivors that the conditions were similar to those in the POW camps examined by the ETO Medical Survey, except that they were worse nutritionally.[59]

The doctors noted laconically, "The situation in these camps was typical of enclosures in the other commands."[60]

Other officers looked indifferently on the dying prisoners in their traps. The dim-witted General Hollar, provost marshal of the Advance Section, Communications Zone, discussed the situation in the prisoner of war temporary enclosures at a meeting on May 28. He opened the meeting with the statement that the reports from the 106th Division showed progress. "The overall population will drop some 25,000 on this day's report on account of evacuation, discharges, losses etc."[61] However, the reports later issued by his own provost marshal office for that day show no discharges, no evacuations, and a maximum of transfers to the French of 1,374.[62] The provost marshal's reports are so sloppily done that it is impossible to say from reference to them if Hollar's predicted decline ever took place, but in the four days May 27 – 30, no drop occurred of the size reported by Hollar.

At the same meeting under Hollar, burials at Rheinberg on the 27th, presumably for men who died on the 26th, were reported to be 10, at Sinzig 32, at Bingen 24 (meaning annual burial rates* of 6.7 percent up to 27 percent). The term "burial" may have been a euphemism for burial in common graves[63] because the figures for POW deaths are different in the provost marshal report. These were for May 25–26 either zero or 191, depending on which page of the TPM (theater provost marshal) report you believe. The report offers both figures: but at Hollar's meeting the reported burials total 66. Also, in the reports from Hollar's provost marshal office, deaths which had been originally reported as 156 for May 26 were corrected soon to only 60. The one comment of General Hollar on these whirling death totals was, "I wonder whether or not Sinzig has received the supply of Physcological [*sic*] Warfare newspapers in the last couple of days. Will you check?" To a colonel in charge of the fatally absent supplies, he said, "Was there anything at that meeting yesterday, G4, that would be of interest to this meeting?" And Colonel Lockett replied, "Nothing of interest."

The quality of thought given to the problem may be seen in the exchange between Colonel Stedman and General Hollar. Stedman remarked that the 106th Division had been ordered to release prisoners in categories that "include almost every PW."

* The annual rate is given only so the reader can compare with other statistics. (A single day's figure cannot normally be extrapolated to a year.)

He asks, "I wonder if we are not bogging the Division down?" General Hollar appears not even to notice what Stedman is saying, because he replies that the 106th has been advised of the definition of categories, missing completely the point that the release of almost all the prisoners has apparently just been ordered. Then he adds "I would be willing to let them get their machinery set up before bogging them down." To which Colonel Viney adds that they also had "a large amount of civilians" on hand. Hollar says that the civilians will be evacuated as soon as there is a report about them. The report was never written or else never implemented, because civilians, including women and children, were still in these camps when the French started taking them over in July and August. In the midst of chaos, General Hollar stood firm for the status quo.

Lieutenant R. H. Burbage wrote of a visit to Charles von Luttichau's camp that "the Surgeon and Chief of Preventive Medicine returned yesterday from a two (2) day trip to the REMAGEN PWTE [prisoner of war temporary enclosure]. It was found that a large number of prisoners had been located deep in foxholes from which they had not moved for days either to report on sick call or to eat." The report goes on to enumerate various remedies that were planned, but not taken.[64]

Rumors of the devastation in the camps ran through the army, making every man shun them if he could. "Boy, those camps were bad news," said B. K. Zobrist, a technical sergeant in the Medical Corps. "We were warned to stay as far away from them as we could, because they were so badly organized and short of supplies."[65]

The censorship imposed by SHAEF after VE Day was stricter than it had been during the actual fighting. The *New York Times* argued vigorously with this policy in a front page news story on May 27: "The American people are being deprived of information to which they are entitled . . . . It seems almost as though now that there is no enemy to fight, high Army officers are spending a large part of their time writing directives to circumscribe the movements and activities of war correspondents."

Eisenhower was fairly open about this. "I have always considered as quasi-staff officers, correspondents accredited to my headquarters," he told a meeting of American newspaper editors.[66] "This wasn't good journalism," said Charles Lynch, the Canadian war correspondent. "It wasn't journalism at all."[67]

By the end of May more people had died in the U.S. camps than died in the atomic blast at Hiroshima. Not a word reached the press.

6

KEEPING HELP AWAY

THE UNITED STATES GOVERNMENT REFUSED to allow the International Committee of the Red Cross inside the camps to visit the prisoners, in direct defiance of American obligations under the Geneva Convention. The ICRC, under the Convention, was supposed to visit the POWs in their camps, then report in secret to the Holding Power and to the Protecting Power. When the German government began to disintegrate toward the end of the war, the United States authorized the Swiss government to take over from the Germans the role of Protecting Power,[1] thus apparently ensuring that the ICRC would continue to visit the camps and report to the Swiss government after the war. This was what had to be stopped. The first day when it was possible to do this was May 8, VE Day, when the German government was abolished. The State Department note[2] telling the Swiss minister in Washington that his government had been dismissed as Protecting Power was dated May 8. With this done, the State Department was able to inform the ICRC that there was no point to continued visits, as there was no

Protecting Power to report to. Only a few days after the end of the war, Marshall signaled to Eisenhower that "there is no longer any protecting power representing German interests. Hence matters pertaining to German prisoners of war cannot be forwarded."[3] In its haste, the State Department was ignoring the fact that the Swiss government was already the Protecting Power to whom the ICRC was reporting. The disappearance of the German government made the role of the Protecting Power more necessary, not less, but the State Department paid no attention to that. Nor was there any mention of the U.S.-British requirement, so embarrassing to the French, that the French government observe the Geneva Convention for prisoners transferred to them for reparations labor. While ignoring the Convention completely, the State Department airily told the Swiss that the U.S. would continue to treat the prisoners "in accordance with the provisions of the Geneva Convention."[4] This ambivalent attitude, eliminating the Convention while confirming it, was typical of the way that the State and War Departments double-crossed the ICRC and the Swiss government about the Convention throughout 1945 and some of 1946.

This policy had catastrophic consequences for the Germans. Lost to the prisoners was the crucial right to tell impartial observers in private what was happening to them.[5] Now that the Allied prisoners had been released, the only protection for the German prisoners, apart from the fundamental decency of the Allied commanders, was the public opinion of the West. Because the State Department, the War Department and SHAEF knew that this opinion was critically dangerous they moved swiftly and secretly together to cut it off.

The western reporting from Germany was heavily censored and biased, allowing the business in both the POW and DEF camps to be conducted in a secrecy that was maintained against all but the victims for many years. One other important right disappeared with the Swiss, the right to mail, which abolished the only chance the prisoners had to get sufficient food as well as the right to give news of themselves and get news of home.[6] No news would leak out of the camps to impartial observers. Little help could get into the camps.

The only important protest on the Allied side against the removal of the ICRC came from the prime minister of Canada, William Lyon Mackenzie King. After discussions with Anthony Eden at the United Nations founding conference in San Francisco in May, he protested in writing to the Foreign Office in London that he didn't want the Swiss to be removed from the role of Protecting Power. King argued, "There is implicit in the Convention the assumption that prisoners of war will always have a protecting power to whom they can submit complaints and enquiries. It is an advantage to the Detaining Power that there should be a neutral agent to deal with the prisoners . . . as well as that there should be a clear record that there has been no misuse of arbitrary power by the Detaining Power." He told the Foreign Office that he wanted the Swiss to "continue to interest themselves in the welfare of German prisoners of war and internees in Canada until such time as there may be a German government." If the Swiss weren't interested in that, he continued, then he wanted them to detach the responsible officer to continue surveys unofficially. He concluded, "May I add that the Canadian government is encouraged to make this request of the Swiss government because of the unfailing interest which the Swiss government have always shown in humanitarian activities and the zeal with which their representatives have continued in all countries during the past years of conflict to carry out their humanitarian missions."[7]

The ingenious colonial was quickly squelched by the British, who patiently pointed out that the USSR, UK, USA and the French provisional government had all agreed that the German government was to be extinguished. To leave alive even an ember such as provisional representation of POW interests by the Swiss might be dangerous. What it would be dangerous to, of course, were the French and American governments. With dignified condescension, W. St. C. H. Roberts, Esquire, C.M.G., M.C., of the Foreign Office in London, pointed out that everything to do with policy towards Germany depended on "the disappearance of the German government" as if it had fallen into a hole. This entailed the assumption by the governments of the UK, USSR, France and the USA of "supreme authority with respect to Germany including all the powers possessed by the German government." Any inconsistency of position would flaw the legal arrangement, according to the FO. "These reasons, as you see, are of a general nature, and apply as much to the protection of the interests of the German prisoners of war as to that of other German interests." How high the Foreign Office balloon floated over rough reality is displayed here in the blithe assumption that the Canadians would believe that the Germans were better protected by their enemies than by themselves. W. St. C. H. Roberts didn't seem to realize that he was advancing the notion that removal of safeguards for the victims was for the good of the victims. Considering what was happening to the prisoners in Rheinberg and Thorée, there can be hardly any doubt that these squeamish legalisms were advanced cynically to protect the Americans and French, not the German prisoners. Roberts neglected to discuss with Mackenzie King the odd fact that the U.S. government, which insisted on receiving reports of the ICRC visits to the prisoners transferred from the U.S. to French camps, had assumed the role of the Protecting Power, keeping alive that dangerous ember of German government.

The cynicism of Roberts's letter was revealed within a few months in a statement in the British House of Commons by the under-secretary of state for foreign affairs who said that "Germany has not ceased to exist as a state, though the exercise of supreme authority in Germany has been assumed by the Allied Powers. His Majesty's Government consider that it is right that the standards of the Geneva Convention should, so far as practicable in present circumstances, continue to apply to German prisoners."[8]

Regardless of the complicated shenanigans with the Convention, the British and the Canadians preserved the POW status and humane treatment of virtually all Germans who were held in Canada or the UK. The Americans did not preserve the right of the small number of prisoners they held in the USA, UK and Italy to visits from the Red Cross, but in general, these prisoners were well treated. Questioned by the ICRC, the U.S. replied that it had no intention of treating the prisoners other than in strict accordance with the Convention.[9] The doubletalk went on, to prevent help reaching civilian Germans as well. The ICRC was in a double bind: if it made a public protest about the treatment of the prisoners, or about the dismissal of the Protecting Power, then the Allies might retaliate by forbidding them to help POWs or civilians elsewhere. The ICRC confined itself to private protests, so the Allies were able to ignore it.[10] As late as February 1946, the ICRC — along with other relief agencies — was still prevented by the U.S. from "bringing help to German children and sick persons in the U.S. zone."[11]

The U.S. War Department, according to Charles Fairman, a colonel in the International Law section of the Judge Advocate General's division, was still maintaining "the theory that the Geneva Convention is still applicable, although the German Armed Forces have surrendered unconditionally and the German government has been extinguished." But Fairman was not satisfied. "On the other hand, the War Department has authorized action which implies a departure from some of the requirements of the Convention. The PW is certainly not being fed a ration 'equal in quantity and quality to that of troops of base camps.'"

Fairman lived up to his name at least in his letter. He finished ringingly with point 15: "The German nation — civilians, disarmed German units and prisoners of war — are now in the hands of the allied nations. They should be treated justly and according to an intelligent and consistent plan. If as this section has argued from the first, not all the provisions of the Geneva Convention are applicable to this new situation, it is nonetheless true that our system of control should be rational and fair. The legal situation at the moment has become so confused that it is difficult to give sound advice on problems that are referred to this section for an opinion. It is believed therefore the entire matter should be reviewed in order that the policies to be pursued may be rational, just and based upon some consistent theory."[12] Nobody paid any attention to Fairman.

As the French, American, British and Canadian prisoners numbering about 2,000,000 were leaving German barbed wire for freedom that spring, the Red Cross was there to welcome them with food parcels drawn from the millions still in storage in their warehouses in Switzerland. The returning prisoners thanked the Red Cross for saving their lives with the food parcels mailed to them in the camps. From the Germans they had received about 1,500 calories per day. Another life-saving 2,000 arrived by mail, mainly from France, Canada and the USA. French families for years had deprived themselves to mail parcels to their 1,500,000 soldiers imprisoned in Germany. Production of these parcels ceased in the USA in April 1945, while roughly 10,000,000 were still in the pipeline from the USA to Europe.[13]

The effectiveness of the Red Cross care was demonstrated in a single figure: over 98 percent of the captured men were coming home safe, according to a news release of the American Red Cross in May 1945.[14] They were in good health thanks not only to the food but also the clothing and medicine which had arrived safely by mail.

Other relief agencies such as the YMCA, the Unitarians, various church groups and the American Friends Service Committee (the Quakers) were also attempting to send teams into Germany. The British Friends and the national Red Cross Societies from Britain, France and Canada by now all had observers or workers helping civilians in their zones of Germany, but the U.S. Army informed American relief teams that they could not go into the U.S. zone.[15] U.S. teams which were already in Europe working in France, Italy or Belgium suddenly found that they were no longer allowed to buy gasoline or tires for their trucks from the U.S. Army, which had been selling them supplies all through the war.[16] The U.S. zone of Germany was closed to all relief shipments until December 1945, when a slight relaxation came into effect.[17]

In response to questions about this policy, the U.S. Army informed the relief agencies that it had taken on the role of supplier of relief to German civilians in the U.S. zone. The question of relief to the prisoners was not allowed to arise, because none of the relief agencies was allowed to know what the situation was. The army said that in the future, under an army-sponsored agency, Council for Relief Agencies Licensed to Operate in Germany (CRALOG), relief agencies might be allowed to carry out their functions. In the meantime, the army would carry on alone, until the United Nations Relief and Rehabilitation Agency (UNRRA) could get rolling. Neither CRALOG nor UNRRA contributed anything to relief of German civilians in 1945. UNRRA was in any case treated as an agency of the U.S. Army, completely subject to army control.

The U.S. War Department had banned[18] all mail to or from all German prisoners of war in U.S. hands on May 4, 1945, so that when the International Committee of the Red Cross suggested[19] a plan for restoring mail to the prisoners in July, it was rejected. While the Red Cross was prevented from sending food into the U.S. camps as it had to camps for Allied prisoners in Germany, the British re-opened mail communications in July–August.[20]

The ICRC in Geneva believed at first that the destruction of Nazism with the success of the democracies would improve the situation of all the prisoners in Europe.[21] They also expected to step in to help the millions of homeless men, women and children in central Europe, especially in Germany. One of the first ominous signs of the future came curiously from North America, where their delegation reported that German prisoners' rations had been cut as soon as the Allied prisoners had been released.[22] Then, in late May or early June, the International Committee of the Red Cross loaded two freight trains with food from their warehouses in Switzerland, where they had over 100,000 tons in storage.[23] They sent these trains via the normal route prescribed by the German government during the war, one to Mannheim and one to Augsburg, both in the American sector. The trains reached their destinations, where the officials accompanying them were informed by U.S. Army officers that the warehouses were full and the train would have to return. They were returned full to Switzerland. Puzzled, Max Huber, the head of the International Committee of the Red Cross, began inquiries.

After a long investigation, in August Huber finally wrote to the State Department perhaps the most wounding letter the Red

Cross has ever sent to a major power. It was couched in language that was remarkably tolerant, considering the situation. Huber referred to the Red Cross food trains that were returned to Switzerland full in the spring of 1945 on the orders of SHAEF.

Huber said:

> When hostilities in Europe ceased, the International Committee of the Red Cross made every effort to improve the situation of prisoners of all categories whose status after the liberation by the Allied Armies became that of "ex prisoner of war." Anticipating the difficulties which would result from these circumstances, the Committee hoped to alleviate as much as possible the hardships of the former internee by working out a relief scheme with the Allied military authorities which, while bringing a considerable measure of aid, would also prove to be a rational means of liquidating the accumulated stocks in Switzerland and other countries.
>
> [He outlined the difficulties placed by SHAEF in the way of the International Red Cross in attempting to help United Nations displaced personnel — that is, all non-Germans.]
>
> Meanwhile, the numerous communications from Allied officers in charge of assembly areas and camps for Displaced Persons; the reports of our delegates on medical missions in Germany; and especially the many direct requests addressed to us from the Camps themselves, bear witness to the fact that tens if not hundreds of thousands of displaced persons in Germany are still in dire need of aid. From all this we are bound to recognize that the demands made upon the Anglo-American pool by the competent sections of the Allied armies are not proportionate to the prevailing need . . . . In consequence, the humanitarian work of the International Committee is in danger of becoming discredited.* Our responsibility for the proper use of relief supplies placed in our care is

* The common report in one part of Germany was that "the Red Cross can do nothing" for the prisoners or civilians. (Author's interview with Peter Hoffman, 1988, who lived near a camp in Germany in 1945. Professor Hoffman now lives in Montreal.)

incompatible with a restriction to the fulfilment of orders which render us powerless to furnish relief which we ourselves judge necessary.

The anticipated requisitions either were not made at all, or else came in with much delay. Having effected delivery with our own trains in Germany in default of those promised by the Allied armies in Germany but never placed at our disposal, we would then find that the receiving personnel at the various destinations were without proper instructions as to the handling of these consignments. If the warehouse happened to be full, our trains would be refused there in turn. That the warehouses were still filled to overflowing was proof positive that the distributions in view of which previous requisitions had been made were still in abeyance. (Experiences made in Mannheim and Augsburg)* . . . The Allied authorities' dispositions . . . of Anglo-American stocks . . . have failed to achieve relief in reasonable proportion to the extent of these stocks and degree of transport facilities available.

Practical experience showed . . . that in consequence of the general food shortage caused by the occupation army's normal requisitions and the dislocation of transport, the [armies] were unable to allot even a minimum ration to the Balts, Bulgarians, Hungarians, Italians, Rumanians and *apatrides* [stateless people] on German territory.

Thus, stating our case fully to the governments and Red Cross Societies concerned, we desire to stress the fact that the conditions set forth above leave us no alternative but to express our grave concern for the immediate future. To stand passively by whilst holding large quantities of immediately available relief supplies and knowing the plight of many camps of Displaced persons of all categories in Germany, growing steadily more alarming, is not compatible with the tradition of our institution.[24]

Albert E. Clattenburg at the State Department recommended that Huber's letter be passed on without comment to the army.

* Huber means that these incidents occurred in these cities.

Months later a response to Huber arrived in Washington, filled with evasions and misinformation. Signed "Eisenhower," it told the army chief of staff in November that the army's agreement with the American and British Red Crosses prohibited use of Red Cross food for enemy personnel.[25] No such prohibition appears in the agreement. In fact, the British were already feeding everyone regardless of nationality, drawing on their share of thirteen million parcels, each one enough to feed one person for one week.[26] Referring to Red Cross "food stocks in Switzerland which have not yet been required," the writer grandly pretended to offer help to the ICRC who he said were "anxious to liquidate warehouses in Switzerland," — as if the liquidation of warehouses were the purpose of the Red Cross.

The charge that the ICRC lacked an agreement to work in Germany was incorrect. The ICRC had an agreement with UNRRA, the agency authorized by the U.S. Army to licence relief to non-Germans in Germany.[27] This work was recognized by the authority on refugees, Malcolm J. Proudfoot, who wrote, "These voluntary relief agencies made a very valuable contribution to the welfare work done and in the provision of supplies for the displaced persons in western zones of Germany and Austria."[28]

The author of the deceitful USFET message to Marshall also professed ignorance of Huber's difficulties, saying: "Reference Mister HUBERS statement that he has been unable to obtain authorization to use part of pooled stock to meet needs of ex-enemy Displaced Persons of non-German nationality in Germany, no knowledge here of any such request from International Committee Red Cross. If such request were received it could not be considered favorably since use Red Cross supplies by enemy or ex-enemy persons prohibited by agreement." This was certainly not true for the agreement of June 15 among SHAEF, the British Red Cross and the American Red Cross, which specifically stated that "the parcels are intended to be distributed in due course through . . . military channels to DPs or in emergency to other recipients after consultation with" the Red Cross. In another section the agreement also said that the parcels might be given "in emergency to other recipients."[29] If there were some other agreement not to feed starving people because of their nationality, which was against all the traditions of the Red Cross, it was surely imposed on them by the army which banned all relief intended for Germans. In any case, the British program was already at work for 40 nationalities in Germany, without excluding Germans.[30] The USFET message comes very close to a harsh libel of all the Red Crosses, with its implication that the Red Cross had agreed to withhold food from starving people. Huber's letter precisely and strongly contradicted this, saying that owing to the severe "restriction to the fulfilment of orders which render us powerless to furnish relief," the humanitarian work of the Red Cross had been compromised and was in danger of being discredited because "hundreds of thousands of displaced persons in Germany are still in dire need of aid, [while the Red Cross was holding] large quantities of immediately available relief supplies."[31]

Huber was now forced to return the food to its original donors, because the army refused to distribute it. There was so much of this food that it would take thousands of train cars to return it to its sources in Paris and Brussels. He apologized for clogging the rail system of France with this unnecessary work. He also had to ask for extra trucks, beyond the 500 belonging to the ICRC in Geneva, to take away from Geneva over 30,000 tons of stock for return to the original donors.[32]

USFET, over Eisenhower's signature, calmly ignored everything that Huber was saying, although he was only reporting the experiences of people who had nothing to gain, and a lot to lose, by slandering the U.S. Army or Eisenhower. Marshall was told by USFET that "Movements from International Committee Red Cross warehouse SWITZERLAND were discontinued owing to insufficient transportation and covered storage space and availability of sufficient stocks in GERMANY and Liberated Areas to meet current requirements."[33] These blithe lies prompted no response from Marshall, or any further correspondence that has survived.

The "World Food Shortage" had now become the Red Cross Food Surplus.

For the crucial months until November while Eisenhower was military governor of the U.S. zone of Germany, the army made it difficult if not impossible for welfare of any kind to reach Germans. Eisenhower's correspondence with Clarence E. Pickett, executive secretary of the American Society of Friends (Quakers), which has survived the purging of the papers in the forties, fifties and seventies, shows clearly how the punishment policy was spread to German civilians. Pickett asked permission for the Quakers to come to Germany to do service and relief work, at which they were very experienced, having helped refugees including Jews and political prisoners destined for the death camps of the east. The Quakers wanted to go to Germany to feed children, and to reunite them with their parents if possible. They intended to find adoptive parents for the many orphans, because, Pickett argued, the children were the main hope for the future of Germany. Eisenhower passed the request up the line to Marshall in Washington, asking, in effect, to be ordered to refuse permission: "It appears unwise to complicate the organization for German welfare by placing certain responsibilities in the hands of American Civilian Agencies, which will require to be supported by the army .... While it is realized that such organizations as the American Friends Service Committee have demonstrated in the past their ability to handle such matters of public welfare and that they have trained staffs of relief personnel . . . it is believed that German Public Welfare Agencies should be charged with this duty."[34]

So vengeance assumed the name of duty. In order to keep Quakers from helping children, Eisenhower invokes the "duty" of the Germans to do what they were prevented from doing. The "German Agencies" that he mentioned to Marshall did not exist, because they were forbidden or drastically curtailed in the U.S. zone of Germany and remained so for over a year. "Strictly speaking, there is no German Red Cross," because it had been abolished by the Allies, said a Red Cross representative at a meeting in Geneva in January 1946.[35] The Germans in the American zone had made three attempts to re-establish it, all of which had failed, according to a second American delegate. But in the French and British zones, both the ICRC and the local

German Red Cross were operating. In any case, the Germans generally were already starving on official rations of less than 1,550 calories per day, which they did not get in full,[36] so they couldn't find enough food for children, future or not. As for the load on the army, which then numbered over a million men, the Quakers were only proposing to send a few dozen workers. At the end of his message to Marshall, Eisenhower gives us an idea of what he really thinks of these arguments he has just advanced, by marking his cable "Confidential" — "Because matters of this kind may react on American public opinion, would like to have a statement of War Department policy to guide me in handling this and other requests of like nature which no doubt will follow."

Marshall presented this to the American Joint Chiefs of Staff. They told him to order Eisenhower to keep the American Quakers out of the U.S. zone.[37] Eisenhower then informed Pickett that the "care of German nationals has been made a responsibility of German public welfare agencies under Military Government supervision. A directive is now being issued which authorizes the reactivation of the private German welfare organizations." He expressed his appreciation of the offer that he had caused to be refused, signing the letter "sincerely." The letter was sent. No Quakers went.[38]

Eisenhower was right in thinking that American public opinion would disapprove of such policies. In a poll taken in the fall of 1945 in the army in Europe, 58 percent of U.S. soldiers approved donations of food as emergency relief to the Germans.[39]

Like the Red Cross, the YMCA visited camps for prisoners all during the war, helping them "irrespective of their nationality, race or creed," in the words of Tracy Strong, head of the YMCA team in France in the summer of 1945.[40] When the YMCA attempted to buy some tires and gasoline from the army, as it had been doing all during the fighting on the continent, the request was refused. Puzzled, D. A. Davis of the War Prisoners Aid of the YMCA in New York wrote to the State Department on July 9, proposing to pay for all goods received from the army so that it could feed German prisoners in U.S. camps in France.[41] The permission was refused by the U.S. Army. As is the case with many potentially interesting documents, the army's reply is missing from the State Department files, but it is clear that although Strong's section was operating in France, it fell under the ban universally applied to all "non-German voluntary welfare agencies" seeking to operate for "the benefit of German nationals."[42] It did not matter that the YMCA was already operating in France; the army was able to extend its ban on helping prisoners simply by refusing the necessary supplies, which at that date could be obtained nowhere else.

The general attitude of the army towards civilian relief agencies entering Germany with the intention of helping people "irrespective of their nationality" was clear from the opinion expressed by Stephen Cary, European Commissioner of the American Friends Service Committee who recalled, "We were very unhappy with their heavy-handed and restrictive treatment." The American Friends had to sit by and watch as their brethren in England and France went into the British and French zones to work.[43]

Eisenhower's successor as military governor of Germany, Lucius Clay, who came in November 1945, wrote: "Germany would starve unless it could produce for export . . . [but] we were not only prevented from taking such steps but also required to stop production in many fields until agreement could be obtained in the Control Council, and such agreement could be blocked indefinitely by a single veto." The efforts that Clay made to modify JCS 1067 "were succesful in limited degree only." He received permission only to make changes in monetary policy to prevent inflation. "There was no doubt that JCS 1067 contemplated the Carthaginian peace which dominated our operations in Germany during the early months of the occupation."[44]

The destruction of German production proposed by Morgenthau deprived the U.S. of the advantage of local low-cost supplies while at the same time forcing starving Germans to think of the communist alternative. The Americans needed or wanted

German oil and gasoline, replacement parts for the trucks and cars they had captured, German labor, either civilian or prisoner, and food. Thus the waste of life and labor in the prison camps punished not only the Germans but the Americans as well. Some of this was thrashed out in a tense meeting in Washington in the summer of 1945 among Morgenthau, General Brehon Somervell, the War Department's chief of supply and procurement, and members of Morgenthau's staff. Somervell was negotiating a list of about 500 items, among them oil, which the Germans were prevented from producing. Somervell replied, "I should think that . . . you wouldn't worry too much about that one [item] out of five hundred," after Morgenthau objected to allowing this item to be left off the banned list. The dialogue continued:

> Morgenthau: I don't like to do business that way.
> Somervell: As far as I can see, it is a pretty straightforward business: you believe one thing and we believe another.
> Morgenthau: It isn't a question of confidence. I put it on the question now of having confidence in me as to my reasonableness.
> Somervell: Well, I don't think there is any question about your reasonableness, but there may be some question as to what you think is reasonable and what we think is reasonable.
> Morgenthau: There is no request from General Eisenhower for this . . .
> Somervell: I am just at sea . . . as to what all the argument is about. Hilldring* called me up late this morning and I told him I didn't know what you were arguing about. In other words, if I could find out — if your committee is willing to continue this oil production, I am sure we would have no special views with respect to the protocol which was used to accomplish that end . . . . The only thing we are looking for is an agreement that the oil will be continued. That is all . . .
> Morgenthau: You can't single out oil when there are so

* Major General J. H. Hilldring was head of the Civil Affairs Division of the U.S. War Department from 1943.

many other important things; lots of other important things.
Somervell: I think we would be very remiss if we failed to utilize any resources in oil that exist. I don't see how you can explain it to this country or to any other country at all . . . .
Morgenthau: [This has] left a very bad taste in my mouth as far as dealing with the army was concerned.
Somervell: All of us regret that . . . . There is certainly no reason why there should be any hard feelings about it.

But Morgenthau seemed determined to see himself in the worst possible light. Frustrated in his attempts to punish Germans, he burst out, "Don't you see, I've learned this thing. I'm not going to take it any more. I hold these meetings for two months and at the end of it all these articles come out. The French are starving and freezing, and I'm the one who is holding this up, and this is wrong and that is wrong, and Churchill gets on the floor in Parliament and thanks Lord Keynes for the wonderful job he did, and I never get even a line. I'm not going to take it."[45] Soon after this, Harry Truman calmly accepted his resignation.

The bewilderment of General Somervell typifies the reaction of a very large number of Americans who were being kept in the dark. Another was General Hilldring, an advocate of harsh treatment for the Germans who nevertheless pointed out that it was in the interests of the USA to permit some production. "In Germany there is some prospect of building up sufficient exchange to reimburse the U.S. for imports . . . . In order to do this, we must promote and stimulate exports that don't jeopardize our demilitarization program. Some opposition will arise at home; [this idea] will be supported by FEA [Foreign Economic Administration], but opposed by the Treasury."[46]

"Starving the Germans is morally damaging to us," was the theme of a few far-sighted men like the English publisher Victor Gollancz, who visited civilians in the British zone in 1946. "I want to feed starving Germans and I want to feed them not as a matter of policy but because I am sorry for them. And I am quite certain that I am not singular," he wrote in a passionate pamphlet entitled *Leaving Them to Their Fate: The Ethics of Starvation*.[47] Gollancz, who had suffered grievously from the anti-Semitism of the Germans, wrote, "If you were to believe our public men, you would think that pity and mercy were positively disgraceful, and that self-interest was a basic ethical duty . . . . I hate the idea of epidemics in Germany . . . because they are a horror to the people who suffer them."

Gollancz thought that Field Marshal Montgomery, the military governor of the British zone in Germany, was perhaps putting on a hypocritical show of brutality to appease vengeful politicians when he said, "The big overgrown Germans have got to tighten their belts. I would not take any food from England to feed the Germans." But it was Montgomery of course who recommended to Prime Minister Clement Attlee that the British must improve the food supply to Germany, which they did. The policies of the French and the Americans meant even greater starvation than in the British zone. When the British were scraping together 1,550 calories per day for the German civilians,[48] the Americans managed only 1,275[49] and the French a mere 950.[50]

In the British zone, widespread starvation among civilians was the result, according to Gollancz. The high civilian death rate, 80 percent above the rate in Britain, where it was 1.2 percent per year,[51] showed that starvation was causing up to 220,080 deaths per year in the British zone alone. This was the zone where U.S. General Hilldring thought the Germans were being treated too lavishly. In the French zone, the official ration was only slightly higher than the ration in the death camp of Belsen.

Gollancz summed up the attitude of more than one writer on the subject with the words, "It has been no pleasure to write all this. I have written it with a mounting sense of shame, which I am sure very many, and I dare to hope the majority, of my readers will share."[52]

The protests by determined men like Gollancz led to improvements in the German rations in the British zone in 1946. A Foreign Office memo in 1946 called the situation "undoubtedly alarming. If further drastic cuts of ration levels have to be enforced, as the Committee has been informed would be the case, having regard to the probability that grain stocks will be virtually exhausted within a month, a catastrophe may follow. The greater part of the population of the larger German towns appears to be facing a nutritional disaster, the magnitude of which and the consequences of which the Committee fears may seriously retard the recovery of Western Europe and probably disturb its political development."[53]

Grain began to flow from North America in larger quantities. By the end of 1946, Canadian grain stocks had fallen to their lowest level in decades, around 67 million bushels. The American surplus also showed a similar sharp drop.[54] The change of mood that led to the Marshall Plan was beginning.

7

THE SLOW DEATH CAMPS

CAPTAIN JULIEN THOUGHT AS HE WALKED gingerly over the scarred terrain among the living dead in the former American camp, "This is just like Buchenwald and Dachau."[1] He had fought with his regiment, the Troisième Régiment de Tirailleurs Algériens, against the Germans because they had ruined France, but he had never imagined any revenge like this, muddy ground "peopled with living skeletons," some of whom died as he watched, others huddled under bits of cardboard which they clutched although the July day was hot. Women lying in holes in the ground stared up at him with hunger edema bulging their bellies in gross parody of pregnancy, old men with long gray hair watched him feebly, children of six or seven with the raccoon rings of starvation looked at him from lifeless eyes. Julien hardly knew where to begin. He could find no food at all in this camp of 32,000 people at Dietersheim. The two German doctors in the "hospital," Kurth and Geck, were trying to care for the many dying patients stretched out on dirty blankets on the ground under the hot July sky, between the marks of the tent which the Americans had taken with them.*

Julien immediately set his officers of the 7th Company to survey the helpless and civilians, to see whom he could release right away. These 103,500 people in the five camps round Dietersheim were supposed to be part of the labor force turned over in July by the U.S. to the French for reparations, but among them the French counted 32,640 old men, women, children under eight years of age, boys of eight to fourteen, terminally sick and cripples. All of these were released immediately. Once the counting was well under way, Julien telephoned to his field headquarters at Neustadt. His CO told him he would send food right away, but that Julien should also seek food in the village.[2]

The Burgermeister in Dietersheim rounded up the women of the village, who immediately brought food out to the camp; the prisoners got a slice of bread and one prune that evening. At Hechtsheim, hundreds of skeletal people dressed in rags crawled across the ground. They too reminded the commanding officer of the Occupying Forces of the victims in concentration camps. In his report he called the camps *"bagnes de mort lents"* or slow death camps.[3] In all, the French found 166,000 men, women and children in the camps they took over from the Americans in Germany that summer, all in "the most lamentable condition." No reports of the hundreds of thousands of other prisoners being turned over in the summer of 1945 by the U.S. have survived at Vincennes, except Julien's and one from the ICRC delegate in France (see below).

A quarrel between Julien and a brother officer, Captain Rousseau, which, according to Julien's superior officer, had been

* A French Army unit under Captain Rousseau took over Dietersheim on July 10, 17 days before Julien walked in. Rousseau claimed the camp was worse when he arrived. The British and Americans turned over about 860,000 captives to the French, most in July – September 1945. The French had requested the prisoners to help repair damage done to their country during the war. The British and Americans agreed, provided that the French adhere strictly to the Geneva Convention. Many of the American-held POWs were in five camps in the section of Germany that became the French zone in July 1945. Most of the rest were in U.S. camps in France such as Thorée les Pins. The exact figure for the total turnover varies by about 10 percent according to various records kept by the French and Americans.

caused by Rousseau's venomous attacks on various officers of the 7th Company, broke out again just after Julien took over from Rousseau. Having heard about what was going on at Dietersheim, Rousseau came round on the pretext of asking about some X-ray equipment which he thought Julien had taken from the hospital at Bingen. Standing near the gate of the camp as some German women were arriving with food, Rousseau sneered at Julien, apparently for mollycoddling the Germans. Julien said something that angered Rousseau, for Rousseau immediately opened fire with his pistol on the women.

Here the French army report[4] breaks off but there is no evidence in the subsequent inquiry that Rousseau was court-martialed for shooting the women. It is the fallout from the officers' quarrel that has like volcanic ash haphazardly preserved the surrounding information, not any desire on the part of French army historians to record French decency or American atrocities.

During the lengthy investigation which dragged on into the winter, Rousseau succeeded in making Julien's conduct towards the Germans part of the proceedings. Asked to explain himself, Julien said that he had fed the Germans "because of the mission assigned to me, not to please the *Boche*, whom I fought and who have ruined us. Besides, I went out of my way to get the donations for a good diet for the prisoners because I was repeatedly urged by the Prisoner Division of the army to do just that. During the first part of the food crisis caused by the chaos in the camp, I made an appeal to the neighboring villages, which I had to repeat because the official army ration was only 800 calories per person per day." This starvation level, the same as at the Nazi concentration camp at Belsen when it was uncovered, was all that the French army allocated to the POWs from its own supplies; anything else would have to come from German sources. Julien said he was helped in his efforts by "German authorities" and by the International Committee of the Red Cross which was operating in the area now that the French had taken over. By August 1, over 90 percent of the prisoners were housed in tents. Within a few weeks, these combined measures had reduced the death toll from about 30 per day where it had peaked as the French arrived, to less than half that.

What saved the prisoners here was basically Julien's belief in the mission which he had been given, which was expressed in the food and care given by the French army, as well as the food given by the local Germans, and the care of the Red Cross. This was the system necessary. That it worked, Julien proved. That it had been prevented by the U.S. Army was clear from the state of the camps when the French walked in.

In the camp at Kripp close to Dietersheim, Charles von Luttichau struggled up one morning in early July resolved to try again to convince his camp commmander that he should be released, not turned over to the French for slave labor. Von Luttichau was sure that the camp commander was deeply prejudiced against all Germans because of the crimes committed by Germany during the war, so he had not much hope of succeeding this time. He did not find out until 1988 to whom he owed his release. He was about to benefit from the sharp eye of Colonel Philip S. Lauben, far away at SHAEF rear headquarters in Paris. Lauben, an impatient, sharply logical officer with a cynical sense of humor, was in charge of the star-marked American trucks that were now transporting home the prisoners who were being discharged. In the same trucks, the unlucky ones would soon cross the border into a new captivity that would go on for years.

These transfers began slowly despite Lauben's skillful organization, partly because his superiors, it seemed, would say anything convenient that came into their heads about the prisoners, without checking the reality. After an American general had promised that the French would find in the zone of Germany they were about to take over, around 275,000 prisoners already in American camps, Lauben had to point out that this figure, which had been "taken as gospel" for a long time by both French and Americans, had appeared for the first time as a guess from afar by a French general who had never seen the camps. Actually, said Lauben, there were only about 170,000 at the time the takeover was due. Lauben also pointed out that

General Blanc's statement that the French army had captured only 100,000 effectives "smacked of grand larceny on an international scale," because SHAEF had reported earlier that French captures were 235,000. Because the U.S. government was basing the number of prisoners to be transferred on the number of prisoners the French had captured themselves, the fewer the French said they had captured, the more the Americans would give them to make up the requested number, which was still under negotiation. Thus, as Lauben saw it, the French were trying to sneak another 135,000 slaves out of the Americans.[5] All this arithmetic, typical of the confusion between the French and the Americans at handover time, ended up to the credit of the prisoners, of whom certainly 35,000 and possibly many more were now deemed not to be owing to the French, but due for release. A few days later, when the trucks were actually rolling up to the gate of the camp, von Luttichau was told that he could go home.

The camps round Dietersheim were much like the other camps taken over that summer by the French army from the Americans. Many complaints flowed to the French army headquarters of the terrible conditions the officers were encountering in the American camps in Germany and in France. Among the 1,000 men received in Marseille, 287 were absolutely incapable of work, even according to the cynical French standards of the time. In the camp at Sainte-Marthe, only 85 of 700 were able to work. The French army report from Siershahn said there were over 400 children under 15 among the prisoners, some of them under eight years of age. There were also women in the camp, and men over 50. At Erbiseul near Mons, Belgium, 25 percent of the men received by the French were *"déchets,"* or garbage, according to their written complaints. Of the people found at the former U.S. camp at Hechtsheim, two-thirds were starving. This time it was Marshal of the French Army Alphonse Juin who complained to the Americans that many of the people there looked like the starving wrecks at Dachau and Buchenwald.[6]

U.S. Army Major William H. Haight, infuriated by his army's callous attitude towards the prisoners whom they were transferring to the French, swore out a deposition in October against an august brigadier general, Charles O. Thrasher, commanding general of the Oise Intermediate Section, who had outraged the French at a meeting about transferring prisoners a month before.[7] Haight swore before Major William G. Downey that Thrasher said to his officers, "Gentlemen, we are to turn over some of our German prisoners of war to the French." He turned to the stenographer adding, "Don't put this down in your notes," then looked round for the French liaison officer. Finding him, he said with a smile, "Well, I'll say it anyway gentlemen. We have some prisoners whom we would like to get rid of. We must keep all of the prisoners who are in the best condition, to get our own work done without difficulty. When we are choosing which prisoners to turn over to the French, let's see if we can't find some old ones or those in poor condition or poor workers — keep the good ones for ourselves. I hope you understand me. Gentlemen, I'm sure you know what to do — I need say no more." He smiled and closed the meeting.[8]

Random shootings appear to have increased under the French, although the coverups carried out by both armies may distort the picture. In any case, Lieutenant Colonel Barnes's "27 deaths by unnatural causes" in April* were far exceeded in one night by drunken French army officers at Andernach, who drove their jeep through the camp laughing and shouting as they blasted the prisoners with their Sten guns. The toll: 47 dead, 55 wounded.[9] One French officer refused to allow the local German Red Cross to feed prisoners on a train although the meal had already been arranged between the Red Cross and the French camp commander.[10] French guards at a camp pretending to notice an escape attempt shot down 10 prisoners in their cages. Lieutenant Soubeiray of the Third Algerians wrote in his own hand a letter of protest to his superior officer denouncing the men who "on the pretext of having suffered from the Germans, show the intolerable inhumanity of the Regular Army."[11] The violence reached such heights in the 108th Infantry Regiment that the commanding officer of the Region, Gen-

* Barnes reported this on May 18. (History of Provost Marshal Section, Ad Sec, Com Z; in RG 332 Box 22, NARS).

eral Billotte, on the advice of the Regiment's CO, Lieutenant Colonel de Champvallier, who had given up attempting to discipline his men, recommended that the regiment be dissolved.[12]

The trains transferring these prisoners from Germany to France were so bad that the commanding officers had standing orders not to allow them to be stopped in stations in France for fear the civilians would see how the prisoners were being treated. Officer Cadet Jean Maurice described one convoy which he led out of Hechtsheim.[13] Maurice reported that it was hard to keep track of the prisoners because the cars were open and the weather was bad. Several times the train was forced to stop in tunnels where the prisoners escaped from the cars. The French opened fire on them in the dark tunnels, killing some — Maurice did not know how many, because their bodies were left there for the dogs. At Willingen, Maurice abandoned one dead body and one dying man "on the station platform."

One train that took prisoners at the end of August to the camp at Thorée les Pins, west of Paris, arrived at the siding in the fields beside the camp with four dead men on board and at least 40 who were immediately "hospitalized." The men here at least had a roof, floor and walls, although they were only horse barns. Originally constructed during the First World War as a cavalry barracks, Thorée had been converted during the war to a POW camp, first for Germans, then for French, then Germans again.* Designed for 12,000, the camp held at least 18,000 from time to time. Many of the guards here lived in the village, so local tradition has preserved considerable intimate knowledge of the conditions. It was here in September 1945 that the seamless censorship covering the prisoners began to split open.

In the late summer of 1945, a man named Jean-Pierre Pradervand, head of the delegations of the ICRC in France,[14] went to inspect the French camp at Thorée les Pins, already

* It is now an army training center. As you enter the camp from a narrow road leading off the main two-lane highway, you cross the railway tracks on your way through the barbed wire gate. To the left is the camp commander's headquarters. Beyond stretch the rows of windowless barns where the prisoners lived.

known in the village nearby as "Buchenwald" after the notorious German death camp.

A crowd of prisoners milled around the windowless sheds as he drove in to Thorée les Pins. Some were lying on the ground, others leaned apathetically against the cement walls. Two thousand men were already so far gone that nothing could save them, according to the French camp commandant Zalay. Twenty of them died that day, while Pradervand was there. No coffins were available for them; they were taken to a farmer's field nearby and buried. Another six thousand or so were in such bad shape that unless they were immediately given food, shelter, clothing and medical care, they would be dead in a couple of months. All the rest were undernourished. Many had just been taken over in this condition from American custody a few days before.

Pradervand decided to appeal directly to de Gaulle, who might be grateful to him because of some amazing rescue work which had been performed by the ICRC near the end of the war. Carl J. Burckhardt, official head of the International Committee of the Red Cross, had met the head of the Reich Security Office, Ernst Kaltenbrunner, in order to discuss repatriating thousands of French civilians, including many women and Jews, from the infamous Nazi camp at Ravensbruck. They met on March 12, 1945, at Feldkirch, an Austrian village near the Liechtenstein border.[15] The meeting, held in secret, had been a success for the French: the Red Cross released more than ten thousand captives from Ravensbruck and other camps many weeks before the end of the war.

De Gaulle had thanked Burckhardt and Pradervand not only for the successful efforts, but also for the added recognition in the eyes of the French people which this affair gave to his provisional government, as yet untried at the polls.[16] All this de Gaulle coldly ignored when Pradervand repeatedly tried to talk to him on the telephone or to see him in his office in September. So Pradervand got in touch with the International Committee of the Red Cross in Geneva, asking for action.

The first significant news of the situation of the prisoners to reach anyone outside the Allied armies arrived on a desk in the

State Department in Washington at 5:05 P.M., September 14, 1945, sent "plain" (not in code) from Geneva, unsigned, but based on what Pradervand had told the International Committee in Geneva.[17] It was a devastating document:

> International Committee Red Cross receive from their delegates France alarming reports health thousands German prisoners transferred from American camps to French authorities during July, August. Large numbers prisoners transferred mainly from camps Germany and Mons, Belgium but also camps in France such as group Normandy base, Delta base and CCE 15 Le Croutoy arrived. French camps state extreme weakness resulting prolonged undernourishment thus rendering impossible their assignment as scheduled by French authorities to labor detachments. Consequence is overpopulation of French camps by unfit for whom detaining authorities lack requisite means of building up their health. Referring memorandum August 21, 1945, International Committee Red Cross anxious United States Government should take necessary emergency measures (firstly) to supply relief many prisoners requiring food, medicants [*sic*] clothing, boots, blankets, soap, (secondly) recommend proceed subsequent transfers only when adequate living conditions guaranteed to war prisoners after transfer, (thirdly) accordance with order June 29, 1945, issued in behalf German prisoners United States, increase prisoners rations in American camps Europe to obviate prolonged undernourishment and aggravation general state health. International Committee Red Cross grateful United States Government's kind consideration this appeal. Intercroix Rouge M976.

This was joined on the desks of officials in Washington within a couple of days by a powerful statement from Henry W. Dunning, elaborating on Pradervand's description. Dunning, in the prisoner of war department of the American Red Cross, wrote to the American Red Cross headquarters in Washington on September 5 that "the situation of the German prisoners of war in France has become desperate and shortly will become an open scandal. During the past week several Frenchmen, who were formerly prisoners of the Germans, have called on me to protest the treatment being given German prisoners of war by the French Government. General Thrasher Commanding the Oise Intermediary sector, asked one of our field workers to come to Paris to see me about the same matter. Mrs Dunning, returning from Bourges, reports that dozens of German prisoners are dying there weekly. I saw Pradervand who told me that the situation of German prisoners in France in many instances is worse than in the former German concentration camps. He showed me photographs of human skeletons and letters from French camp commanders who have asked to be relieved because they can get no help from the French government and cannot stand to see the prisoners dying from lack of food. Pradervand has appealed to everyone in the French government but to no avail."[18]

The U.S. Army now sent Ambassador Jefferson Caffery a copy of the ICRC cable, asking Caffery for help. Caffery cabled Washington saying that he had asked his military attaché to make a "pertinent investigation," which he sent on. The memorandum which Lieutenant Colonel Andrew P. Fuller prepared for the ambassador said that the attaché had talked to General Larkin, who confirmed that the prisoners had indeed been turned over. It claimed that the "generous rations" which had formerly been given them (in 1944) had been so severely criticized by the French authorities and French press that they had been reduced to 2,000 calories per day; adequate rations had been turned over with the POWs, but these had "disappeared" promptly when the prisoners were turned over. The prisoners were inspected and accepted by the French medical authorities as being in good shape when turned over, it went on, and contended that "this Red Cross report was initiated by one of their field men who found prisoners in bad condition and who accepted the statement exactly as given to him." There was a copy of a further memo, also from Fuller, this time to Eisenhower's chief of staff General Walter Bedell Smith, saying that the prisoners were well equipped on turnover, with greatcoats, blankets and medicine, in good physical condition; that the French had agreed to abide by the Geneva Convention; and that the United States Army officers whom he had interviewed "feel that the United States Army is entirely clear with respect to the prisoners turned over."[19]

But rumors of the dreadful conditions in the Allied camps were spreading through Paris, perhaps from one of the 15 delegates assisting Pradervand. A young man named Serge Bromberger was assigned to investigate by one of the most influential newspapers in France, *Le Figaro*.

8

LIMING THE CORPSE

"Thou canst not say I did it: Never shake
Thy gory locks at me . . ."
— MACBETH

LE FIGARO BROUGHT THE NEWS TO the victory celebrations of the Allies, who welcomed it like Banquo's ghost. At first incredulous, the paper had been convinced by the level testimony of impeccable witnesses, such as a priest, Father Le Meur, who had actually seen the men starving in the camps.

Censored and second-hand because the French government refused to allow reporters into the camps, *Le Figaro*'s story, published in September, was nevertheless shocking. The reporter, Serge Bromberger, wrote: "The most serious source confirmed that the physical state of the prisoners was worse than deplorable. People were talking about a horrifying death rate, not from sickness but starvation, and of men who weighed an average 35 – 45 kilos [80 – 100 lbs.]. At first we doubted the truth of all this, but appeals came to us from many sources and we could not disregard the testimony of Father Le Meur, Assistant General Chaplain to the prisoners." *Le Figaro* interviewed French General Buisson, in charge of the French camps, who admitted that the prisoners got only 900 to 1,000 calories per day. "The doctors told us that this was just enough for a man lying in bed never moving not to die too quickly," said Buisson.[1] Having refused *Le Figaro* permission to go into the camps, Buisson nevertheless produced photographs of prisoners for Bromberger to inspect, but not to print. Bromberger wrote that they "looked like skeletons." The General hastened to add, "Since those were taken, there has been improvement." But before that, "it was a catastrophe" on cold days. "I hope it's not too late," he added mysteriously, "and we will be able to get back on course without ravaging losses." Circumspectly, he referred to the Americans only as the source of prisoners transferred to French custody, leaving the cause of their condition implied.

Bromberger gives a hard-hitting summary of the discoveries, also without blaming the Americans. Then, as he interviews the charming and very sympathetic Buisson, Bromberger gradually succumbs to the spell of the man and the prejudice of the time. Buisson has given him *"toutes les précisions désirables,"* all the necessary details. Buisson slyly admits the problem while pretending to deplore it, as he expresses the hope that it will soon be over. It was understood of course, that there was a terrific food shortage everywhere. Not in irony, *Le Figaro* printed the story right beside an announcement of the next races for the well-fed thoroughbreds at Longchamps racetrack.

On September 26 the patient Pradervand tried again to interest de Gaulle, with a remarkable letter which formed the basis of most of the subsequent controversy.[2] Pradervand begins:

> My General.
> On the third of September, I asked you to do me the honor of giving me an audience so that I could tell you about the situation of the German prisoners of war in French hands. These prisoners now number 600,000. Two hundred thousand are now incapable of work, as follows:
>
> a) 50,000 because they should be repatriated under the

terms of the Geneva Convention (amputees, blind, crazy, tubercular, etc.) and

b) 150,000 because they are suffering from severe malnourishment.

The situation of these 200,000 men is so precarious from the point of view of food, clothing and unsanitary conditions that one can say without fear of pessimism, that they will not survive the winter.

To show the general situation, let me tell you about the camp at Thorée les Pins, near La Flèche, which you will find reported here in photographs enclosed. This camp at Thorée contains about 20,000 prisoners, of whom 13,000 are, although underfed, able to work. Seven thousand are very sick, of whom

a) 2,000 are in such bad shape that no matter what care is given them they will probably die in the next few months (even the German doctors have given up caring for them);

b) 2,000 are starvation cases who might be restored by the right kind of feeding, in particular injections of blood plasma;

c) 3,000 are gravely undernourished but might be saved by extra feeding. On the day of the visit by one of my delegates, there were twenty deaths at Thorée, but no more coffins for them.

This camp at Thorée gives a slightly exaggerated picture of the whole situation. To fix this up, urgent and energetic action is necessary. Permit me — because I have been immersed in this problem for more than three months — to suggest to you the following measures:

1) Suspend all further transfers of prisoners until the administration is able to absorb regularly new contingents;

2) Repatriate quickly all the prisoners who are not going to recover, who live in the French, American or British zone, by agreement with military authorities;

3) Give extra food to the prisoners who can be saved, and put to work gradually these prisoners to fulfill the demands for labor;

4) Distribute to some of the prisoners food and clothing

which the administration already has. (The prisoners in general are sleeping on the ground and have on average one blanket for four people.)

Thus the cost to the administration of these 200,000 useless mouths will disappear and the catastrophe which threatens will be averted.

The International Committee of the Red Cross is at your disposal to help as much as it can with its modest means in this heavy task.

The International Committee of the Red Cross has at its disposal some funds left over from the German Red Cross, gifts made to the committee by German prisoners in the USA and some gifts made by prisoners of war in French hands. With these different sums the Committee is ready to buy food, clothing and medicine for the German prisoners in French hands.

He tells de Gaulle that he will place at the French government's disposal three trucks and a big stock of medicine. He asks for gasoline, saying that he has repeatedly requested the Ministry of War for gas, but received none. He points out that there is a large number of food parcels in Geneva belonging to the Ministry of Prisoners of War, Deportees and Refugees, which the Committee is ready to buy to hand over to the prisoners. The government could then use the money to buy clothing for the prisoners. According to international law, he points out, the Americans have not escaped their obligation to the prisoners by handing them over to the French, a fact which he has already pointed out to the different governments, in a memo of August 21, 1945.

In the margin of Pradervand's typed letter, still in the archives at Vincennes, beside the request for gasoline are written in a hand not de Gaulle's the words "*C'est fait.*"[3] But the ICRC was still asking for gasoline three months later.

The scandal breaking over the French army threatened to engulf the Americans at any moment, so all difficulties with the ICRC were swept away immediately. Within a couple of days, General Lee had been ordered to organize a public relations feeding for some prisoners in French hands. The food was being sent, General Lee said, because "International Red Cross state these supplies are required to save life and prevent undue suffering."[4]

Over Eisenhower's signature, orders went to Colonel Lauben to convene a meeting with the French to deal with the problem quickly. Lauben took the chair at a surreal meeting of 20 high U.S. and French officers at 41, rue Cambon, Paris, on September 26. At this meeting, the Americans and French vied in cynical accusations against each other and in hypocritical pleas to treat the prisoners better.[5] Chief representative for the French was Major General Buisson, who had been himself a prisoner of the Germans until recently. He was now director general of Axis prisoners of war. The French repeated their request for 1,750,000 prisoners of war to use as forced labor in France. In turn, Buisson pointed out that of approximately 450,000 who had been transferred already, at least 50,000 "can not be brought up to the necessary physical standard" to work. This astounding statement, which plainly meant that nothing could ever make these men fit to work, that is, they were either dead, or soon would be, was calmly accepted by the Americans.

Colonel Lauben in the chair pressed Buisson to promise to maintain the prisoners according to the Geneva Convention. Buisson asked that the United States provide clothing for the prisoners. Lauben replied that the "United States will accept responsibility" for the initial issue of clothing. Buisson, taking this to mean that the Americans would now supply the clothing that Fuller had said had been supplied with the prisoners already transferred, grew encouraged. He made "an eloquent appeal" to the Americans' "love of humanity." They could demonstrate this, he thought, by confiscating supplies from the starving German civilians to feed prisoners working for the French. He concluded his humanitarian appeal by stating that the French couldn't get any useful work out of the prisoners if they were dead.

For the United States, Colonel Albrecht, whom Lauben thought was a cynical man, replied that he too "hoped the prisoners would not die of cold in France as [he] feared that this might raise the question of turning over additional prisoners." He assured General Buisson that the United States would do everything in its power to avoid such a calamity, because it was worried that prisoners might indeed die of cold — which was not permitted under the Geneva Convention.

The French wanted mail service established between the prisoners and their families, but Colonel Lauben pointed out that he had not been authorized to discuss this. Nor was he allowed to ask the German Red Cross to campaign among civilians for winter clothing for the men. The general effect of the meeting was to neutralize all controversial subjects, while postponing the French requests for more help.

Only a day after this, Pradervand was abruptly invited to Frankfurt to talk to Eisenhower's chief of staff, Bedell Smith. He gave Smith pictures taken at Thorée les Pins, which Smith took in right away to show to Eisenhower in his office.[6] Pradervand describes the meeting: "On September 28, in your office, we attempted to give an exact picture of the situation, attempting to remain inside General Buisson's own statements. We showed you pictures taken at Thorée Camp which we later sent to you and whose receipt Colonel H. E. Kessenger, G1, acknowledged in your name."[7] (These were photographs he had taken of starved, dying prisoners recently transferred from the Americans to the French. They are not preserved among the many photographs of prisoners in the Smith collection at Abilene.)

Pradervand was especially grateful for three actions that Smith had promised to take, the first being the suspension of all new transfers, until the French could live up to the Geneva Convention. He was also pleased because he thought the Americans would take back the 200,000 sick men whom he judged would die during the winter unless they were helped immediately. Pradervand thought that because these men were so sick, they would immediately be repatriated, as prescribed by the Geneva Convention. Finally Pradervand was grateful to Smith for promising to begin "a course of generalized aid" for all the prisoners whom the Americans had turned over to the French. It seemed to him that he had finally been able to persuade the French and the Americans to treat the prisoners humanely. Back in Paris, Pradervand wrote with deep gratitude to Smith for his "humane understanding and for the speed with which you have worked so that the obligations, resulting from signing the Geneva Convention by the United States, might be fulfilled."[8]

These hopes were apparently justified at a meeting of U.S. officers at the American embassy in Paris a few days later, where it was agreed that Colonel Renfroe should ask Colonel Lauben to take up the matter of extra food rations with Theater G4, to supplement the French rations, which were only 1,006 calories per day.[9]

While these discussions were going on, General Littlejohn was trying to get agreement on how to dispose of the surplus "subsistence" with which the army was embarrassed.[10] "There is in this Theater a substantial excess of subsistence in certain items due to the rapid discharge of prisoners of war after VE day, the accelerated deployment of U.S. Military, the sharp decrease in employment by U.S. forces of allied liberated nationals and the ending of the supply responsibilities of the French army. Over 3,000,000 rations a day less than those requisitioned, were issued . . . . I received . . . . concurrence to stop the flow of subsistence [from the U.S.]." The excess rations accumulated to 39 days' supply more than the army liked to keep on hand, which was 100 days. Thus the excess in October 1945 was around 39 percent, for a total of 139 days' supply of food in the Theater. So great was the surplus in the USA that Littlejohn noted that "we have been invited to increase our rations of fruit juices and have been advised that our requirements for fresh eggs, fresh fruits, potatoes and butter can and should be met from U.S. sources." The letter goes on to discuss a policy on how to get rid of the surplus, which some officers wanted to send to the USA.

Nevertheless, the prisoners went on starving. *Le Monde* printed a story by Jacques Fauvet that began passionately: "As one speaks today of Dachau, in ten years people throughout the world will speak about camps like Saint Paul d'Égiaux," where 17,000 people taken over from the Americans in late July were dying so fast that within a few weeks two cemeteries of 200 graves each had been filled. By the end of September, the death rate was 10 per day, or over 21 percent per year. Fauvet attacked head-on the question of revenge: "People will object that the Germans weren't very particular on the matter of feeding our men, but even if they did violate the Geneva Convention, that hardly seems to justify our following their example.... People have often said that the best service we could do the Germans would be to imitate them, so they would one day find us before the judgment of history, but it is to an ideal higher than mere dignity that France should remain faithful; it is to be regretted that the foreign press had to remind us of that.... We didn't suffer and fight to perpetuate the crimes of other times and places."[11]

This was the only press coverage in which the reporter used the kind of language about these camps that was used by people such as Captain Julien who had to go into them. Fauvet was right about everything except the judgment of history, which was apparently beginning with his own words.

Jefferson Caffery, the American ambassador in Paris, was well aware that the situation was heavy with danger to American prestige in Europe, to the reputation of Eisenhower, to the honor of the army. He issued a warning to the State Department at Washington urging extreme caution.[12] With the cooperation of the American embassy, Charles de Gaulle and General Buisson, and cheered on by the sycophantic press, the USFET staff went to work to create history's judgment in advance. They prepared the ground quite carefully. Eisenhower personally announced at the end of September that he had suspended deliveries to the French. This was a double coup, because it showed him protecting the remaining prisoners from the French, who were therefore the ones to blame.

The Americans were risking serious retaliation, because President Truman and Ambassador Caffery had recently humiliated General de Gaulle, who was morbidly sensitive to insult. In fact, Foreign Minister Georges Bidault said that he "fervently hoped [the U.S. government] would take no steps to wound our *amour propre*. Don't face us with any disagreeable *fait accompli* because I want to help on this."[13] The only help he could offer the Americans, of course, was to protect them from the press.

But if de Gaulle told the truth about the Americans now, he risked exposing serious maltreatment by his own army as well. Revenge would cost him dear in prestige, arms, food, and future deliveries of prisoners. De Gaulle had felt the American lash a few months before, after French troops had seized the Val d'Aosta and some other sections of Italy north of Nice at the end of the war. Truman told de Gaulle to order them out, or suffer the loss of all American arms shipments, which de Gaulle desperately needed for his war on Ho Chi Minh in Viet Nam, and to take over Syria from the British. De Gaulle backed down. The arms continued to flow.[14]

Now de Gaulle pulled back again. He took a moderate line in his press conference on the prisoners. The relieved Americans praised his forbearance.[15] The arms as well as the American food continued to flow.

Jefferson Caffery's relief is almost audible from the State Department copy of his cable covering de Gaulle's press conference. Caffery reported, "When questioned about this matter in a press conference, de Gaulle gave a rather restrained reply. He observed that the problem was complicated and that thus far, matter had been presented as being solely fault of French Govt. He denied this and said that 'As a result of the difficult circumstances with which the Allied Armies were faced, a considerable number of prisoners transferred to France were in a very deficient state . . . . We have every right to hope that the goodwill which is being shown on both sides will lead to a humane and practical agreement on this subject.'"

Caffery admitted that "I have been reliably told that there is some truth in French allegations and that in French occupational zone many German POWs whom we transferred to the French were in a very poor physical condition. I believe that understanding and goodwill are being shown by both French and American authorities who are seeking a solution but it is obvious that matters will not be helped if a campaign of mutual recrimination is carried on. There is always a certain danger that the French press might go all out on this problem. I feel that our military authorities should bear this in mind and not try to point finger at French but should point up fact that in an atmosphere of mutual understanding and goodwill a solution of a difficult and complicated problem is being sought."[16]

Caffery's cable limes the corpse. It was obvious by now that the only thing that could possibly have helped the prisoners was precisely a whole lot of recrimination. Caffery, although he pretends to consider the prisoners with a glancing reference to a satisfactory solution according to "the letter and spirit of the Geneva Convention," is only discussing the prestige of the "high levels" involved. To preserve this prestige is everything; the prisoners mean nothing.

The Americans had agreed only to supply arms for Viet Nam, not to accept blame for the camps. USFET now pulled off another public relations coup. The army held a hurried investigation which carried in the required buckets of lime. Then the "investigation" was presented over Eisenhower's signature in a toughly-worded statement that minimized the blame while shifting it to the French. The statement said, "With reference to allegation by Intercross [International Red Cross] that large numbers of prisoners were transferred to French camps in state of extreme weakness resulting from prolonged undernourishment, extensive investigation has been made and much evidence collected from American and German personnel of transferring camps. Inescapable conclusion is that present extreme weakness of transferees, including approximately 2,000 desperate cases, is result of nutritional and other maintenance deficiencies experienced while in French custody, subsequent to transfer from American sources. All prisoners transferred for rehabilitation work in France were fully equipped with personal clothing, either two blankets or one blanket and one overcoat, two weeks rations, two weeks medical supplies, and were in physical condition fitting them for labor, except for such negligible number as may have been overlooked by American and French officers charged with delivery and reception."[17]

The testimony of officers who participated in the transfer and this or similar "investigations" shows that none of Eisenhower's statement was true, except what was being denied. Lieutenant Fisher, who had been on a previous investigating board in the spring of 1945, was struck by what a whitewash it was.[18] Colonel Philip Lauben later said the American and French camps in the Vosges region were so bad that "the Vosges was just one big death camp."[19] Even Eisenhower's chief of staff and Jefferson Caffery[20] admitted in secret within a few days that some of the Red Cross allegations were true, but this neither slowed the army in its fierce denying, nor prompted any of the journalists acquainted with the story to investigate further.

What Pradervand thought he had secured from Smith was never done, or cancelled before it could have any lasting effect. The transfers were not stopped, not even when the French themselves requested a suspension because of cold weather.[21] On October 19, 15,000 prisoners were sent by the Americans from Würzburg to a French camp.[22] Conditions in the French camps then were about the same as they had been. A message to Marshall signed "Eisenhower" recommended resumption of the transfers on November 1, while Pradervand's letter of thanks for Smith's humane understanding was still in the mail to Frankfurt. Marshall approved the USFET message the next day.[23] At least 20,000 more German prisoners were ordered transferred on November 29 to mine coal for the French.[24] Another 100,000 were on their way at the end of the year, despite the starvation and foulness of the French camps.[25] Deep into 1946, as the transfers went on and on, men went on dying of starvation and disease in the French camps. The ICRC delegate in France in October 1946 warned the War Department of the gravity of the situation in the French camps, complaining of "the absence of improvement in conditions in the last six months." The report offered "a grave warning" to the War Department that "because of reduced diet and insufficient clothing . . . many of the prisoners may not be expected to endure the rigors of winter."[26]

The number of the sick to be returned to the Americans kept dropping from Pradervand's original 200,000, loudly proclaimed, to 100,000, quietly admitted, to a final 52,000, never publicized.[27]

Pradervand had imagined that returning the men to U.S. camps would help them, but the likelihood is that the conditions they met were as bad as they had been in September, and were to be again in 1946. They were thus exposed to a death rate of 2.6 percent per week, which was as bad as in the worst French camps.[28] The generalized aid promised by Smith turned out to be soap, louse powder and a little food. Smith claimed that it would provide five ounces per day for 13 days for about 606,000 men,[29] but General Lee, who was in charge of actually issuing the food, said on November 10 that only 100,000 prisoners would receive extra rations. He was so wary of the way orders for prisoner rations had been given so far, once again "by winks and nods," that he would not continue the special feeding, which had scarcely begun, unless he got "orders in writing."[30] Colonel Lauben recollected in 1987: "I was rather appalled over the state of the prisoners, but I have no memory of the matter of bringing in extra food."[31] In any case, the "extra" food would not be continued for any prisoners returned to U.S. camps. No one mentioned this to Pradervand, because it meant that the food offered would only prolong life for a few weeks. Then the men would begin starving again.[32] The news of the extra food was more news than food.

The cynicism with which the Red Cross and Pradervand were treated by the U.S Army was evident in army warehouses in Europe which still contained the 13,500,000 high-protein Red Cross food parcels taken over from the ICRC in May, but never distributed. On November 17, the army was still wondering what to do with them.[33] Each parcel contained on average 12,000 calories, so there was enough food in them to have given the 700,000 or so Germans who had by now died a supplementary 1,000 calories per day for about eight months. The ICRC parcels alone would probably have kept alive most of those men until spring 1946.

The *New York Times*, which had thundered against censorship in May, did not use its precious freedom now to investigate the story on its own. The *Times* summed it all up while dismissing it in four stories beginning October 11.[34] One of the paper's stars, Drew Middleton, opened the coverage of this major discovery by tamely summarizing the *Figaro* story. No one from the *Times* bothered to go and interview Pradervand, the prime source of the news. On October 13, 14 and 20, stories from Frankfurt and Paris inflated the myth that was being created with the help of Caffery and Bedell Smith. In the October stories from Frankfurt, what officers at USFET told the *Times* was accepted and printed by the paper. No other source was named. This whitewash was called "hundreds of interviews with American officers, non-commissioned officers and enlisted men from all over the theater who remained in the camps for four to six weeks after the French took over." The customary "unimpeachable source," according to Drew Middleton, said that these interviews were supplemented by interviews with German officers and men. Middleton must have known that millions of these German officers and men were in easy range at the 50 U.S. camps within 38 miles of his desk in Frankfurt, and another million or so were back at their homes in Germany, but he nowhere explains why it was necessary for him to accept the army's word for research he could have done himself.[35]

Middleton reports that the French had stolen food from the prisoners, but that the Americans had agreed to take back about 90,000 who had been maltreated by the French, to restore them to life with extra food. The *Times* informs us not only that the United States observes the Geneva Convention, but that the army had turned over "large stocks of army rations" to the International Committee of the Red Cross for the prisoners, "because General Eisenhower and his senior staff officers feel strongly that the United States army is obligated to watch over the welfare of the prisoners that it captured." The *Times* had found "one source" who likened photographs taken in French camps of rows of emaciated prisoners to photographs taken at Dachau. Along with the description of the photographs, which sound like Pradervand's, Captain Julien's observation about the American camp resembling Dachau and Buchenwald now turns up amazingly in the *Times* — only this time turned against the French. Now it is only attributed to "one source." Why was this source so shy? The *Times* does not explain, although it knows that "feelings at USFET have been sharpened by the inspection of these photographs." The officers were now deeply wounded by the sight of the rows of emaciated prisoners in the

French camps. "It is not exaggerating to say that many high officers feel that the army's honor has been sullied by the manner in which the French have treated the prisoners that it captured."

The *Times*'s man could detect honor being sullied in army Headquarters, but missed seeing the starved corpses in the camps that he said he had visited.

Why did Middleton accept so tamely what USFET officers said? Discussing the camps in 1988, Middleton told the author that he had visited two camps in the summer of 1945, one near Gotha, the other at Bad Kreuznach. He at first said the prisoners were well fed. The author then told him that he had discovered that over half a million prisoners had died in the U.S. camps, and offered to let him read the manuscript before publication so he might defend himself. Middleton replied, "Don't worry about me." He explained that he wasn't surprised that the author had been "able to dig up some bad things from that time." He now added that he had not actually visited the camps themselves, but only "driven by."[36]

It is remarkable that no one disputed Pradervand's statements. For months after, in cables from embassies to home, or between armies, the figures are quoted as absolutely true. The only question was, who was the accused? No one else did a survey to find out who was responsible. Not the French army, nor the Red Cross, nor any journalist and of course, no German. Pradervand makes his one brief blazing appearance in history and then disappears.

It would have been easy for a reporter, after Pradervand's revelations, to visit a village near a camp to talk to the villagers, in France or in Germany. But no one wrote about such a visit, either to challenge Pradervand or to confirm his information. Nothing appeared in *Le Monde* or the *Times* from the "unimpeachable source" at USFET, about the sensational betrayal of Smith's promises, which assured the deaths of thousands of men. By August 30, more than two million men had been discharged but apparently not a single interview was reported in the press west of the Rhine. No one interviewed a camp commander, or guard, or any of the thousands of priests, professors, ministers, teachers, doctors, women and children who by now had emerged from the camps. No one thought to ask for the death certificates in the *mairies* or the *Rathaüser* (town halls) where by law they had to be recorded. The way things began in 1945 was the way they continued for 43 years. Charles von Luttichau, who during the Pradervand episode was living not far from Frankfurt, was among the millions not interviewed. Nor did any Americans ever believe his story about his experience when he repeated it to them years later in the U.S., although by then von Luttichau was a U.S. citizen writing history for the U.S. Army. The attitude created in the heat of the moment cooled and hardened and became history.

In Germany there were over 200 U.S. camps; in the French zone of Germany plus France itself there were over 1,600 French camps. That the camps were disaster areas was widely known in both armies, but never reported outside, apart from the three-week sensation caused by *Le Figaro* and Pradervand. They had revealed in embryo the monstrous atrocity. The reporters had only to strip the caul from it to get the story of their lives, but they would not.

Why was there such aversion to continuing this major story with its truly unimpeachable source? Unless the journalists are willing to say, like Hitler's Germans, "we didn't know," there can be only two reasons. They didn't care. Or they approved.

9

INSIDE THE GREENHOUSE

"The French prison system is a glass house where there is nothing to hide."

— MAJOR-GENERAL BUISSON

THE INTERNATIONAL COMMITTEE OF THE Red Cross, inspecting the French camps, reported time after time in 1945 and 1946 that conditions were "unsatisfactory," "disturbing," "alarming," very seldom that they were satisfactory. Two camps were notorious to the Red Cross, at La Chauvinerie and Montreuil-Bellay, where, in September 1945, there were thousands of women and children who had been originally imprisoned by the Americans. The ICRC complained to the French that these old men, women and childen were dying of typhus that would soon spread to the surrounding French civilians.[1]

At the end of October 1946, the International Committee of the Red Cross reported that "the situation at present is more than alarming. More than half the German POWs working are insufficiently clad and will not be able to stand up to the rigors of a winter without running the gravest risks of disease. In such conditions a high number of deaths in the course of the winter must be expected."[2] The same sort of report was repeated in 1947, with the same dire warnings.[3] Any reports of satisfactory conditions usually came from French army officers who had just been asked by High French Levels to respond to charges by some outside agency, such as the Red Cross or the U.S. Army. Despite all this, the U.S. Army handed over at least 101,000 more prisoners in early 1946. The British also handed over another 30,000 in January 1946.[4] That the Americans knew they were delivering these men to disaster is clear in the complaints the army made through the period about the failure of the French to live up to their previous commitments to improve conditions. "Owing to the continuing inertia of the French authorities to correct deficiencies which have been repeatedly brought to their attention, it is further recommended" that the army try to get the State Department to correct the deficiencies to meet the standards of the Geneva Convention, and also to repatriate soon all the ones who have just been transferred.[5] General John T. Lewis, who wrote that, must have made these recommendations only to cover his exposed flanks, because there was no chance the French would accept criticism from the Americans for failure to respect the Geneva Convention. There was no chance that they would soon repatriate men whom they had frequently said were being taken in to work, not to be sent home. Lewis was obviously looking to improve the image of the U.S. Army: he was only repeating recommendations that had already failed.

The first faint hint of America's future involvement in the Viet Nam War appears in these camps. The French deliberately starved some of these prisoners in order to force them to "volunteer" to serve in the French Foreign Legion. Many of the Legionnaires who fought in Viet Nam were Germans handed over by Americans to the French in 1945 and 1946.[6]

All through 1945 and much of 1946, Pradervand struggled in the ever-changing net of American bureaucracy, trying to help the prisoners of the French. His approach was ingenuous. He reminded the generals and diplomats of their principles of justice, decency, generosity, pointed out the obligations these entailed, then offered to help fill them, always with a sense of the urgent need of the prisoners themselves. Afraid to denounce the principles, ignorant of the reality they were supposed to administer, the diplomats squirmed away, inventing new difficulties.

Prompted by Pradervand, International Committee President Max Huber wrote to the new Secretary of State James F. Byrnes in January, to "note with gratification" Byrnes's claim that the U.S. government's policy towards prisoners of war "is in complete conformity with the spirit of the Geneva Convention, and that transfer is allowed by the United States authorities only when there is sufficient assurance that the terms of the Convention are adequately observed by the other Power."[7]

Pradervand devised an ingenious plan which he outlined in a letter to Eldred D. Kuppinger of Special Projects at the State Department.[8] He began as usual by giving the Americans what might be called "the benefit of the no doubt," saying, "As you no doubt are aware, the situation of the German prisoners of war now in French custody has become very critical." The International Committee of the Red Cross, through Pradervand, was attempting to help the prisoners, partly by using money given him by the prisoners themselves, to buy food. This was probably the hardest-earned money in the history of the world. According to one prisoner, he had to save for six months to buy a tube of toothpaste.

Pradervand's problem was currency restrictions. Could Kuppinger help find a way round these? Pradervand suggested a way, promising as well not to treat any consideration granted this time as a precedent for another appeal. Kuppinger routed this to Byrnes, who then wrote to the new Secretary of War, Robert Patterson, suggesting that it "would be appropriate at this time for the American military authorities at Paris to enter into discussions with the French military authorities in order to ameliorate if necessary the condition of those prisoners of war already transferred . . ." and so on.

Other discussions followed as the prisoners died, until June 13, 1946, when Kuppinger, with a prodigious squirm, denied

Pradervand on the ground that "the American authorities are not in a position to turn over the items desired by the Committee against payment in French francs." Then he howevered "it is believed that the Committee's desires in this connection have been substantially met by the inclusion in Section Nine" of a clause which might or might not permit the prisoners to buy — in competition with the civilian black market — food which had already been allotted to them.

The total number of prisoners on hand in France at its peak of about 800,000 represented about 2 percent of the total population of France (which in 1945 was about 40,000,000). If, as many prisoners contend, their ration was about half the minimum needed to sustain life, then just 1 percent of the total food consumed in France would have saved them all from starvation. This food would have turned the dying people — on whom French food was ultimately wasted — into productive workers contributing to French recovery, as was initially intended.

Once the depredations by the Germans stopped in August 1944, the production of food in France in effect grew as French supplies now remained at home. The German requirement for certain goods had been extremely high and amounted to one quarter of all French meat production and some 13 percent of French wheat.[9] Nevertheless, French wheat production in 1944 was 500,000 tonnes higher than consumption, which was about 6,500,000 tonnes;[10] this production total of 7,000,000 tonnes was approximately 1,310,000 tonnes higher than production in 1941 of about 5,690,000 tonnes.[11] Although production of potatoes in France fell by about one third from the average before the war, the reduction of German demands again eased the strain on the French. The production of meat rose by so much, that in 1946 it was 48 percent higher than the consumption of meat had been in France in 1941.[12] In Germany itself, the French Army confiscated so much food from German civilians that massive food shortages were caused.[13] Confiscation of "this very considerable total"[14] soon resulted in widespread starvation.[15] "In the French zone, what weighs heaviest on the people are the enormous requisitions of the

French Army," General de Gaulle was told by one of his representatives in December 1945.[16]

The little French or American food that was doled out to the camps was depleted by theft on its way to the prisoners. It then appeared on the black market.[17] Raoul Laporterie, mayor of Bascons southeast of Bordeaux, who had given work to two German prisoners of war in his chain of haberdashery stores, wrote a stinging letter to General de Gaulle about the situation in the Landes, southeast of Bordeaux, where there were many prison camps. Heedless of the reprisal that was likely to come, and did, Laporterie wrote, "The French army amazes and disappoints the farmers, who see that the requisitions levied on them don't relieve the painful situation in the cities. The explanation for this is the fact that the military administration which takes for its so-called needs a large part of the requisitions, greatly exaggerates the amount of supplies required, and it seems from all the evidence that all the army's surplus ends up in the black market."

In May 1946, the State Department was still gingerly considering the possibility of opening mail service to the prisoners in U.S. and French camps. Acting Secretary of State Dean Acheson wrote to Henry A. Wallace, Secretary of Commerce, that "there is considerable demand among people in the United States for the opening of a channel whereby they might send parcels of food and clothing."[18] How was it that the august Acheson had discovered this "considerable demand among people in the United States" while firmly seated behind his desk in Washington? He had found out from Pradervand, who had detected, and perhaps even generated, this hitherto unknown demand. Further, Acheson was able to tell Secretary of State Byrnes, the French would be glad to cooperate in satisfying the Americans.[19] He enclosed a copy of a letter from Marshal Juin to Pradervand saying there was no objection to the proposal. And that was how, more than a year after the war ended, the prisoners finally started getting mail. "The joy of some of these men who had been waiting for news for months was beyond description," one Quaker observer said.[20]

The French made little use of their starvelings. In France, in January 1946, just over half a million men were nominally at work for the armies or the civilian economy. Most of these, underfed, badly clothed, weak, worked at far less than normal efficiency. Another 124,000 were so sick they couldn't work.[21] When 600 dying men fell off the train at Buglose near Bordeaux in the summer of 1945 before the shocked population of the village, 87 men were in such bad shape that the two-kilometer hike to the camp killed them. In camp, the rest of the men in their indecent rags stared through the cracked and dirty windows into the wet pine woods, perhaps thinking of the pretty story the French guards had told them back in Rennes: "You're going south to pick grapes." It was easy to imagine themselves among the sunny vines popping ripe grapes into their mouths. As the grapes ripened, and no one came for them, they realized that their only purpose here was to die. Many did. In Labouheyre, a work camp nearby, 25 percent of the men died in January, of starvation, dysentery or disease.[22] The dysentery was so bad that the French came down with it.

The work at Labouheyre was called forestry, but it was a ghastly charade of the conventional picture of burly woodsmen chopping down trees. Many of the guards were ashamed of the condition of the prisoners whom they had to lead into the woods to work.[23] Most of the prisoners had little or no experience, so they were already at risk. Starved, with bad boots or none, ignorant of the process, they were often injured. Once injured, such men died quickly. There were many who died on those work teams.

These guards, mostly decent men recruited from the villages and farms round about, did not think of vengeance, although many of them had recently been prisoners themselves in Germany. They did not torture or maltreat the men, but left them alone as much as they could. Some of the guards brought a little food from their homes to feed the famished Germans. Two of the Germans said they would have died without the liter of milk brought to them every day by a guard who lived on a farm nearby.[24]

Heinz T. had left Bad Kreuznach in May thinking his trainload of sick, starving comrades was a strange gift for the Americans to give the French. He was still wearing the same shorts he had on when he was captured in hospital. He was barefoot. He was cheerful. He was 18 years old.

> I went with people who had just been operated on in hospital but that didn't matter, they loaded us all up. We crossed the Rhine by the Roosevelt Memorial Bridge, which was temporary. I remember being in open wagons looking straight down at the water which was frightening as the bridge wasn't very solid. That was on the eighth of May, and there were a lot of American aviators around who were celebrating their victory.
>
> I only had one piece of ID showing my birthdate, 1927. I thought they might release me if they thought I was only 16, so I changed the seven to a nine, but it made no difference. That didn't stop them, I was taken to France too. We heard that there were American camps in France where the prisoners were well treated. We heard that in Reims, the Germans controlled the traffic, they even scolded the French drivers, which made the French angry. We went to Rennes but it wasn't until two months had gone by that we were handed over to the French.
>
> They put some food on the train with us, the labels said 10 and one so we thought they meant enough food for 10 people for one day and we were about 30 people so we thought we would be one day on the road, but we traveled for over three days, without getting out, completely locked in. We would look through the little cracks to see where we were. At one point someone said he saw the Eiffel Tower, but he couldn't see Paris. Then after the three days we arrived in Rennes. There were more than 100,000 prisoners in the camp, about the same as in the city. In the barracks were beds, the first we had seen for many weeks, three levels high, made of wood with nothing else, no straw or anything. We slept on the boards. This was the first time we were covered by a roof since we were cap-

tured. We had spent three weeks at Kreuznach on the ground, not allowed to make a fire or dig a hole, and our work during the day was to line up for a bit of water. It was brought by farmers and put in barrels, but it didn't even have time to be put in the barrels before it was all gone, because sometimes people would make holes in the pipes and get at it first. It's always the same wherever there is hardship.

There was a real shortage of food. When the peas arrived, they were divided and once they had been shared out some were still left. Everyone counted and if we had six each, then we'd wait till we got six and a half.

We stayed at Rennes almost eight months. In those months we understood why we had been brought to France. France needed soldiers. They had a big problem in Indo-China, in Algeria and they wanted to staff their Foreign Legion. We were infiltrated by German agents who worked for the French to round up soldiers.

When the Americans left the camp they did shitty things to the French. The French revenged themselves on us. The first thing the Americans did was to take everything out of the military hospital. They broke the windows so they could also take the heating system. The French watched them do all this. And they also took a whole load of cement and dumped it into the river. The Americans were real bastards. The prisoners that the French had taken by themselves fared much better.

There was another group of prisoners who arrived from Norway. They were taken across Germany by the British and they thought they were going home so they carried huge sacks with them, but then they arrived in France. That was in 1946. When they got to our camp they were well fed and we asked them if they had been through Germany and they said yes, but the British didn't care if some got away, they looked the other way and if some got away that was too bad. In Norway they were still armed four months after the war. They were confined to an area but they still had all their belongings.

The soldiers who did join the Foreign Legion were put in another camp nearby where we could see them, and in a couple of weeks they were well fed and looked stronger, but we became weaker and weaker. We could see them starting to play football and singing and we were right beside them.

I met a university math professor and he gave me private tutoring in mathematics. I got a piece of canvas from one of the barracks and I could write on that. I found that I understood everything I wrote but as soon as I erased it I erased it from my memory, so that was the first sign of fatigue, not to remember things. It was terrible, I erased it and I was no longer able to remember what I had just written and understood. I was not depressed, it was just malnutrition. My friends in the camp who were older wrote to my parents when they got back to Germany and they said I was incredibly cheerful and that I had raised their spirits because I was not depressed. I don't know how I did it. I had developed a philosophy of protection when we found ourselves in that camp for the winter. We thought they were going to ship us off to the States. I understood we were in for a long time and everyone has his own defense system so I said to myself OK, we're making a film, it's captivity, I am an actor, I can get out when I want but I won't be paid so I'll stay for the whole thing. As I had done a bit of acting in youth films in Berlin I knew a little bit how it worked so I said that's what it was. A lot of the French would go by on the road near the railway at Rennes who would stare at us and we would look at them and finally I said to myself it was like a zoo except we don't know which side the monkeys are on.

So finally I viewed the barbed wire not as something to prevent us from leaving but as something to prevent those we didn't want from entering. Those were little crutches, when it goes on like that you have to grab on to something. But later when the weakness really came and the slightest movement made you faint, we could calculate how many hours we would pass out. The malnutrition got to such a stage that the smallest gesture done too quickly would cause us to faint. The first time it happened to me, we were sitting down in the sun with nothing to do, absolutely nothing. I can remember saying to myself, as we all sat on the ground in the sun, OK, there is still six hours until the soup, and since there is nothing to do, no books or anything, I said, OK if I do this quick little movement with my arm I'll be out for three hours, if I do it again, that's another three hours, so six hours altogether. I'd be out for six hours which didn't get counted in my captivity period.

Food was so scarce that people were usually sick and when you got sick they took you to hospital. When people were taken to hospital you never saw them come back. Of the hundred thousand prisoners at Rennes there was certainly a percentage who died which would make a fair number. But I've never been able to find a cemetery.

We never saw the Red Cross, nobody came to inspect us until two years later, to bring us blankets. That was the first time they came, in 1947. We were eating the grass between the buildings. The French were not solely responsible for what happened in the camps in France because they received a huge number of Germans who were already handicapped by bad treatment in Germany. When you round up hundreds of thousands of people into an area and you don't think about how you are going to feed them, that is very serious.

We were finally sent to a work commando in a village. There were 20 of us, one supposed to be the cook, but each time the rest of the group came back from work the cook would have eaten everything. At the beginning of one day, the guard who was responsible for us said OK, I'll try to round up some food for you but for now there are potatoes in that room. There was a huge pile in there and we said how many can we have and he said take all you want. So we each took two kilos of potatoes, put them in water, then put them on the fire to cook them and I think we ate all the potatoes in one day. The guard came back and saw there were no more potatoes and said that there had to have been at least 150 kilograms. All of them gone between 20 of us. There was no salt so we took wood ashes to put on them. We were sick from eating so many, with huge stomachs.

When we arrived at Rennes, the Germans amongst themselves decided that since the food shortage was so serious, they would give double rations to those under 18 years of age and in the 3,000 at our cage there were about 150 guys who were 15, 16 or 17. I am an honest man, I had always lied to the French and the Americans but with my own compatriots I could not, so I told them I was 18, I swear it didn't really matter because two times nothing is not much either. And to those young guys we gave all the teachers and we tried to interest them in lectures and so on but most of them weren't interested. At the beginning, I went to some of the lectures, everybody took turns giving a presentation but when the young guys saw me in there they said what is this guy doing here?

I told myself I would never join the Foreign Legion, this is the end, even if I die here. After having survived the war and being in Berlin during the bombings, and fighting the Americans in Germany with almost no weapons, I was so happy to have survived that I didn't even think of captivity as punishment.[25]

Prisoner number 1503477, Werner Steckelings, had strong reason to hate France and Frenchmen for the rest of his life, which in 1945 didn't promise to be long.[26] Transferred from the big American camp at Heilbronn, where he had starved in a hole in the ground, he arrived at Rivesaltes in the south of France in August. Water was scarce. Once the French driver of the water truck opened the tank outside the gate, laughing at the screams of the thirsty prisoners inside as the water gushed into the dirt. Every day, three or four or five men died in his barracks of about 80 men. Some days he helped to drag as many as 20 bodies to the camp entrance.

In November, he was transferred to Aubagne in the Bouches du Rhône. When the truck stopped in a town, Steckelings noticed a crust of bread on the pavement. Frantically he signaled to a passing Frenchman, who handed it to him between the slats saying, *"Monsieur, je connais la vie."*

The new camp at Aubagne was nicknamed "The Organ of Death" because the barracks moaned in the wind. Steckelings' head was shaved, "only because the French hated us. It was pure hatred." He was bald, he weighed about 36 kilos (80 pounds), he was 19 years old. But he still had his sense of humor. An illiterate young prisoner who had received a letter from his mother asked Steckelings to read it for him. They sat down together, Steckelings began to read aloud, the other boy reached out and covered Steckelings's ears with his hands. Steckelings asked, "Why are you doing that?" The other replied, "You shouldn't hear what my mother is saying to me."

His life was saved when he was shipped north with about a dozen other prisoners to work, eventually at a fertilizer factory. Here he was befriended by a French family who took care of him, giving him clothes, food, friendship. They invited him to the wedding of their daughter. He worked in that place for three years, until he was released. His attitude to France was completely changed by his experiences with the family at Sorgues. "They were very kind to me. Although the French in the camps were very cruel to us, I have put that aside because so many French people were kind to us once we got out. In a family you find out what a nation is." Steckelings has visited these people many times since, always taking presents with him, always bringing presents home.*

Many prisoners passed from death to life once the camp gates opened to let them into homes in the villages or on the farms of France. It is a fair guess that the majority of the prisoners who survived French camps were saved by the generosity of French civilians, mainly farmers and villagers.

About 900,000 prisoners were taken in by the French by capture or by transfer from the British and Americans by November 1945. Of these, 255,953 were no longer being accounted

---

* Before granting an interview to the author, Steckelings said, "I'm going to tell you some terrible things, and something good. You must promise to print the good as well as the bad."

for in November, after only a few months of captivity.[27] In March 1946, a new category appears in the French statistics, *"Perdus Pour Raisons Diverses,"* listing 167,000 people. What fate did this term indicate?

There are a number of possible fates. One is that they were discharged without being counted, in the chaos following the turnover of the camps by the Americans. This is highly unlikely, because the French always intended to use these men for labor, so they wanted to keep them on hand. Besides, in order to be discharged, they had to be transported home to Germany, so the travel had to be arranged, meaning they had to be counted.

Another possible fate is that the missing men escaped. The French reported a number of escapes from trains, trucks and so on, but the majority of prisoners was handed over to them very sick, in France, lacking papers, in rags. They spoke no French, they had no money, they didn't know where they were, and the local population was at first very hostile.

Paratrooper Alfred Tappen was such a man. Captured north of Paris in August 1944, Tappen actually escaped from his camp, then re-entered it willingly, at the risk of his life. In October 1944, he was in an American camp near Alençon where they were well treated but very hungry. With the help of another prisoner, he slithered under the barbed wire out into a ditch at dusk, collected apples in an orchard near the wire, then went back near the wire in the dark. He flung an apple over the fence onto the roof of his friend's tent. The friend lifted the wire for him as he tried to slide back in. His paratrooper trousers, stuffed with apples, were much bulkier than before, so he caught the fabric on the barbed wire. For a moment he tore frantically at the wire, fearing the smash of a bullet into him from the guard whom he could hear returning. At last, the material ripped and he slithered in safely.

Tappen went back in because "I couldn't see any point in trying to get away without any help."[28] During the war or afterwards, the danger to escapees was the same. To believe that a large number escaped without help through hostile France, over a guarded border, is to wish them safely home, rather than to make a judgment about possibilities. The likelihood is that the escapes from French camps, as from American, are statistically negligible.

Another possible source of error is that they were miscounted. Juin refers to errors in reporting by the Americans of up to 30 percent, without saying whether the errors over- or underestimated the men being turned over. In the case of such confusion no sensible allowance can be made. It is even possible that the numbers are correct by mistake, if the many errors canceled each other out. The rough agreement of the French and Americans on the total number transferred suggests that the number is accurate. The ease of counting such a small number of men static in camps makes it likely that the French did count accurately, once the prisoners had stopped traveling. In any case, these figures are, as with the American figures, not only the best we have, but the most authoritative figures that we could have, because they come from the highest sources on either side and because they roughly confirm each other. No quarrel ever developed between the Americans and the French about the totals received, for Juin accepted the errors without disputing the totals, so these figures have at least enough credibility to give us a general view.

The last possible fate is death. At Thorée les Pins, the population dropped from about 20,000 remarked by Pradervand in late summer, to 15,600 on November 10, as reported by the regional commander.[29] None of the 4,400 missing men was returned to the Americans. It is not certain but it seems likely that none was shipped out to other camps before November 1, because the Americans said in October that they would take back the sick ones, of whom Thorée had a big supply. The French wanted to get rid of these useless men, not ship them on to other camps.

The commandant, Zalay, told Pradervand in August that at least 2,000 of the men were so sick there was no hope left for them. A list for only one section of the camp, kept by a German prisoner, confirms by name over 400 dead in the period August—October.[30] The camp guard Robert Langlais of Thorée, who was one of the gravediggers at Thorée for six months, helped to bury on average about 15 bodies per day in August through October.[31]

Of the 200,000 men likely to die according to Pradervand, approximately 52,000[32] were returned to the Americans, leaving 148,000 in French camps. There was no improvement in the French camps that winter, as we know from the Americans, the Red Cross and some French complaints as well, so it seems certain that all the 148,000 leftovers died as predicted.

The feeble vacillations of French policy, between pusillanimous vengeance and the hypocritical concern that was usually triggered by the threat of the press, were embodied in the story of a single person, l'Abbé Franz Stock, a German priest.[33] Stock had come to France during the war, ministering to French people in German jails in France. Shocked at the un-Christian behavior of his countrymen, he secretly made notes of the circumstances of the deaths of each Resistance person shot. Hundreds of deaths were detailed in his book, which after the war became a useful source of information for the families of the dead. He pleaded with the Germans to improve conditions for the prisoners, and personally brought them relief and religious comfort. As the Allies began winning, and Germans poured into the camps, changing places with their enemies, he followed his compatriots into captivity himself. Because of his ambivalent role during the occupation, he was not treated as a full-fledged German, but allowed enough liberty to seek help for a small seminary he set up amongst the German POWs. The French army let other chaplains minister to the prisoners, apparently in the thought that they would help the prisoners to die politely. But Stock would not let himself be limited by the narrowness of hatred, either French or German. He saw not the barbed wire but the spaces between. His young students, soon numbering a thousand, returned to Germany to re-establish the Christianity which had been destroyed.

Stock spent three years despite his bad heart and the horrible living conditions of the camps, training the seminarists and doing everything he could to re-establish the mail service, get better food and clothing, exactly as he had for the French in their years of pain. At last, exhausted, emaciated, he died in a hospital attached to a prison on the Boulevard Saint-Germain in Paris, in 1948. Major General Buisson, who had presided over the conditions that drove Stock and so many others to a premature grave, came like a vulture to the funeral. Monsignor Roncalli, later Pope John XXIII, spoke at the graveside of the strength and kindness of Stock, but Buisson forbade the newspapers to report the remarks, or the death of Stock. An old woman who had known Stock stood nearby saying aloud over and over "*Scandale, scandale.*"

For years the source of the statistics about German prisoners in French hands has been a self-lauding tract by Major General Buisson, head of the Prisoner of War Service, who briskly set the tone of his whole book with the epigraph saying the French prison system was a glass house in which there was nothing to hide.[34]

Let us peer inside.

As we approach the glass house, it disappears, revealing Buisson standing in its place with his description of it. He says it is an open greenhouse (which we cannot visit), buzzing with visiting journalists (although we cannot see them), who are eagerly interviewing the prisoners about their glowing testimonials (unfortunately not available), given in grateful recognition of their comfortable conditions — which the Red Cross has described as "catastrophic."

Buisson tends to succumb to his own propaganda. For instance, after saying that in March 1946 the "number of prisoners of war attained its apogee, just over 800,000," it only takes another 39 pages of his prose to expunge this entirely from memory. Then he tells us that "October 1945, marked the extreme summit attained by the number of prisoners on hand in French captivity — 870,000." Onwards another 174 pages; here we find a different October total, this time 741,239.

Buisson failed to count 65,000 men given by the British and Americans before February, 1946. The total for prisoners on hand in October, 1945, is about 150,000 lower than the number confirmed by his chief, General Juin.[35] Buisson also conjures up some soothing death totals for us, on page 221. In the five years 1944 through 1948, he says, 24,161 prisoners died.

Given that he was accounting for more than 2,000,000 prisoner-years (that is, one million held for two years), this death toll would amount to 1.2 percent per year, which speaks volumes for the prisoners' ability to live without food, clothing, medicine and so on. But Buisson is not content with 1.2 percent: he attributes 18,416 of the deaths to war wounds, reducing the non-wounded total to 5,745. This produces a number satisfying to Buisson but incredible to everyone else, a death rate for these unwounded prisoners of 0.28 percent per year. The comparable death rate for resting U.S. Army personnel was 0.38 percent.[36] So anyone who believes Buisson, must also believe that starving, sick men in rags without medicine, far from home in the despair of defeat with no news of their families, doomed to a captivity whose end they could not see, lived longer than rested, victorious, well-fed U.S. troops in peacetime. It is a novel argument against war, that the loser wins.

It is clear that Buisson is not a reliable witness, nor are the writers who have depended on him, such as Kurt Böhme in the Maschke series, who reproduces many of Buisson's agile statistics, expressing here and there some doubts.[37]

Finding the death total for the French camps begins with determining the Missing/Not Accounted For, because here the French, like the Americans, appear to have been unwary. The total intake of the French at November 1, 1945, stood at 280,629 captured by themselves according to SHAEF, plus a further 724,442 turned over to them by the Americans,[38] plus the 25,000 from the British and Canadians, for a total of 1,030,071. In the *Notes Documentaires et Études* of the Secrétariat d'État, the total number on hand is given as 719,936, leaving 310,135 to account for.[39] Approximately 30,000 to 60,000 had been released on the spot in Germany from U.S. camps taken over there, leaving between 250,135 and 280,135 Missing/Not Accounted For.

At February 1946, the total intake, down slightly because of returns to the Americans, is now 1,009,629, made up of a reduced total American-British cession of 729,000[40] plus the original captures. But only 770,000 can be accounted for at this date,[41] leaving a total Missing/Not Accounted For of 239,629.

Here the French government pamphlet, perhaps inadvertently, uses language eerily similar to the USFET phraseology, for 167,000 of the Missing/Not Accounted For are termed *Perdus Pour Raisons Diverses,* Lost For Various Reasons.

An important clue to deciphering *Perdus Pour Raisons Diverses* is Pradervand's prediction that of 600,000 men he had surveyed, 200,000 were sure to die in the winter if conditions didn't improve. It is certain that conditions did not significantly improve, so it is more than likely that Pradervand's prediction came true.

The overall final figures as of 1948 based in part on Buisson, in part on SHAEF, and on the *Notes Documentaires et Études,* show that the total of prisoners taken by the French on the field, plus net from the Americans, plus the British transfer, plus the North African transfers, is 1,072,629, the difference from figures quoted above being due mainly to the prisoners in North Africa, taken over from the Allies after the German defeat there in 1943.* Buisson says that final repatriations were 628,388, and the number released to Free Worker status was 130,000. This total of 758,388 leaves 314,241 Missing/Not Accounted For.

At this point anyone looking to find what actually happened is stopped by Buisson's shifty phrase that of the 314,241, "dozens of thousands" were repatriated uncounted and unaccounted for.[42] This phrase, so vague it could mean as few as 24,000 or as many as 100,000, destroys the Big Number and thus prevents us from seeing clearly the exact size of the atrocity. This is how history was managed.

Luckily, we can prove that the omission of the number of men repatriated but not accounted for is deliberate and therefore intended to hide something.

The number of prisoners was quite important to the French.

---

* The British apparently transferred a further 30,000 prisoners to the French in 1946, and the U.S. a further 101,000. Because so many records are missing, it is impossible to say if any or all of these turn up in the totals quoted of the French intake. The figure used above is the lowest of several possible choices.

Time after time from late 1944 onwards, they asked their allies for prisoners to help rebuild France. They first asked for 1,750,000, but later accepted whatever they could get from the Americans. The reports from Buisson, from the Chef de Bureau in the Labor Ministry, M. Simon, and in the *Notes Documentaires*, show month after month how many prisoners were working throughout France in each of dozens of categories. They give these totals to the last digit, without rounding off. So we know not only that the French were capable of counting masses of men in their camps, but that they did. That they failed to count — or report the count of — the repatriates, who were being subtracted from the totals they were printing, and which they were always trying to increase to the benefit of France, cannot be unintended. The only reason not to report the repatriates when all other subtotals are being assiduously noted, is to hide the true totals. And the only credible reason for that is to hide the deaths, which therefore must have been high enough to be worth hiding. Thus, although it is impossible to say with great accuracy how many people died in these camps, it is certain that it was enough to cause concern and embarrassment to the French.

Other evidence enables us to focus this picture a little more sharply. The following table supports in detail what Pradervand found:[43]

Mortality in six French camps surveyed by James Bacque, 1986, plus one reported by *Le Monde*, September 1945.

	Complement	Deaths	Death Rate (annual)	Period (months)
Thorée les Pins	12,000	2,520	42 percent	5-6
Marseille (Hospital)	800	450	100 percent	3
Buglose	800	250	37.5 percent	10
Labouheyre	600	221	37 percent	12
Daugnague/Pissos	800	400	100 percent	6
Rivesaltes	2,400	1,350	100 percent	3
Saint Paul d'Égiaux	17,000	400	9.4	3
Saint Paul d'Égiaux	(17,000)	300	21.4	1
Totals	34,400	5,891	30 percent	

In addition, a secret French government report said that at the army camp at Barlin, where 3,000 men were held, the death rate was 17 percent per year.[44] At a camp of 2,000 people near Toulouse in January 1946, a Quaker relief team found that 600 men had died in three weeks.[45]

Including both of *Le Monde*'s reports on Saint Paul d'Egiaux, the total surveyed is 51,400.[46]

Although the two reports on Saint Paul d'Égiaux may be used for the death rate, only one visit should be used to determine the size of the sample. Accordingly, this size is 34,400 or approximately 3.4 percent of the total ever held. The size of Pradervand's Red Cross sample was around 80 percent of the total holdings at the time, or about 60 percent of the number of captives who passed through the French system at some time.

The overall death rate produced when the prisoner-months (number of prisoners times number of months captivity) are scored against total deaths shown, is 41.7 percent per year, or .8 percent per week. These samples taken together with all the other information above, show beyond reasonable doubt that the French camps were a catastrophe for the prisoners. A number somewhere between the total Missing/Not Accounted For, and the total predicted by Pradervand, died as a result of that captivity, or as the result of disease and weakness following American captivity. Following Pradervand and the table above, we can be sure the total falls within a range of certainties: not more than 314,241 prisoners and no fewer than 167,000 died in French captivity between 1945 and 1948.

10

THE BRITISH AND CANADIANS

AT THE END OF THE WAR, THE BRITISH and Canadians in north Germany were faced with an amazing situation: they were far outnumbered by the Germans who were eagerly surrendering to them. Hundreds of thousands of Germans were hiding in the woods, in cellars, "hungry and frightened, lying in grain fields within fifty feet of us, awaiting the appropriate time to jump up with their hands in the air." The description[1] of the fighting in the north by Captain H. F. McCullough of the 2d anti-Tank Regiment of the 2d Canadian Division ends with the chaos at the time of the German surrender: "It was a strange situation in that they wandered about the countryside, no enclosures, sleeping in barns, fields, etc. We naturally had commandeered houses and took over the hotel on Wangerooge Island. The Germans were very disciplined and no animosity existed between our side and theirs. We of course were far less in numbers but were armed and they were not. We paid very little attention to them."

In these bizarre conditions McCullough believed without

question the story he heard that after VE Day, May 8, an armed German soldier and a Canadian stood guard together outside an ammunition dump. He was told that the Canadians reasoned, "The war is over, it will give confidence to the civilian population . . . the troops will not act aggressively as they have too much to lose with final release so close at hand."[2]

During the war, the Canadians quickly threw up for their prisoners barbed wire cages that lacked shelter or good kitchens for the first few days. In one of these camps near Dieppe in the fall of 1944, there were "many thousands of men crowded into the cages built in the fields." These prisoners were fed immediately, given enough to drink, and within a few days, got tents. The German who reported this, Werner Heyne of Toronto, said that there were no deaths in this camp. After a month, they were shipped to better camps in England.[3]

Like the Americans, the British and Canadians at the end of the war in north Germany were at first short of food and shelter for their astounding numbers of Wehrmacht prisoners. In a day and a half, Field Marshal Montgomery reported, half a million Germans surrendered to his 21st Army Group in north Germany.[4] Soon after VE Day, the British-Canadian total catch came to more than 2,000,000 captives. The looting which had already begun in the areas conquered by the Canadian army was quickly quelled by Montgomery, who directed "urgent action to stop this looting of food and livestock. It will be explained to the soldiers that any food they take from the Germans now may well be at the expense of the UK at a later date."[5] With the exception of the British camp at Overijsche (see below), the British and Canadian camps soon provided just enough food and shelter for the prisoners to survive in fair health.

Although the British had said they would refuse to accept any DEFs from the Americans, they in fact did accept hundreds of thousands of sick, starved men from American POW camps. Among them was Corporal Helmut Liebich, shivering with dysentery and typhus in the camp at Rheinberg.[6] Liebich, who had been working in an anti-aircraft experimental group at Peenemunde on the Baltic, was captured near Gotha in central Germany by the Americans on April 17. There were no tents in the Gotha DEF camp, only the usual barbed wire fences round a field soon churned to mud. On the first day, they received a small ration of food, which was then cut in half. In order to get it, they were forced to run a gauntlet. Hunched over, they ran between lines of guards who hit them with sticks as they scurried towards their food. On April 27, they were transferred to the U.S. camp at Heidesheim further west, where there was no food at all for days, then very little. Exposed, starving and thirsty, the men started to die. One night, when it rained, Liebich saw the sides of the earth-holes, dug in soft sandy earth, collapse on men who were too weak to struggle out. He tried to dig them out, but there were too many. They smothered before the others could get to them. Liebich sat down and wept. "I could hardly believe men could be so cruel to each other." He watched about 10 to 30 bodies per day being dragged out of his section, Camp B, which held at first around 5,200 men. He saw one prisoner beat another prisoner to death to get his little piece of bread.

Typhus broke out in Heidesheim about the beginning of May. On the 13th, Liebich was transferred to another U.S. POW camp at Bingen-Budesheim near Bad Kreuznach where he was told that the prisoners numbered between 200,000 and 400,000, all without shelter, food, water, medicine, or sufficient space.

Soon he fell sick with dysentery. He was also told he had typhus. Delirious with fever, he was nevertheless told to help sort out prisoners according to their birthplace. He noticed that all the men who had lived east of the Elbe river were being sent to truck convoys destined for France. Liebich told the guards at the end of the shift that he was from Westphalia, which was in the British zone.

He put away his diary now, because he was too weak to write. He was moved again, semi-conscious, in an open-topped railway car with about 60 other prisoners, down the Rhine, on a detour through Holland, where the Dutch stood on bridges to smash stones down on the heads of the prisoners. Sometimes the American guards fired warning shots near the Dutch to keep them off. After three nights, his fellow prisoners helped him stagger into the huge U.S. camp at Rheinberg, again without shelter or food.

When a little food finally did arrive, it was rotten. The men said that at Rheinberg, they had "35 days of starvation and 15 days of no food at all." The death rate in camps such as Rheinberg at this point, May 1945, was about 30 percent per year.[7] In none of the camps had he seen any shelter for the prisoners. In none of the camps had Liebich been registered or counted. Men keeping diaries wrote only information they thought would not offend the guards, because they had heard that prisoners would be punished if they took notes of what was going on.[8]

One day in June, Liebich saw the "Tommies" (British) coming in through the hallucinations of his fever. "We were counted, then counted again, I think six or seven times in the first week. I was shipped to the hospital at Lintfort." At this point, Liebich, who is 176 centimeters high (5 feet 10 inches) weighed 44 kilos (97 pounds). The life-saving care he received at the hospital of Brandt, Schweitzer and Borgmann he remembered with gratitude for the rest of his life. He attributed much of the good work to the British. "It was wonderful to be under a roof in a real bed. We were treated like human beings again. The Tommies treated us like comrades."

According to stories told by ex-prisoners in Rheinberg to this day, the last act of the Americans at Rheinberg before the British took over in mid-June was to bulldoze one section of the camp level while there were still living men in their holes in the ground.[9] Nothing of this has ever been known outside the stories of the prisoners, which have taken 44 years to reach print. It is a safe guess therefore, that none of the British officers reported this to the press. Certainly no report of the conditions at Rheinberg was made public, although an ICRC delegate apparently visited it in May.[10]

At Linfort the men received food every day, but it was too late for many of them. The dying continued for some weeks there. In Liebich's room, he was the only survivor, although each bed was filled three or four times during the few weeks he was there. Liebich did not blame the Tommies for this. He thought that "with the Tommies came order. The difference was like night and day. They saved my life." Cured, he was sent back to Rheinberg, counted again, then released a few weeks later.

The Americans told the British 21st Army Group commanders that they were turning over more prisoners than the British actually found in the camps. The discrepancy was probably due to deaths that had gone uncounted.[11] Once this "British Discrepancy" is taken into account, there is a low variance in the totals of those accounted for among the 21st Army Group prisoners, indicating a low level of deaths in their camps. A further indication of low deaths in British camps is that among the prisoners in the Bremen enclave in British hands, the USFET G3 records show no significant drop in the number of captives accounted for, through August and September 1945.[12] Most significant of all, the USFET records show no Other Losses at all during periods when very high figures of Other Losses are recorded in the U.S. camps.

Among two dozen witnesses, chiefly German, but including several Canadians who guarded prisoners of war or SEPs (surrendered enemy personnel — prisoners without prisoner of war status), all but one report no maltreatment, enough food to live, and, after the first two or three days, sufficient space, enough water, and enough tents to shelter them all. Former prisoner A. Bodmar, now of Markham, Ontario, who was well treated himself, heard of a British camp where, rumor said, between a thousand and five thousand men died very quickly.[13]

The news of these starving men spread not only through the camp system but out of it, probably by mail, for the British began re-establishing mail service for all the prisoners in August of 1945.[14] The Markgraf von Baden in Germany wrote to the editor of the *Times*, Robert Barrington-Ward, in April 1946, complaining about conditions in the British camp noticed by prisoner Bodmar. The Markgraf said:

> I am writing to you because I have received most distressing news about conditions in certain camps under British Control. The information refers to a camp near Ostende

which houses Senior German officers and also to political prisoner camps in the North of Germany. Authentic details are available: a film if it were made would rival the Belsen film.

My chief anxiety is the saving of lives. A number of the prisoners may be guilty but surely not all guilty enough to deserve death by starvation: many however are innocent.

But I am concerned also about England's good name — we need it to heal and to enlighten the Young of Germany. They ask us again and again: are the Allies in earnest about their Christianity?

Yours faithfully

BERTHOLD
Markgraf von Baden

This letter produced results, partly because Barrington-Ward made sure it got wide circulation in the old boys' network. The Lord Bishop of Chichester got up in the House of Lords to ask a question about it:

> My Lords, I beg to ask His Majesty's Government a question of which I have given private notice. The question is: Whether their attention has been called to statements made in the Press and elsewhere about conditions in certain camps under British control for German civilian internees and for German prisoners of war in Belgium and in the British zone of Germany; whether investigations are being made as to the accuracy of such statements; and whether the results of such investigations will be made public as soon as possible.

To which Lord Nathan responded, as parliamentary undersecretary of state for war: "As far as prisoner of war camps in Belgium are concerned, inquiries were instituted immediately reports of irregularities had been brought to notice. A Court of Inquiry is now sitting in Belgium under the auspices of the General Officer Commanding-in-Chief of the British Army of

Three days after the end of the war in Europe, prisoners dig earth holes for shelter at Dallien in the U.S. zone. *(U.S. Army photo)*

In camps like this one at Sinzig on the Rhine on May 12, the death rate observed by U.S. Army doctors was 30 percent per year. *(U.S. Army photo)*

Lineups for scarce water in camps beside the Rhine sometimes lasted all night. *(Rheinberg Town Archives)*

After it rained, deaths greatly increased in camps due to the lack of shelter. Along the Rhine the spring of 1945 was abnormally wet and cold.

The U.S. Army provided few or no cooking facilities, so prisoners improvised.
(Rheinberg Town Archives)

The prisoner's caption reads, "My village, Rheinberg." *(Rheinberg Town Archives)*

The tent in the distance may be a "hospital." *(Rheinberg Town Archives)*

The perimeter fence at Rheinberg was nine kilometers long. *(Rheinberg Town Archives)*

Weakened prisoners often fell off the slippery, narrow mud paths between earth holes. *(Rheinberg Town Archives)*

Many prisoners died lying in their earth holes. *(Rheinberg Town Archives)*

Searchlights picked out one young prisoner climbing the wire at night. He was shot. Other prisoners shouted "murderers, murderers," so the camp commander cut off their food for three days, resulting in many more deaths.

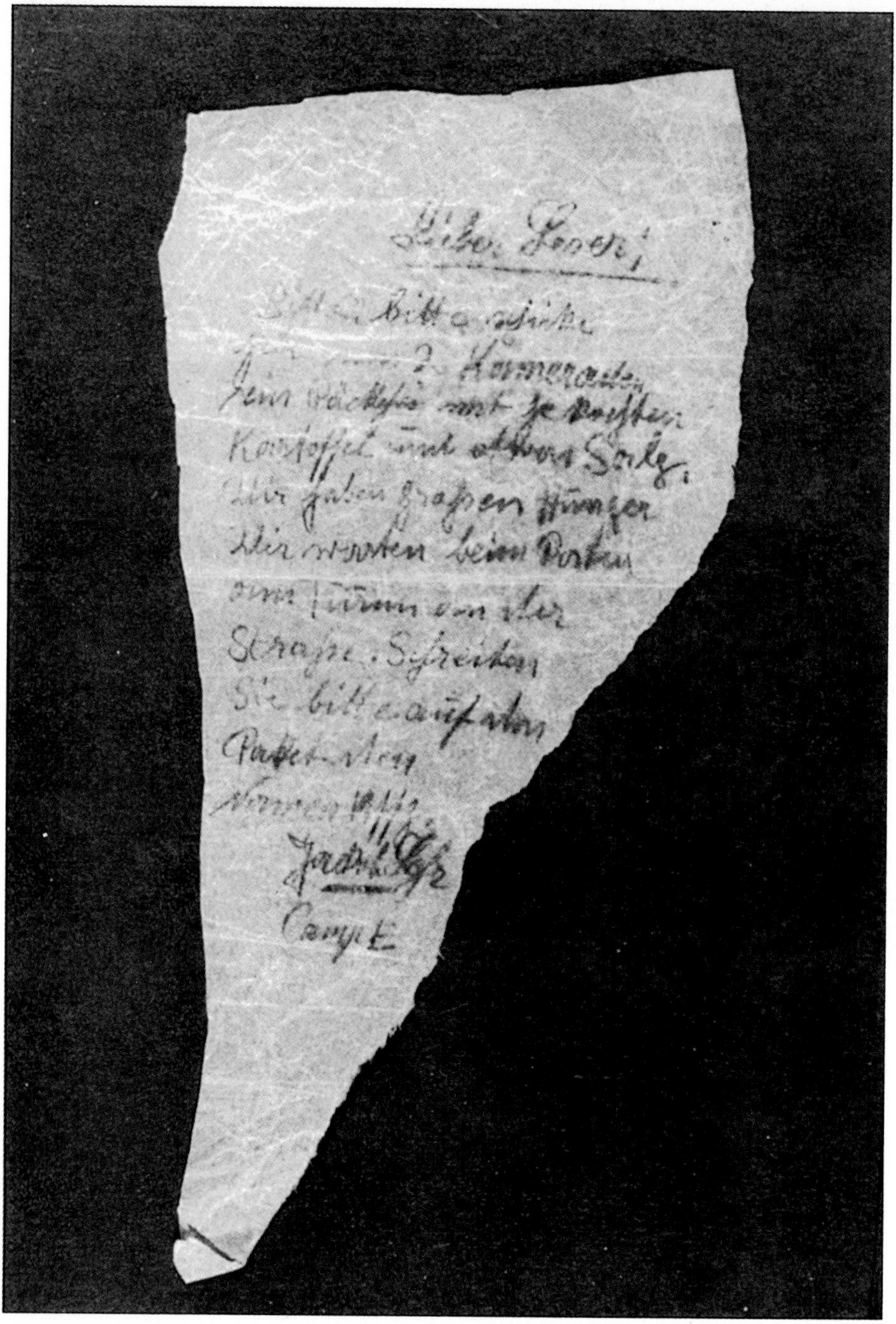

Denied mail, a prisoner in a U.S. camp at Rheinberg threw a note wrapped around a rock over the perimeter fence. The note begs the reader to bring salt and cooked potatoes because, "We are terribly hungry." Signed Jakob Lohr, the note, on brown wrapping paper, is preserved in the town archives of Rheinberg. It is not known if Lohr survived.

the Rhine, and . . . a report is likely to be rendered shortly."[15]

What had happened was that the rations of prisoners in one camp for one month had been reduced by bureaucratic mistake to a disastrously low level.[16] "At least" 200 men died in a few weeks, according to the ICRC observer, M. E. Aeberhard. He visited a few British SEP camps in Belgium, where he found "very painful conditions," notably at Overijsche in December 1945.*[17]

Prodded by the House of Commons, the House of Lords, the *Times* and by articles in the *Observer*, the investigating officers produced results. The accusations by von Baden were publicly confirmed, although one official called his comparison with Belsen nonsensical. It was now revealed that the ration had been restored before the publicity; the dying had stopped within a month. The Red Cross reported, "After our intervention, we were pleased to note that the British authorities energetically went to work to fix this in the second week of December 1945."[18]

There was no whitewash because there was no need for one, according to Colonel Henry Faulk, who was in charge of the re-education of German prisoners of war in British camps in the United Kingdom during and after the war. Faulk is certain that the men running the British camp system in Belgium and Germany kept their prisoners in fair health. The ICRC reports for the British camps in Belgium in the main confirm this, with significant exceptions. In his book, Faulk quotes a report by the German writer A. Mitscherlich in which German prisoners complained bitterly of the wretched conditions in one or two Allied camps in Belgium, which probably included an exceptional British camp: "That they were treated inhumanly, that they starved in wretched conditions and were tormented, is regarded [by the prisoners] as injustice, as a crime against humanity . . . that puts them on the same footing as the victims of the concentration camps. And it leads to the conclusion that The Others do the same things for which they are blamed."[19]

The publicity surrounding the Markgraf von Baden incident makes it seem highly unlikely that the SEP camps were the

* This visit was one of a few exceptions to the general exclusion of ICRC delegates from British camps on the continent in 1945.

scenes of any unnecessary deaths beyond those at Overijsche. There is no reason to suppose that the censorship varied from camp to camp, because mail was allowed freely. It is virtually certain that the Markgraf von Baden discovered Overijsche through a letter from a prisoner.[20] Publicity was not what was needed to move the British, as the Red Cross letter shows: the situation was rectified before the questions were asked in the House.

All this goes far to show that the reason the British members of the Combined Chiefs of Staff refused in April to accept Germans from the DEF camps of the Americans was that they did not intend to allow their own prisoners to suffer the exposure and starvation that were inevitable in the DEF camps. If the British in April had planned to keep their SEPs in the conditions described for American DEFs in Eisenhower's messages of March 10 and in later orders, there would have been no reason to object to receiving captives subject to the same conditions. In other words, the British would scarcely have objected to taking in dying Germans from the Americans if they had been planning to mistreat Germans themselves. Their treatment of Corporal Liebich and thousands of others at Rheinberg shows that even if they were forced to accept dying Germans from the Americans, they did not continue the American treatment of them.

The British policy was not pure devotion to humanitarian principles, or sporting defense of a gallant enemy in defeat. There was cynical self-interest in preserving the strength of the Germans now under Allied control. Like George S. Patton, the British were aware that they might be forced to ally themselves with the Germans against Russia in the coming struggle for Europe. And like Patton, who rapidly discharged his Germans in May 1945,[21] the British did the same with their surrendered enemy personnel, until there were only 68,000 left in the spring of 1946.[22] The British went Patton one further: for several months they kept intact in their formations with their arms, about 300,000 to 400,000 Germans captured in Norway. Stalin taunted Churchill about this at Potsdam.[23] Disingenuously, Churchill denied all knowledge of them. Soon after, some of these men were sent by train to British camps in north Germany and some to French camps in France. As Heinz T. has said, despite their status as SEPs, they were healthy and well fed when they arrived among the ghostly remnants of their army in the French camp at Rennes in August.[24]

Unlike the Americans, the British made sure nearly all the time that their SEPs got food from German sources in quantity and quality equal to the rations of the prisoners of war, which were themselves adequate. They also supplied as a matter of policy enough space, tents, water and other necessities.[25]

Colonel Faulk confirmed that the policy was very evident even at his level. "The War Office was always thinking of the next war. Therefore they were very very careful not to do anything that would set a precedent for mishandling British POWs in the next war. That's why they got rid of the SEPs so quickly."[26]

Ruling millions of civilians from his isolated HQ in the painful chaos of postwar Germany, Montgomery soon lost his wartime urge to "knock the Hun about." He telegraphed London in October: "I wanted to make sure the Control Office has all the facts about the future repercussions of the food situation. I think it is my duty to do this. I hold no brief for the Germans except humane treatment and they will have to tighten their belts. But I do not think we should provide a ration less than Belsen."[27]

British policy stirred deep resentment in U.S. General Hilldring who was director of the Civil Affairs Division of the War Department. He told the State Department on September 4, 1945, that "in direct violation of Combined Chiefs of Staff's instructions, the British are lavish in the use of supplies, particularly food, in their zone." He contended that in order to avoid four-way competition to outdo one another in feeding the Germans, "the Americans must be sure that food bought in the USA" was controlled by the army. He was worried that the British would get the credit for good work in their zone, because they had the coal of the Ruhr with which to pay for food imports. "General Clay sees in this a great danger to the U.S. Army's position in Germany." The Americans should not permit the British a free hand in the distribution of food in Germany, he continued: "I share General Clay's views most strongly."[28]

One objective view of the British policy was provided to General de Gaulle by a French diplomat who reported in December 1945 that the German civilians in the British zone "appreciate the firm but gentle British policy. In the City of Hamburg, although the population has risen by 400,000 people in the last three months, the food situation is better than fair."[29]

Because the British and Canadians were busy stockpiling 500,000 tons of Canadian wheat against possible shortages, the U.S. Army challenged them as to how a shortage of this amount could possibly arise. It was not able to get an answer. "I am completely satisfied that only the U.S. Military Government authorities in Germany have any genuine desire to hold rations [for Germans] down to a reasonable level," said General Hilldring. For Hilldring this was a matter of policy. He was not justifying his attitude by the World Food Shortage, for he frankly admitted to the State Department that there was a surplus of flour in the U.S.

At the start of the British occupation, the soldiers of the 21st Army Group dreaded their civil administration work, thinking it would be boring and frustrating. Their attitude changed rapidly as they attempted like Gollancz, to alleviate the suffering they saw all around them. They made it very clear to one of the most respected and authoritative experts on the subject, F. S. V. Donnison, that "by the time their connection with military government was to be severed, they had come to feel it was the most rewarding work they had ever undertaken. One, a man of penetrating honesty and exacting standards with a record of valuable service behind him, wrote that he 'privately and quite honestly has always considered it the only really worthwhile thing he ever did in his life.' It is hard to believe that work which yielded such satisfaction and fulfilment was anything but worth while and well done."[30]

11

MYTH, LIES AND HISTORY

"What may not be, can not be."
— CHRISTIAN MORGENSTERN

MASS MAKES HISTORY. IN HISTORY we see the crowd, in art we see the face. In art, a single person is enough to animate a painting, a play, a movie, a book; but in history, the individual is important mainly as the symbol of mass.

Without the Big Number of deaths in the camps, there could be no history of the camps. All the Americans and French had to do was to suppress the Big Number to prevent knowledge of their crime from spreading and becoming history. This was easy to do because they were the only ones who knew the Big Number. This was done.

Having suppressed the Big Number, the Americans and French then had to supply some other number, because it was not credible that no one had died or that there had been no count — unless there was a strong reason for there not to have been a count, which could only have been the monstrous number that must not leave the caul. Therefore, they supplied the Small Number. This number was so small that no one with elementary arithmetic and knowledge of comparative death rates could believe it for a moment. For men Buisson had said were starving, he announced a death rate that was below the death rate among well-fed soldiers in peacetime. The Americans supplied to the town authorities of Rheinberg the number 614 for the dead in the camp, less than one thirtieth the total their own secret Other Losses figures implied. The Germans accepted the Small Number because they felt guilt about their camps, or about the war, or because the Small Number reduced the evidence of their humiliation. Also, the Germans did not want to offend the conqueror, especially after he had become their ally. One of the many ways to accommodate him was to accept his lies about something that in any case could not be changed, although this argument would of course not be allowed to absolve the Germans of responsibility for the Nazi concentration camps. Within a few years, to doubt the Small Number had become an implied treachery, for any good German who doubted the Americans was *ipso facto* an enemy of both states. So the Americans were in effect forgiven without even being accused.

Many Germans believed that there was a Big Number, but didn't know it; they knew the Small Number but did not believe it. This ambivalence that destroys belief is typical of much German thinking today. Not to be able to speak the truth about the American atrocity is an eerie echo of not knowing about the Nazi camps. A general who knew Eisenhower well wrote in 1945 that Eisenhower was using "practically Gestapo methods" against the Germans. His name was George S. Patton.[1]

The German ambivalence of today appeared in a conversation about prisoners of war at Rheinberg. When I visited the *Rathaus* [town hall] there, I discussed the deaths with the director and several other townspeople. They told me the figure of 614. I said I didn't believe it. They replied that they too did not believe it. I asked, "Why do you give it out then?" and they said, "We have to say something."

Answering questions untruthfully in this case is not exactly lying, because the truth is not known. The people of Rheinberg are telling a story to account for a mystery. In other words, they are creating a myth.

One of the functions of myth in the twentieth century is to glorify the leaders who betray our ideals. The greater the betrayal, the greater the myth erected to hide it. The guilty Hitler sheltered behind the Big Lie; the vast crimes of the gulags were hidden behind Stalin's smiling portrait painted six storeys high. The leaders who betrayed the ideals of French civilization and American generosity in 1945 were apparently protected by several myths, including the lofty war aims of the Allies expressed in the Atlantic Charter, as well as the World Shipping Shortage, and the World Food Shortage. As it was applied in Germany, this myth was many layers deep. There was no fatal food shortage in the western world, except for Germany. The German shortage was caused in part by the Allies themselves, through requisitions of food, labor shortages caused by the imprisonment of workers, and the abolition of export industry. Although the myth was supposed to explain why the Allies could not feed the prisoners, the majority of deaths in the camps was caused not by starvation but by the fatal shortage of readily available goods and services, such as barbed wire, tents, water, guards, the Red Cross, mail and so on.[2]

But no messages crossed the Atlantic bearing news of a World Tent Shortage, or of a World Barbed Wire Shortage, or a World Red Cross Shortage, or a World Guard Shortage, or a World Space Shortage or a World Water Shortage, or a World Mail Shortage. Not only the amount of food in Allied warehouses but also the astounding wealth of North America, especially the USA, should have made the notion of fatal shortages absurd. At the end of World War II, Canada, the third-largest manufacturing nation in the western world, was so wealthy despite its small population that it gave Great Britain huge gifts of food and money, amounting to at least $3,468,000,000, possibly as much as $6,000,000,000 in 1945 currency.[3] In the United States, by 1945 the richest nation ever known, the GNP had risen 50 percent during the war. The USA had more than half the world's ships, more than half the world's manufacturing capacity, the greatest agricultural output, and the biggest gold reserves: $20,000,000,000, almost two-thirds of the world's total.[4] American generosity to Britain reached the astounding sum of $25,000,000,000.[5]

That the Allies could not maintain the Geneva Convention was, according to the SHAEF messages, *only* because of the World Food Shortage and for no other reason. If the intent had been to preserve every measure of humane treatment possible while saving Allied food, so that others who had been robbed for years by the Germans would be fed first, there would have been no need to deny the prisoners anything except their liberty, very briefly. The Allies didn't need to imprison soldiers for more than a week or two in order to begin identifying the war criminals, but the U.S. had discharged only about 36-to-40 percent of its total catch of Wehrmacht soldiers by January 1946.[6]

Once the myth of the World Food Shortage had been established, the small amounts of food that did reach the U.S. and French camps could then be defined as the maximum possible under the "chaotic conditions of the time." That no one remarked on the survival of the prisoners in the British and Canadian camps, which would have been miraculous if the shortage existed, shows how little attention was paid to the prisoners even after Pradervand's revelations. The sub-text of the myth blamed the Germans for their own deaths, for if they had not done such damage, there would have been no World Food Shortage.

When propaganda stories about the camps reached the controlled German press from their American or French sources, German families desperate for news of their men were tempted to believe them. In the absence of news direct from their men, it was hard to resist believing any comforting wisps of information no matter how suspect the sources. There was thus the desire for good news and a strong reason to supply it. Once the half-dead men were discharged, however, conflict between eye-witnesses and propaganda arose. The evidence of the witnesses lost credibility as it was repeated by word of mouth alone. It had the status of doubtful rumor from resentful individuals, lacking the authority of print. What that authority meant is visible in the following report, received by Colonel Lauben on August 11, 1945:

> The following is a news report from the reporter at CAMP SCHALDING GERMANY. "Such is life in SCHALDING! Twenty thousand German PWs pressed together on a small meadow at the edge of a Bavarian small town. Some fences, some tents, that is the embryo of the tittling PWs. Nobody thinks of past times. There is one call only, just a single word: 'Discharge.' Finally came 17 June 1945. The first thousand German PWs leave the camp and go home. Each day new tents, new offices. Each day new men come from all parts of the territory occupied by the US Armies but there are no hindrances. One truck after the other takes off loaded with discharged PWs. During four weeks twenty thousand German PWs were released to their families. Then amid all this uproar moving to SCHALDING near PASSAU. The new place is installed with all available accommodations, big barracks with a bed for each one of the two thousand men. The hygienic necessities were made by the PWs and they did it with interest and fervence. A good cook (formerly Hotel Adlon, BERLIN) takes care of a sufficient and not at all monotonous nouriture for the inhabitants of the camp. The American and German Camp administrators are endeavoring to discharge every PW as soon as possible. Those former German soldiers who, for the time being can not be returned to their next of kin are paroled to local farmers or other vital working places. It is understood that there will be entertainment."[7]

The odd reference to "the reporter at CAMP SCHALDING GERMANY" together with the freaky English suggest that this was written by some tame German for local consumption. *The Stars and Stripes*, the army's own paper, also sang in the chorus. Under the headline "7 GIs and a Colonel Boss 2,000,000 PWs," Na Deane Walker, staff writer, gaily reported on November 20, 1945, that it took only two minutes for the Prisoner of War Information Bureau to locate a prisoner. "Dramatically enough, the young ex-sergeant in charge of PWIB's 'Wanted' section is a German Jew whose entire family was wiped out by the Nazis. Helmut Stern, Frankfurt-born American citizen, has culminated a successful search for his parents' killers by ordering the arrest of two suspects." Walker says the PWIB's "record of finds is good — 80 percent of all witnesses and criminals listed as wanted in queries that pour in from G2, the Judge Advocate, the War Crimes Commission and the Central Register of War Criminals and Security Suspects (CROWCASS) are found in PWIB's master index of 2,000,000 PWs. An additional 500,000 are being reprocessed now as the French return that number of prisoners to American custody." None of this lavishly erroneous report can be trusted.[8] The army did not even know the names, let alone the histories, of many of the people in the DEF cages. The same Prisoner of War Information Bureau praised by Na Deane Walker had just reported to the State Department that it had no idea of the identity of the dead bodies in over 5,000 recent burials at the camps. The bureau told the Special War Problems division of the State Department as it was forwarding 5,122 Reports of Burial of unknown deceased German personnel that "no death list has been transmitted since identity of the deceased is not available. The above reports are fowarded to your office in lieu of a protecting power of German interests."[9]

The first element of the cover-up was to confine knowledge as tightly as possible. How could such widespread events involving millions of men be covered up? The camp at Rheinberg was bordered by the main road through Lintfort. The barbed wire fence around it was nine kilometers long. Inside were over 100,000 men, much of the time. The men released from the camp, or handed to the British or the French, would spread the knowledge of what was happening there. It was clear that news of the camps could not be withheld from the Germans, but all public discussion in the media was prohibited. In the blank that this left, the army printed the myth.

Inside Germany, Eisenhower or his deputies ran everything, so censorship was much easier to maintain. Newspapers, radio stations, book publishers, even movie theaters had to have licences to operate in the U.S. zone. For a long time, they had no freedom, but much free propaganda.

The army controlled information so well that Jean-Pierre Pradervand, head ICRC delegate in France, did not find out until he talked to the author in 1989 that there were American camps there through to the end of 1945. These camps contained over 750,000 captives in May 1945.

The army kept close watch over what the press was saying. Frequent, meticulous and wide ranging, these army reports reflect the interest that Eisenhower and his staff had in how their reputations were being treated by the press which made them. The reports, subdivided under the headings "Favorable" and "Not Favorable," were widely circulated. Patton recorded some remarks of Eisenhower's on the subject at a lunch for his generals: "Ike made the sensational statement that while hostilities were in progress, the one important thing was order and discipline, but now that hostilities were over, the important thing was to stay in with world public opinion — apparently whether it was right or wrong."[10]

Eisenhower was also very clear about the kind of loyalty he expected from his officers whenever any kind of public investigation of the army was proposed, Patton wrote in his diary. "After lunch General Eisenhower talked to us very confidentially on the necessity for solidarity in the event that any of us are called before a Congressional Committee . . . . He outlined . . . a form of organization. While none of us exactly agreed with it, it was not sufficiently contrary to our views to prevent our supporting it in general."[11]

The fear of such Congressional investigation is a logical explanation for the cover-up that was going on even within army headquarters itself. The falsified SHAEF-USFET HQ papers were all marked SECRET, so the falsification must have been designed to deceive people who would have access to these papers despite the secret classification. Those people were of two kinds: Americans with high-level security clearance, and posterity. Whoever did all this must have needed to prevent Americans with top-secret clearance from finding out what was going on.

Not only the Congress had to be deceived. Certain officers

may have presented a security risk as well — for instance, General Patton. For all his prejudices, Patton represented to a high degree the honor of the army and the basic generosity of the American people. He made this very plain in a reply to a question put to him by the army's Theater Judge Advocate: "In all these talks [to the troops] I emphasized the necessity for the proper treatment of prisoners of war, both as to their lives and property. My usual statement was . . . 'Kill all the Germans you can but do not put them up against a wall and kill them. Do your killing while they are still fighting. After a man has surrendered, he should be treated exactly in accordance with the Rules of Land Warfare, and just as you would hope to be treated if you were foolish enough to surrender. Americans do not kick people in the teeth after they are down.'"[12] He openly deplored Eisenhower's anti-German policies: "What we are doing is to utterly destroy the only semi-modern state in Europe so that Russia can swallow the whole."[13]

General Buisson completed his cover-up of the French prison camps in 1948 with his account of the Axis Prisoner of War Service. Discreetly circulated within the French government, it claimed that the men of his prison service "accomplished a work of the highest economic value, and of the highest humanity. They had a heavy responsibility, sometimes a crushing load, because they were so few. But they never lost sight of their soldier's training . . . Justice therefore has been rendered to them — given by those who once criticized them, then spontaneously admitted that the Prisoner Service did honor to the French army." He says, like an ad agency tout, that the service has received from prisoners many unsolicited testimonials to the good treatment they got in the camps.[14] The Americans nourished this kind of jollity as well, spreading the story that some of their camp commanders in Germany were having to turn away released prisoners who were trying to sneak back in for food and shelter.

Civilian governors who believed in freedom of the press and democracy, instead of censorship and authoritarian rule, took a different line towards the beaten Germans. Robert Murphy, who was the civilian political advisor to Eisenhower while he served for a few months as Military Governor,* "was startled to see," on a visit to one camp, "that our prisoners were almost as weak and emaciated as those I had observed in Nazi prison camps. The youthful commandant calmly told us that he had deliberately kept the inmates on starvation diet, explaining 'These Nazis are getting a dose of their own medicine.' He so obviously believed that he was behaving correctly that we did not discuss the matter with him. After we left, the medical director asked me, 'Does that camp represent American policy in Germany?' I replied that of course it was contrary to our policy, and the situation would be quickly corrected. When I described the camp's condition to [General Lucius] Clay, he quietly transferred the grim young officer."[15] It is as stupid to let generals run a country as it is to let politicians lead an army.

In Germany after 1945, there were millions of biographies; there was no history. When the nation was cut in four, its history was fragmented by the political division, censorship, coverup and fear of criticizing the USA and France. No intelligent public opinion was formed on the subject because no expression of it was allowed. The occupation of Germany resulted in an occupied mentality, which attempted to subject reason to unreasoning discipline.

This was the easier to impose because of the unquestioning belief in authority in which Germans were trained. This is brilliantly satirized by the Bavarian poet Christian Morgenstern in a poem about a solid burgher named Korf who is walking along a street when he is hit by a car. Korf, dazed, bruised, staggers home wondering what happened. Wrapped in damp towels, he studies his law books, where he discovers that cars are forbidden to drive on that street. Korf therefore decides that it was not a car that hit him because "what may not be can not be." He tells himself it was a dream. So the wounded Germans, as convinced as we are ourselves that we *could* not do such

* General Lucius Clay succeeded Eisenhower in November 1945.

things, believed as we have believed that we *did* not do such things.

In the general bewilderment after the Occupation began, a campaign against rumors was initiated by the British. At a meeting held to discuss the importance of the campaign, a German Burgermeister got up to proclaim, "Herr Oberstleutnant, I have the solution to the problem. Let official denials of each rumor be published in the *Neue Hannoversche Kurier* and the *Nachrichtenblatt*. Let the Military Government issue an order that the people should read the denials.[16] Then let the Military Government issue a separate order that they should believe the denials." After the zones and overt censorship were abolished, the situation was not much improved, because the attitudes formed under that regime had already become part of the people's history.

Despite that history, wives and husbands, brothers and sisters, children and parents wanted to find out what had happened to their relatives whose fate was still unknown in 1947. During June and July, the three south German *Länder* in the U.S. zone tried to carry out the first comprehensive postwar registration of returned German POWs. They gathered data on POWs still interned, listed as dead, missing or discharged.[17] The survey showed that at least 2,107,500 persons born in prewar Germany were still not home. About half a million were listed as prisoners of war, the rest were simply missing. The survey seemed to show that about 90 percent of the missing had last been seen on the eastern front. But there were several important inadequacies in this survey. One was that the figure for the missing was only a projection for the whole armed forces based on partial figures collected in the American zone, which was the homeland of only a small minority of prewar Germans.[18] The second was that none of the figures was from the German army order of battle records and *Kriegstagbuch* (war diary), showing the disposition of all German units into April 1945, although these were in the hands of the U.S. Army. The survey depended only on voluntary responses to notices posted in public places in the U.S. zone, such as post offices. It was based mainly on the last news of the missing man received by his family, which might have been months old when received. It also reported sightings made by friends in the army, which of course could not reveal what the missing man had done after the sighting. Nor was a tabulation made of how much time had elapsed between the last sighting or letter, and the surrender of the man's unit. The survey encouraged the belief among Germans, now divided along Cold War lines, that most of their missing relatives had died in Russian captivity, or were still being held incommunicado in the Soviet Union.

This belief did not accord with the reality of the end of the war. The OKW (Wehrmacht supreme command) had been ordered by Hitler's successor, Grand Admiral Doenitz, to hold the eastern front with as few men as possible in order to surrender as many as possible in the west.[19] All told, about 9,000,000[20] Germans were rounded up in camps of the western Allies during the war, over 7,600,000 being counted as prisoners of war, surrendered enemy personnel or disarmed enemy forces captured in Germany and northern Europe, whereas the Russians reported taking only between 1,700,000 and 2,500,000.[21] The Americans, British and French, accusing the Russians of taking far more than they reported, hinted that these men were dead. The Russians were criticized for their POW policies in Allied Control Council meetings in 1946 and 1947,[22] and through the United Nations and the U.S. Senate in later years.[23]

At first, the Americans tended to deflect blame onto the broad shoulders of the French. U.S. Senator Knowland, speaking in the Senate in 1947, had a near miss with the dangerous truth when he said of the French camps, "If we are not very careful, there may arise to embarrass us in later years a situation in which it can be shown that some prisoners captured by American forces are being treated not a great deal better than were some other prisoners who were thrown into concentration camps in Nazi Germany."[24] Senator Morse then read into the record an article by the famous columnist Dorothy Thompson, who also expressed shock and horror about the situation in the French camps: "That country, with our consent and connivance, and in defiance of the Geneva Convention, has been employing [prisoners] as slave labor under the same definition of slave labor as that used against Herr Sauckel in Nuremberg [who was executed] . . . Few care to recall that President Roosevelt gave a specific pledge to the German people in September 1944: 'The Allies do not traffic in human slavery.'" She went on to ask pointedly: "Do only a handful of people see that if, having defeated Germany, we accept for ourselves Hitler's standards and Hitler's methods, Hitler has conquered?"

The War Department slyly informed Senator Knowland that 2,216,000 prisoners had been discharged while 24,834 remained in U.S. custody in 1947. A further "600,000" had been sent to the French. In his speech, Knowland did not refer to the true capture figure, presumably because the War Department did not tell him. This would have risked revealing the death toll.

The ICRC was also given misleading information that threw the Germans off the trail. In response to inquiries from German families, in 1948 the ICRC asked the U.S. Army for records of the missing, and were told that only 3.5 million DEF had been taken, with about 600,000 POWs.[25] This omitted about 1.8 million captives of the total U.S. wartime catch. Together with the 1947 survey, this created a deadly suspicion that settled like radioactive fallout on the Russians. To give this lie the character of truth, the original letter to the ICRC was photocopied by the U.S. and sent with other "documents" as a gift to the Bundesarchiv in Koblenz, where it is handed out as truth to the public to this day.

Thus the impression was imposed on Knowland, the U.S. Senate, the ICRC and the world, that the Americans had captured between 1,800,000 and 3,100,000 fewer than the true figure.

No organization dared to challenge these figures. It seemed that everyone was afraid to speak about the missing.

But the families of the dead spoke. After the creation of the Government of the Federal Republic of Germany, their collective voice began to be heard. The (West German) Government Ministry for Refugees announced on 31 March 1950 that in the Western Zones of Germany and in West Berlin there were still missing from their West German homes, their fate unknown, 1,407,000 persons. There were believed to be 69,000 ex-soldiers still in prison, 1,148,000 soldiers reported missing, and 190,000 missing civilians.[26]

As the Cold War grew colder in the 1950s, the original concealment by the SHAEF-USFET officers became much more important. Because national guilt had been buried along with personal, the U.S. and France could heap their own atrocity on top of the dead in the Russian gulags. Now the belief flourished that most of the missing men were the responsibility of the Russians. In Germany, as Arthur Smith wrote in his book *Heimkehr aus dem Zweiten Weltkrieg,* "The mystery about the location of Germany's POWs ceased to be."[27] Of course, there never would have been such a mystery if the French and Americans had told the truth about their camps.

In 1972 the distinguished Senator James O. Eastland rose in the Senate chamber to denounce the Russians for secretly holding millions of German POWs in "grisly" conditions. Following the research of Samuel C. Oglesby, foreign affairs analyst in the Library of Congress, Eastland righteously denounced the Communists: "The records of the Soviet treatment of POWs in World War Two and of the Chinese-Korean treatment of POWs during the Korean War are even more grisly than the dismal record established by the Vietnamese Communists." According to his advisor Oglesby, the USSR "was holding or had failed to account for, approximately 1,952,000 German POWs in 1950."[28] If true, this would be about 100 percent dead or missing among the POWs the Russians said they had.[29]

Cold War recrimination did not interest the German families and friends who still wanted to find their relatives and friends, or at least know their fate. The government supported the series of books to be edited by Dr Erich Maschke, which would answer all questions. This series was financed by the West German Government and censored by the Foreign Office under Willy Brandt. The purpose of the series was clear to see in Brandt's statement to the Bundestag on April 25, 1969. Brandt said: "After the first two volumes appeared, it was decided with the approval of the Foreign Office to print them [the books] with the FO's stamp of approval . . . to exclude misunderstanding, with a modest publication . . . and to avoid provoking a public discussion at home and abroad . . . [which would] open old wounds and would not serve the reconciliation efforts of the Federal Republic's foreign policy."[30]

In this series, the book *Die deutschen Kriegsgefangenen in amerikanischer Hand* by Kurt W. Böhme quoted the U.S. Army as saying that the total U.S. wartime capture figure was 3,761,431, more than 2,000,000 lower than the true total capture of the U.S. in North Africa, Italy and northern Europe. The U.S. Army also told the German author that at Rheinberg only 438 people died in the eight weeks the camp was under American control,[31] which means the death rate was about 3.16 percent per year in the same weeks when U.S. Army doctors secretly reported deaths in nearby POW camps to be 30.6 percent per year.

The bias of the author is evident from the fact that he reports death "rates" of various percentages for six camps, without mentioning the time period. Because the time period discussed, though never precisely defined, was far less than a year, this statement produces a spuriously low rate.[32] Thus the author brings us to his conclusion that although "one can't find out the exact death rate, there is absolutely no reason to believe in mass killings." A few lines later, he contradicts himself by citing an overall rate in his summary of the whole situation: "Compared to the east where four-fifths of the POWs died, in the west it was only one percent. Conclusions: no mass deaths in the west, a statement which is confirmed by local administrations."

The French cooperated with the Germans in what was by now becoming serious Cold War propaganda.[33] General Buisson told Böhme that by 1948 the French had accounted for all the prisoners taken by them. This was loyally reported in the book paid for by France's ally Germany, whereas there was nothing about the report of the Secrétariat d'État in March 1946 that the total of Prisoners Lost For Various Reasons (*Perdus Pours Raisons Diverses*) had already risen to 167,000 by February 1946.[34] Böhme allowed himself one plaintive question about Buisson's absurd statistics: "What about the number of missing men who are not accounted for by escapes?" There was of course no answer.

So, like Buisson's own book, Maschke's series was not allowed to inflame the public. On their trip through the death camps, the German writers saw mainly night, heard mainly fog. "Modest publication" was prepared. Only 431 copies were sold, mainly to universities and research libraries. No discussion was provoked.

Inconvenient truths were whited out of the record in American books as well. Eisenhower's postscript to Marshall in May 1943, that "it is a pity that we could not have killed more" Germans was cut from printed versions of the letter in the supposedly authoritative *Papers of Dwight David Eisenhower*, probably by order of the Defense Department. The note has also been deleted from the book of Eisenhower's correspondence with Marshall entitled *Dear General*.[35]

In a thick biography of General Eisenhower, grandson David Eisenhower writes: "The situation in Germany was grim. Eisenhower presented the facts: Food stocks were low. There was need for 175,000 tons of wheat and flour monthly . . . . German military prisoners were a special case. Under the Geneva Convention, POWs were entitled to the same rations given depot troops and civilians and could legally be cut from the allotted 2,000 calories to 1,500 calories. Since the troops were performing heavy labor, in Eisenhower's opinion a ration of 1,500 calories per day was inadequate."[36] As the reader discovers in surprise that Eisenhower is a quotable authority on human nutrition, he is steered away from the inconvenient fact that the American food standard that was supposed to determine the POW ration under the Geneva Convention was the 4,000 calories per day given to U.S. base troops, not 2,000 or 1,500. To this the grandchild adds the loyal hint that General Eisenhower somehow improved the rations which the general himself had told Churchill he had cut.[37]

The myth-making was extended a little further by Professor Arthur L. Smith, who describes the situation of the returning German prisoners of war in his book. Smith deplores the lack of a Protecting Power for the Germans, which he attributes to "the large number of participants in World War II."[38] In this he follows Maschke, not the State Department's decision of May 9, 1945, which removed the Swiss government from the role. In a long discussion of the difficulties of starting Germany's postal service again, he does not mention that the British re-established mail, even to the camps, in July — August 1945. Nor do we hear that the lack of mail in the U.S. camps was caused by the ban imposed by the State Department. Smith, a defender of American generosity and decency, finds these qualities even in the DEF policy, which he says was "a blessing in disguise,"[39] because it meant a quick return home for many prisoners. He does not notice that 60 to 64 percent of the prisoners were still in prison or dead in January 1946. In general, the faults of the French and the Russians are plain to see in this book, not those of the U.S. Nothing about the appalling condition of the U.S. camps appears, although a few hints had turned up even in Maschke's soothing series.

In the absence of truth, Germans began very early to believe myths. One was that the starvation, which was in any case inadvertent because of the chaos and the food shortage, was alleviated as much as possible by the kindhearted Americans, who did their best in impossible conditions. One German archivist and historian told the author that the Americans did not have enough food for themselves. He had never seen any books or documents supporting this, he admitted.[40]

When this particular scar over the German wound is touched today, the reaction is usually guilty anger. "Look at what *we* did during the war," is a common reply. Just as blind vengeance replaced justice in the camps, so guilt has replaced justice in such Germans. Another confusion in the minds of some otherwise responsible Germans is the notion that it is more important to avoid encouraging the tiny neo-Nazi party than to publish the truth about such things as the death camps of France and America. According to this curious analysis, which has been repeated to the author in Toronto, Washington, Zurich, New York, London and Paris, as well as Germany, the danger of Nazism is so great that we must stick to our lies no matter what they hide. This bizarre notion, which supposes a Truth Convenient and a Truth Inconvenient, means that one of the characteristics of truth is that it can be defined to your advantage. So much does that war still corrupt our minds.

The only useful aspect to all this mythopoeia has been to hammer deeper into German consciousness a sense of guilt for what that nation had done. But guilt about the Nazi camps inevitably became associated in their minds with hatred for the Allied camps. The Germans who know what the camps were like, because they were in them, find justification for themselves in what the Americans and French did. If they accept that the Allies were justified in punishing them for their crimes, then they are also justified in seeking revenge against the Allies for their unpunished war crimes. Because this desire for revenge is impossible to satisfy, it seeks scapegoats. It also appears in neo-Nazism, and in anti-Americanism.

What many Germans feel now is not that the camps were a just punishment from which they learned a painful lesson, but that they were an unjust punishment which they dare not protest. This was hardly the intention of the French or the Americans, who if they intended anything more useful than blind vengeance, wanted the Germans to go and never sin again.

"The Others [Allies] do the very same things for which they [Germans] are blamed," said prisoners returning from Allied camps. "And this crime against humanity very often is not only considered unforgiveable and denounced as deception and hypocrisy, but also serves as exculpation for themselves in the guilt question. They don't forget the injustice they suffered, and a great many of them do not wish to forget it. But they do expect others to forget their own transgressions. This negative attitude, to which they are grimly attached with might and main, was driven so far, that they even refused to listen to lectures by Germans on conditions at home [that is, what the Nazis did to civilians in the extermination camps]."[41]

The punishment policy deeply betrayed the will of the American people against indiscriminate vengeance, which had been demonstrated in the nationwide condemnation of the Morgenthau Plan. The mass resignations of French camp commanders in 1945, as well as the kindness of French families to emerging German prisoners, is significant evidence of a similar widespread attitude in France, although the French had suffered incomparably more. The punishment policy also contradicted itself. The secrecy meant that young Germans were not to learn publicly the lesson supposedly being taught to their elders. No respect was possible for the teaching of the hypocritical conqueror, whether French or American, who condemned German death camps from the mire of his own.

It must have been obvious to even the most vengeful officers that although they were risking the honor and security of their countries, there was no benefit to France or America in these camps. Only their own feelings would be assuaged: everyone else was deprived of the gratifications of vengeance.

The camps taught no useful lesson, unless that they were useless. No one learns justice from cruelty. But the camps and the cover-up have been dangerous for the Allies as well. The responsible officers were beyond control, unrepresentative and deadly dangerous to the security and honor of the U.S. and France. Like Sergeant Zobrist who had been warned to stay away from the camps if he could because they were so horrible, many brave men in the U.S. Army were sent home with a fear of knowing the truth about their own leaders. Can anyone be certain that this secret abuse of power was not related to the unprecedented attempts by cliques of officers and high state officials to subvert their governments in both the U.S. and France in the last 40 years?

Even in Germany the cover-up has been a success. If a German researcher hears about the atrocity in some camps from witnesses, he finds in the German archives evidence that is hard to refute, that the Americans either obeyed the Geneva Convention, or tried to. Thus, it is possible to believe, after a visit to Koblenz, that the testimony of the witnesses may well be correct, but that even if their death rates are prorated over the whole American or French camp system, thereby suggesting mass killings, the Americans and French were not responsible, because official policy, recorded in documents of the period, preserved in the national archives, confirmed in books and never challenged, was to treat the prisoners as correctly as possible, in painful circumstances created mainly by the Germans themselves. It seems pointless to pursue the quest, even to someone who believes that there was a disaster.[42]

If Germans could not do this work, there were still French, Americans, English and Canadians. That this work was for so long left undone, while dozens of admiring volumes about de Gaulle and Eisenhower have been published, shows the truth in Lewis Lapham's brilliant phrase: "Beyond the ceaseless murmuring of a lickspittle press, the mode of feeling is trivial and cruel."[43]

The writers artfully setting the haloes on the heads of heroes can not tell the truth without destroying the meaning of their work. Without heroes, these writers are nothing, because the truth means nothing to them. Elias Canetti comments on the way that conquerors are viewed by historians: "Truth has no dignity whatsoever here. It is as shameful as it was destructive."[44] The dead were "slaughtered for nothing, absolutely nothing." Not even revenge is sufficient explanation, for the killers hiding in shame what they were doing could neither boast nor gloat. Canetti said, "The terror that power wants to arouse, that power is actually after, is contingent on the mass number of victims . . . . [The general's] fame and his power grow with the number of dead. The famous conquerors in history all went this way. All kinds of virtues were later attributed to them."

"It is a pity we could not have killed more."

12

BY WINKS AND NODS

WERE THESE DEATHS CAUSED DELIBERATELY, or was it beyond the power of France and the United States to keep the prisoners alive? If it was beyond their power, why did they not release them immediately?

The DEF message of March 10, 1945, shows that American policy was planned well in advance,* before the large captures had actually been made. It was U.S. Army policy to deprive the captives of shelter and of army food as soon as the war was over. The actual deprivation of food, water, shelter and so on had begun weeks before that, as Beasley and Mason saw to their awe. Although there were plenty of surplus tents in the U.S. Army, it was policy to construct the PWTE cages without shelter as of May 1.[1] The first captives were deprived of POW status on May 4, four days before VE Day. It became general policy in May to deprive prisoners of war of their status and hence of the food which they had already been getting. It was policy that

* The original of this message is initialled DE.

deprived all remaining prisoners of their status on August 4. It was policy to prevent civilian food and relief agencies from helping prisoners of war, DEF and the civilians of Germany.[2]

All the decisions about prisoner welfare in U.S. camps up to July 14 were made in the U.S. Army headquarters at SHAEF. When SHAEF was disbanded on July 14, the U.S. Army continued under the same command as it had had before. Eisenhower, who had held two commands, one as Supreme Commander at SHAEF, the other as the Commanding General of the United States Forces in the European Theater (USFET), now had only his American command. Similarly General Smith, former Chief of Staff at SHAEF, also Chief of Staff to Eisenhower at USFET, continued in the second role. There was thus continuity of command in the American forces in Europe through the changeover of July 14.

Both the organization of SHAEF and the way in which Eisenhower ran that organization, and later USFET, made it highly unlikely that any major decision would be taken, or any major policy implemented, without the knowledge of the Supreme Commander. "Eisenhower and his staff are cool and confident, carrying out an affair of incredible magnitude and complication with superlative efficiency," said General George C. Marshall, who knew efficiency when he saw it.[3] Certainly few things escaped his notice, or the notice of subordinate officers who were loyal and efficient. Eisenhower took care of such details as the sponsorship of dances for enlisted men[4] and what make of car should be driven by what rank of officer in which area.[5] He read all the important cables which he had not written or drafted himself. Returning to his office after a trip, one of the first things he did was to read over the log of incoming or outgoing cables, which contained the messages themselves, not just the list of subjects.[6]

All the Allies chose to have prisoners, once the war had been over for more than a few weeks. Nothing compelled any army or government to keep large numbers of Germans, including many women and children, in these camps. The French, especially, could have adjusted their intake to the number they could usefully employ.

That the armies were not simply overwhelmed by prisoners is clear from all this.

Although the DEFs undoubtedly died in large numbers directly as a result of starvation, it was lack of sanitation and overcrowding that caused most of the deaths among the POWs and DEFs. A relatively small percentage died from "emaciation or exhaustion" — about 10-to-15 percent — and a very high number from diseases directly associated with unsanitary conditions or exposure, such as pneumonia, dysentery and diarrhea, respiratory sickness, and so forth. What can explain the refusal to supply goods and services readily available that would have prevented these things?

Two of the three major political decisions made by the Combined Chiefs of Staff — about their transfer to other nations and removal of the ICRC's protection through removal of the Swiss — did not condemn the prisoners to an early grave. The acceptance of the DEF status, although made in the belief that the Germans probably could not feed the prisoners, meant the acceptance of a high risk of starvation, but not of mass deaths through exposure, dysentery or overcrowding. No message ever crossed the Atlantic ordering the army to eliminate masses of prisoners. Mass killings could not have been War Department or government policy, or the German prisoners in Italy would also have died *en masse*. The American Chiefs of Staff plainly expected that the men in the camps would be weak, but there is no proof that they expected anything worse, whereas the officers in Europe on the spot said in several messages that the situation in the camps was "critical" and "very serious." It is difficult to see any basis for these messages except that the officers wanted to record that they had warned against the disaster. The warnings can hardly be sincere, in view of the fact that the necessary supplies were all available. Nothing has yet been discovered to show that the War Department or the Chiefs ordered the army not to use the supplies it had for the benefit of the prisoners. In fact, the reverse is suggested in the Quartermaster Reports, because food actually sent by Washington, or "procured" in Germany, is withheld by the army, creating a surplus in storage.

Was the army only saving food in order to feed the hungry civilians of Europe? If that were the case, the prisoners would have been discharged immediately, or tents would have been routinely issued to the prisoners, along with clean water and medicine, because lack of food is much more dangerous for men who are exposed or weakened by minor illnesses. A much better way to save army food supplies would have been to release the prisoners quickly, but only about 36-to-40 percent of the total U.S. capture figure of about 5,900,000 in the three Theaters had been discharged at January 1, 1946.[7] The rest were in French camps, or dead, or in British camps, or on hand. That it was possible for commanders in the U.S. Army in Europe in 1945 to keep prisoners alive without "spoiling" them was shown by the experience of the 291,000 prisoners in the hands of the U.S. Army under General Mark Clark in Italy.[8] No mistreatment of these prisoners has ever been alleged by anyone. When these prisoners were weighed in a U.S. camp in Germany soon after their return from Italy, none was underweight, whereas of those kept in Germany "all were below standard."[9]

That it was possible to keep millions of prisoners alive in Germany in 1945 was shown by the British and Canadian experience. No peacetime atrocity has ever been alleged against the British or Canadians, except for the apparently inadvertent starvation of about 200-400 prisoners on the British camp in Overijsche, Belgium, in 1945–6.

That the prisoners in the U.S. camps would have had a much better chance had they been released into the civilian population is shown by the 3.5-to-5 percent civilian death rate[10] in the British zone in 1945–46, compared to the rate in the U.S. camps of around 30 percent or worse during that period.

That the army *in Germany* was responsible is clear; that this was not an accident is also clear. Who then in the army in Germany was responsible?

Eisenhower was responsible. Only the army handled the imprisoning, feeding, discharge and transfer of the German army. The initials DE on the SHAEF Cable Logs prove that he knew from the beginning of the DEF policy and probably drafted it.[11]

Eisenhower frequently used his power to control rations, as we see in messages or orders bearing the personal pronoun, such as his message of May 16 saying, "In view of the critical food situation in Germany, it is necessary for me to take timely action to meet emergency conditions." He asked for permission to issue imported food "in Germany" without further permission from the Chiefs, "if in my opinion the situation so requires." This was not to mollycoddle the Germans, but to prevent food riots in Germany that might "result in conditions prejudicial to military operations." Permission was given on June 6.[12] In response to President Truman's investigation of displaced persons camps in October, Eisenhower commissioned an investigation of his own, which prompted him to tell Truman, "I have recently raised the daily calorie food value per person for ordinary displaced persons in approved centers to 2,300."[13]

General Littlejohn was facing a dilemma when he wrote his letter of August 27 about the 1,550,000 unfed people in the camps. If he said too much, he threatened his colleagues; to say too little meant that people continued to starve unnecessarily. His motive may have been simply to protect his flanks, or it may have been to rectify the situation; either way, Littlejohn's solution to the food problem was clear. All the army had to do to get more food from the USA for the unfed was to ask for it. There was no point to such a recommendation if there was no possibility of getting the food from the USA. Whether the memo was cynical or sincere about feeding the unfed, Littlejohn still wanted to leave the impression that he genuinely tried to do something. No such impression would be left if he recommended a solution to the problem that everyone in army, government and press knew could not work.

Littlejohn nowhere mentions finding out who was responsible for the disaster. He comments only that the army data were "inaccurate." There is no hint of investigation, responsibility, discipline, court martial. Surely, if Littlejohn had suspected that junior officers had done this against the will of the Commanding General, endangering the army by creating the conditions for civil unrest through the food shortages caused by the army's unnecessary requisitions, he would have ordered an investigation. That Littlejohn did nothing shows perhaps that he didn't care, because he already knew, and was therefore partly responsible himself, or perhaps that he knew that whoever had done this was too high to touch. In other words, Eisenhower.

Nevertheless, the United States Army in Europe was still huge, with many complicated tasks, including some for which it had never been designed, such as feeding large numbers of civilians. Was it possible that somehow a cabal of officers invented and carried out this policy without Eisenhower's knowledge or permission?

This theory is in trouble as soon as it is formulated, for several reasons, the first being that Eisenhower certainly knew of and probably created the DEF policy in March. In his message to the CCS, he accurately predicted that the Germans would not be able to feed the DEFs. He also knew that the CCS had approved the policy, the British with ominous reservations.

If such a cabal existed, it must have included Hughes, who was so interested in POW rations. It must have been numerous, because the circulation lists of the SHAEF–USFET reports that used the euphemism Other Losses to record the prisoners' deaths every week show that two generals, one brigadier, four colonels, three majors, one captain, plus nine unnamed heads of department, regularly received this damning information. Besides them, Smith, Littlejohn, Hughes, Barker and Crawford all must have known what was going on. The commanding generals of the armies must also have known, because it was from their headquarters that the first lists of Other Losses came to SHAEF. Therefore, a minimum of 23 officers knew.

If he did act alone, or with this cabal, Hughes would have known that he was creating a terrible risk for his friend, against his friend's wishes. He would have been doing this to satisfy only himself. He would have been betraying the trust that Eisenhower had clearly placed in him, a trust that Eisenhower continued to place in Hughes even after the camps had been silhouetted by Jean Pierre Pradervand, *Le Figaro* and *Le Monde*.

The cabal also had to make sure that the officers in charge of tentage issued no tents from their ample stores.[14] Engineers who knew there was enough barbed wire, and lumber, and water pipes and pumps and so on, had to be prevented from issuing them. The Medical Corps had to be persuaded or ordered not to put up enough field hospitals. Someone had to make sure that sick prisoners did not get into those empty beds. Someone had to prevent mail from going in and out. Someone else made sure that German food did not reach many of the camps, including the three in the Dietersheim complex uncovered by Captain Julien of the Third Algerians, one at Kripp, one at Rheinberg, and one near Gotha. Reporters had to be kept out of all the camps. Records had to be inspected and destroyed, in 1945 and later in Washington. Someone at SHAEF, unknown to Eisenhower, had to get the War Department to ask the State Department to make sure the International Committee of the Red Cross did not visit the camps. Someone else coordinated this with the British, who squelched the protest of the Canadian prime minister. All this required "strenuous efforts" according to Littlejohn, who in October congratulated his staff for the fine job they had done in reducing "the burden on U.S. food resources by eliminating from the ration returns as many as possible."[15]

The theory that someone in the army other than Eisenhower was responsible also means that after Pradervand's revelations, Eisenhower ordered an investigation which did not find out the truth, but published a series of lies, which Eisenhower did not know were lies. Still unaware of all that his subordinates were doing, Eisenhower must then have let things go on as before, because it is clear from several reports that starvation conditions continued in many of the camps in Germany after the exposure. Yet Eisenhower wrote in his book *Crusade in Europe*, long after the war, "We had by this time [spring 1945] a logistic and administrative organization capable of handling such numbers of prisoners and these captives interfered only temporarily with troop manoeuvres and offensives."[16]

And all of this would have to have happened under the rule of the man whom General MacArthur had called "the best officer in the Army."

Because the Combined Chiefs of Staff approved of the DEF

policy on April 26, there can be no doubt that Eisenhower believed he was following orders not to feed the prisoners.* The CCS were undoubtedly responsible for the DEF policy along with Eisenhower. Nor is there doubt that Eisenhower wrote those orders for himself, then carried them out for seven weeks before receiving approval.

Eisenhower was not alone in believing that the prisoners' rations should be reduced. At the meeting with Churchill on May 15, the Chief of the Imperial General Staff, Sir Alan Brooke, said "that under present conditions when it was known that there was an overall shortage of food, it would be wrong to feed German prisoners of war on the same scale as British and American troops. If widespread starvation was to be avoided, it was essential that the rations of enemy troops should be reduced to the bare minimum." He pointed out in this connection "that the scale for German civilians under Allied Military government was 1,550 calories."[17]

Obviously the difference between the British-Canadian camps and the American was not due solely to better nourishment in the British-Canadian camps. It is virtually certain although not proven that the higher survival rate in the British-Canadian camps was due to factors that had nothing to do with the supposed World Food Shortage. The captives in the British-Canadian camps got shelter, space, enough clean water, better hospital care and so on. Prisoners in American camps were still furtively throwing messages wrapped round rocks at night out of their camps begging for food, when prisoners in the British camps were receiving mail regularly. The Canadian army permitted at least one German unit to retain all its telephone equipment and even to continue operating a radio transmitter.[18] Within a few months, prisoners were receiving visitors in British and Canadian camps.[19]

In all this sorry record, the only important thing lacking is evidence showing who was responsible for preventing German

* Several U.S. officers complained in May that their requisitions "to the War Department" for essential supplies had been denied. It is not clear who denied them, but it must have been someone in SHAEF at Frankfurt, or at the War Department in Washington.

civilians from sharing their own meager rations with the prisoners. That Germans were prevented, we have seen; that we do not see an order from anyone keeping civilians from helping is not surprising, in view of the wide-ranging and persistent cover-up continuing to this day. That the order was given by someone, somehow, is plain from the evidence of the camps.

Guilt for all this rests primarily on Eisenhower, together with Smith and Hughes.[20] Simply to have allowed the junior officers to get what they needed from the stores would have saved many lives. To have allowed the distribution of the 13,500,000 Red Cross food parcels designed for prisoners would have kept alive for many months, perhaps over a year, all those who starved to death. A single order to release all those who were never needed for labor would have quickly reduced the death rate from over 30 percent per year to the civilian rate of about 3.5 percent. Granting permission for the welfare agencies to visit the camps would have led to a storm of public protest against the atrocious conditions, while at the same time producing the workers and political will needed to alleviate them. It can hardly be doubted that this was why permission was not given. It is quite clear from the record above that Eisenhower, aided by Smith and Hughes, played the leading role in preventing all this from happening. The deadly conditions, as Littlejohn said, were created by "strenuous efforts."

General Littlejohn certainly knew by August, and probably earlier, what was going on, but did little to prevent it. General Lee appears to have done all that he could, consistent with keeping his job. General Patton seems to have done as much as he could to liberate the dying, despite the difficulties placed in his way. Morgenthau did as much as he could to punish the Germans. Hull, Somervell and Stimson in varying ways sought more constructive remedies to the German problem. Roosevelt, inscrutable because so changeable, seems to have had no firm policy at the end of his days, unless to keep Morgenthau, Hull and Stimson from useless disputes over a beaten enemy. Nothing has been turned up so far in the records to indicate what Marshall or Truman knew of all this. Both were technically responsible; it is likely, but not proven, that neither of them knew what was going on.

Buisson in his book accepts complete responsibility for the French camps. That this was not an acknowledgment of guilt was plain through every claim he made that the camps were run as well as possible in difficult times. The records of Deputy Labor Minister Simon and the Ministère des Affaires Étrangères have helped to expose him, inadvertently, because the bureaucrats had to base their work on known facts, not on Buisson's dreams of innocence.

That de Gaulle knew about the camps before Pradervand wrote to him on September 26, 1945, seems highly likely, not only because he was commander of the army, but also because Pradervand phoned him after visiting the camps. De Gaulle knew and remembered Pradervand for the help that Pradervand had given him during the wartime negotiations for releasing French civilians from Ravensbruck.

As head of government and commander of the army, de Gaulle must have discussed the matter with his chief of staff, Marshal Alphonse Juin, who was well informed about the sensitive situation in the camps. De Gaulle, briefed by Juin, refused to see Pradervand; briefed by Juin, he gave his remarkably restrained performance to the world press in early October about the camp situation. This was the performance praised by U.S. Ambassador Caffery for its restraint towards the USA, not unlikely in a man dependent on the Americans for thousands of tons of war material and food arriving every day. This restraint translated into a campaign to extend his control over turbulent France while winning back all the colonial *gloire* lost in 1940. This was the mission of de Gaulle; the fate of a million or so German prisoners was of little consequence.

Juin ordered any number of reports from the army of the situation in the autumn of 1945, few of which survive at Vincennes. All of these, not surprisingly, report that the camps were improving, that great efforts were being made, and so forth. Most of the camps in the score or so of the military districts of France remain unrepresented here, notably the "one big death camp" of the Vosges, as described by Colonel Lauben.

Juin was not in principle out for revenge against the Germans, according to General George S. Patton. He saw, like Churchill and Patton, some use for the Germans. "It is indeed unfortunate," Alphonse told George at dinner in Paris in August 1945, "that the English and Americans have destroyed the only sound country in Europe — and I do not mean France — therefore the road is now open for the advent of Russian communism."[21]

Most of the prisoners in French camps, probably all, had a roof over their heads, but many were in rags in the fall of 1945 as a result of their exposure in American camps. Some got some clothing through a small campaign instituted by de Gaulle in Germany in late 1945. The International Committee of the Red Cross was permitted to inspect a minority of camps, but not all the 1,600. From the few inspected[22] they reported that starvation and malnutrition went on and on as France recovered, into 1947. There was food for the men who starved, but much of it was sold on the black market in France by the officers, to the amazement and disappointment of honest men like Mayor Raoul Laporterie of Bascons, who risked his career to criticize de Gaulle, and who suffered for it.

So in a sense, all of French society was guilty. Certainly most Frenchmen knew about the suffering in the camps and did nothing. The protest in the newspapers was as nothing compared to the outrages in the camps. The resistance to this shadowy atrocity was nowhere near enough to stir the conscience of the nation which prided itself on *la mission civilisatrice*.

De Gaulle could have prevented many deaths very easily by ceasing to add new prisoners to those who were already starving. Juin might have persuaded him to do this. Buisson to some degree was a victim, along with his prisoners, of a futile and vicious policy inflicted by the top men. These were de Gaulle and Juin. To whom belongs the glory, belongs the shame.

The Rules of Land Warfare, the Geneva Convention, the International Committee of the Red Cross, the common decency of the enormous majority of Americans and French people, the honesty of the British and Canadians, the free press, all failed. They failed because men who were heroes to us secretly seized the power of death over people who were helpless in our hands. Their superior officers failed to stop them, or to tell the public. Their peers or subordinates said nothing. The French press said little, or lied. The American press said nothing, or lied. The British and Canadians stood by and watched. The only people who spoke up when it counted were Jean-Pierre Pradervand, Jacques Fauvet and Victor Gollancz.

These people and a few others, such as the Abbé Stock and the Markgraf von Baden, continued to believe in the ideals so cynically exploited by the others. Believing, they felt the good of them, like the anonymous British soldier who had dreaded doing relief work for the Germans but said when it was over, "It was the only really worthwhile thing I've ever done in my life." For the U.S. and French commanders, committing their vengeful atrocities, keeping even the gratifications of wickedness to themselves, there was a sinking toward the evil which we had all supposed we were fighting.

Among all these people thought to be of good will and decent principles, there was almost no one to protect the men in whose dying flesh was our deadly hypocrisy. As we celebrated the victory of our virtue in public, we began to lose it in secret.

EPILOGUE

THE SURVIVORS OF THE CAMPS have ceased to suffer physically, but they are still being tortured spiritually by those who deny that they have suffered at all. As a result of the cover-up, their dead comrades continue to lie in unmarked graves, a perpetual accusation: *You have forgotten us.*

Approximately 2,000 of the survivors have written or called me, my publishers and the press, almost all of them expressing profound relief that the truth about their suffering has at last been published outside Germany. Children who did not believe what their fathers told them, now know. Knowing, they understand better their fathers, and us. Guards in the French and American camps have relieved their consciences. Nearly every new witness or survivor who has stepped forward has expressed heartfelt thanks that the truth has come out. No one has called for revenge.

The resistance to the first edition of this book was fierce. The French government flew two secret agents down to Mont de Marsan to harass M. Raoul Laporterie, aged 93, *Chevalier de la*

Légion d'Honneur, demanding to see the secret documents he had shown me that revealed the existence of the French death camps. The U.S. Army and the State Department have issued press releases filled with incorrect information ignoring the book's massive evidence of brutal conditions in the camps. A Pentagon representative, desperately searching for a way to exculpate Eisenhower, has tried to shift some of the blame to another American general, who in fact took good care of his prisoners. Academics in Canada, the U.S.A., France, Germany and the UK have denounced the book with a ferocity unimpeded by any weight of evidence. One such academic, a professor at York University in Toronto, told *Time* magazine that "Bacque's data are completely fallacious." My publisher immediately wrote to him asking for the errors, and the corrections. That was more than a year ago, and there has been no reply.

Most authors emerging from public excoriation claim they have been reviewed without first having been read. It is often true. The author of a review in *Le Figaro* proudly annnounced to a friend of mine that he had been able to denounce my book on the basis of the blurb alone. "Why didn't you read it?" my friend asked. "I didn't need to. I knew it couldn't be true," the reviewer replied.

In May 1990, the French writer Jean-Louis Cremieux-Brilhac wrote a letter to *Le Monde* saying that my book, *Morts Pour Raisons Diverse*, was false. Through a friend, I got a copy of the letter before publication. In my reply, I quoted from French and American army documents, showing that Cremieux-Brilhac was quite wrong. My letter went by fax through my friend to *Le Monde*, with a note saying that if Cremieux-Brilhac's letter appeared, mine should be on the facing page. In the end, *Le Monde* printed neither. Who can explain this? One is left to assume that Cremieux-Brilhac, on reading mine, withdrew his letter to *Le Monde*. My French publisher has since told me that the word in French journalism now is that even to notice *Morts Pour Raisons Diverses* is *"pas bon pour la carrière."*

Reaction has been violent because my book appears to attack a myth in which we have all participated for decades. North Americans and Western Europeans believe that one of the proofs of our virtue is that we killed the devil named Hitler, conquering a horrible tyranny that then reappeared in the body of our former ally. Uncle Joe Stalin, our smiling ally against evil, became evil himself. The democracies that fought to liberate the world from Hitler united against the treacherous Russian, who we now admitted used secret police, huge standing armies, death camps and a single-party dictatorship to maintain his evil empire. The enormous crimes that we committed against the Germans after the war were lacquered with self-righteous hypocrisy.

Our sense of virtue was secretly fed on hatred. This was an evil deeper than hypocrisy because virtue is not nurtured but sickened by hatred.

As the Communists finally began to free themselves from their own bondage in recent years, we grew freer ourselves. The Iron Curtain was raised, the Berlin Wall came down, painful truths were revealed in Russia, Poland, Czechoslovakia. And in Western Europe and North America. If truth shall make us free, then we soon should be the freest generation.

Whoever controls the press proclaims that it is free. Those to whom this freedom is denied have no means to deny it. In Russia for many years the editors proclaimed the press to be free. Only through the underground press, *samiszdat*, did we know it was not free to all. This is bound to be the way as long as the press is run for only some of the people in the society it nominally serves. True freedom of the press is not owned. It is not divisible. It is not deniable. It belongs to all of us.

What was the situation in Germany after 1945? At first, the press was directly licensed and censored by the victors. After the Allies established a client government, journalists, writers, artists, academics all supported "the West." This was expressed somewhat euphemistically by Willy Brandt in the Bundestag when he explained the government's reasons for taking over the editing, financing and publication of the Erich Maschke series about German prisoners of war in Allied hands.* If such a thing had happened in the West — a government taking over an important literary-historical research project to make sure it

* See pp. 155–57 above.

published soothing conclusions — there would have been an outcry. There was none in Germany. The client-academics tamely published a series that reproduced lies by the French and Americans, omitting vast tracts of history, statistics and experience that millions of ex-prisoners and their families knew were crucially important.

The result of this control of the client press was the emergence of a small, semi-furtive *samiszdat* (which literally means "self-published"). Dozens of books and pamphlets published in small editions by local publishers described the individual suffering of survivors of one camp or another. Our client-Germans, in control of the powerful national media, condemned the *samiszdat* as irresponsible or Nazi-inspired. So all of this went unknown in the West. Only if a fearless writer west of the Rhine took the initiative was something published that was truthful, and therefore revolutionary in this context. Such were the books by the American scholar Alfred De Zayas, which sold in the hundreds of thousands in Germany, because they told truths the Germans had not yet seen in print. These books, *Nemesis at Potsdam* and *The Wehrmacht War Crimes Bureau,*[1] described deportations, robberies, murders, atrocities leading to millions of deaths, committed by the Allies against millions of Germans, mainly women and children, in peacetime. Rejected some eighty times in the United States through ten years, but finally published in the U.S., Canada and England, these books were ignored by all the major English-speaking reviewing media and academics, who nevertheless had plenty of space or time to re-expose, hundreds of times, the crimes of Germans who had already been caught and punished.

To the extent that Germany was of the West, the German press was not free; to the extent that Germans were free, they were not of the West.

But it was not just in Germany that the press deceived, or was deceived. The U.S. Army has kept up its propaganda steadily if stealthily since 1945. The authors of various histories have done all in their power to minimize the damage to the reputation of the U.S. Army wrought by Eisenhower's policies. This is shamefacedly hinted by the author of an article on preventive medicine for prisoners of war, which appeared in the official U.S. Army history of World War II.[2] The author, Brigadier-General Stanhope Bayne-Jones, describes the difficulties he faced in attempting to get accurate statistics on the number of prisoners of war held by the Army. Saying that he failed completely (though the author of this present book found the basic figure in his first day's search in 1986), he concluded that the figure was not obtainable:

> Although the author spent much time examining various records in the attempts to reconcile . . . discrepancies, and although several explanations were furnished personally by former provost marshals, he was not able to discover all the reasons for the disparities. He came to the conclusion that corrected figures do not exist and that adjustments cannot be made from the available records.

His attempt to exculpate the Army for the cover-up he has just defined, while avoiding entanglement himself, is a masterpiece of historical tomfoolery:

> (I) concluded further that for the purposes of this chapter, the magnitudes, which were real and confirmed by all eyewitnesses, are all that matters. Little would be gained for the comprehension of the medical and sanitary problems of such multitudes of prisoners of war by refinement of statistics to the point of numerical accuracy.

This is the sort of balloony nonsense constantly employed by apologists to this day. Army apologist Stephen Ambrose, asked for the source of his figure of "about 50,000 starved to death," brought to perfection the notion that "numerical accuracy" is not important. He tells us that his source is a guess.[3] No such tendentious tergiversation exists in his and other historians' writings with regard to the vast numbers of U.S. troops employed in the theater; accuracy is sought and found among the millions of shifting masses of DPs and Allied prisoners of war being repatriated at the time, who were much harder to track because many of them simply walked home freely. The explanation for Bayne-Jones's failure to believe in "numerical accuracy," even though he reproduced hospital admissions rates to the second decimal place, is murkily hinted at in his conclusion:

> Although the terminal date for the official history of the Medical Department of the U.S. Army in World War II is 31 December 1945, the author of this chapter felt that it would be better to end it as of about 30 June 1945 after introducing accounts of a few episodes needed to complete bits of an ongoing record. Actually, after V-E Day, 8 May 1945, there were, technically speaking, no more German prisoners of war in the European Theater. The remnants of the German Army were classed as surrendered military personnel or disarmed enemy forces (at no little strain upon provisions of the Geneva Convention). Although these people were discharged and disbanded as rapidly as possible, a year or more was required to complete the process, during which much of the misery in the enclosures, previously described, was repeated. Another volume . . . would be needed to record the events in the immediate aftermath of the war relative to former enemy prisoners of war.

Well well. Accuracy, whether numerical, historical, historical-numerical or numerical-historical, is now so unimportant that the six months during which conditions were at their worst, deaths at their highest and Bayne-Jones's subject most important can be jettisoned without any reason. Except that it makes Bayne-Jones feel better.

Bayne-Jones casually dismisses the Allied contravention of the Geneva Convention. He says the convention is "strained," without revealing that it was unilaterally denounced by both British and Americans over the protests of Canada. And now, in 1991, the Americans and their Allies properly demand that the Geneva Convention be applied to their prisoners in Iraqi hands. Righteousness is only a myth if the Convention that embodies it is discarded whenever it is inconvenient.

Bayne-Jones admits that one of the causes of disaster in the camps was that the prisoners were deprived of their messing equipment so that food could not be cooked or distributed properly. "Admittedly, however, the lack of these implements and facilities was frequently caused by the fact that U.S. supply could not furnish them in the numbers needed. Whatever the reasons, numerous reports and photographs testify to those deprivations." He then tells an anecdote about two U.S. Generals trying their best to deal with the masses of prisoners of war arriving in April 1945. One General says that a German offer of surrender should only be accepted if the Germans can bring with them their "own kitchens and can take care of (themselves)." To cite this is just sanctimonious pleading for the Army, as we can see from the fact that Bayne-Jones does not reveal information that is very easy to discover: that the U.S. Army captured and held but never distributed vast quantities of German messing and cooking equipment. Under "German mess equipment" in late August 1945 there were still in U.S. Army warehouses 778,000 items, plus 2,106,000 items of cleaning equipment, 99,000 personal mess kits, almost six million toilet articles and 227,000 items of barracks equipment.

This sort of *trompe l'oeil* is still going on. Colonel Philip Lauben told me in 1987 not to give his address to any journalist because "when this book comes out, the shit is really going to hit the fan." But the British Broadcasting Corporation nevertheless did get his address — not from me — and his agreement to be interviewed, after Lauben had been briefed for the interview by a representative of the Pentagon. In this briefing, Lauben was warned that he had not understood his own experiences. The Pentagon representative explained everything to him anew. The BBC later would come to do an interview in which he would deny everything. According to Professor Ambrose, the BBC producer later would claim that Bacque had browbeaten Lauben into saying things he didn't mean. Lauben himself did not say this.

It is a singular idea that a Pentagon representative in 1990 who had not been on the scene in 1945 would be able to explain

Lauben's own experiences to him. Lauben was the Head of the German Affairs Branch of SHAEF. He was the officer in charge of repatriations and transfers who helped prepare the forms that used the term Other Losses. He went to Norway to arrange for the return of hundreds of thousands of Germans. He wrote detailed memoranda intelligently demonstrating how the French were attempting "larceny" in seeking prisoners to whom they were not entitled. He was trusted by Eisenhower with chairing a delicate meeting with the French at the moment when the Red Cross and the French press were threatening to expose the disaster in the camps.[4]

Lauben worked regularly with the Weekly PW/DEF documents, and when he discussed them with me during our interview in 1987, he said that Other Losses meant deaths and escapes. I did not suggest this to him. I did not "explain" this to him. He volunteered the information from his own first-hand knowledge.[5]

It is of course a comical notion that a strange foreign writer could walk into Lauben's living room and make him give evidence against his will in front of his wife for publication in a book proving that he and his army had committed a vast atrocity which had never occurred. There are other things to consider. Lauben gave me permission to tape the interview and, for safety's sake, repeated a second time that Other Losses means deaths and escapes. Weeks later in his house and far from my presence, he signed a transcript of this statement and returned it to me. More than a month later, and knowing that Colonel Ernest F. Fisher had been an Army historian, Lauben told Fisher that Other Losses means deaths and escapes. Lauben volunteered the comment that "the Vosges was just one big death camp." He wrote me a letter wishing me the best of luck with my book. Was Lauben browbeaten by me and by Colonel Fisher?

Lauben told the naive BBC interviewer that the Pentagon representative "explained to me" that the term Other Losses meant mainly transfers to "other U.S. army commands" and thus could not mean many deaths. This notion was based on the fact that under the heading Other Losses for the PW-DEF report of August 4, 1945, 132,262 men were footnoted as "turned over to" U.S. Forces Austria. "I made a mistake," Lauben said.

In his Monthly Governor's Report, Eisenhower also says these 132,262 DEF prisoners shown under Other Losses had long since been transferred from Germany to Austria. However, the U.S. political commissioner in Austria, General Mark Clark, issued a report in November 1945 stating the number of DEFs who had entered Austria in August 1945.[6] The number of DEFs transferred from Germany to Austria in August 1945 was 17,953. Eisenhower says they were transferred; Clark says most of them never got to Austria. A hundred and fourteen thousand men were no longer in Germany, they didn't arrive in Austria and they could not all have escaped. There's only one way to leave a place and not to arrive anywhere else, and that is to die. There is no other possibility. So from Eisenhower and Clark we have proof that even transfers under Other Losses hid a huge proportion of dead. In this case, 87 percent of the "transferred" were dead.[7]

Lauben was persuaded to change his mind by false information difficult to distinguish from a lie. Lauben's original explanation that Other Losses means deaths and escapes now stands confirmed by Clark's denial of Eisenhower's "transfer."

It is also true that apart from Eisenhower there was no other U.S. Army command in the European Theater of Operations responsible for prisoners. General Eisenhower was the commander of the United States Army in the whole European Theater including the forces in Austria. Prisoners transferred to Austria were still under his command. General Clark was subordinate to Eisenhower on all matters involving control of the Army, including supply, which was assigned to Eisenhower by the JCS in June 1945.[8] If the Army was correct in its "explanation" to Lauben in 1990, then weekly reports for those 132,262 men would have been issued by Clark. But there are no separate Weekly PW/DEF reports of any prisoners in Austria. They just disappear.[9]

Not that a transfer would have made much difference to these men. The Austrian camps were themselves so dreadful that a special investigation into starvation conditions there was held in September 1945 under the command of Lieutenant

Colonel Herbert Pollack, who found severe malnutrition problems among many of the prisoners.[10]

If the "explanation" given to Lauben in 1990 is correct, the camps in Austria were under the sole command of General Clark, who arrived there to take charge on August 12, after a brief preliminary visit in July. The Army story presupposes that what Clark found on arriving in Austria were prisoners in fairly well-run camps with no excessive death rate. The Army story means that Clark immediately ordered overcrowding and starvation to be imposed on these camps, formerly well-run under Eisenhower. This must have happened as a result of a complete change in Clark's character, because while in Italy he had kept his hundreds of thousands of prisoners well enough that when they were examined on discharge they were all of normal weight.

In fact, the truth about Clark is radically different from the Pentagon story. When Clark arrived in Austria,[11] he was horrified by the conditions he discovered. He took the unusual step of writing a memo "for files." This was probably to exculpate himself before history, without embarrassing his commanding officer, General Eisenhower. Clark wrote:

> When I first came to Austria from Italy, General Keyes told me of the deplorable conditions which existed in the Ebensee Camp, mostly due to over-crowding and to lack of proper nourishment. He told me he was taking corrective steps. . . . I . . . sent for Colonel Lloyd, my Inspector-General, and told him to make an inspection at this camp. Later General Hume came in with a detailed report showing the critical situation which exists there. I immediately directed the overcrowding be released, and that the caloric value of the ration be increased to approximately 2800 calories. I am not sure that I have the authority to do this, but will do it anyway because some immediate action must be taken. What astounds me is my lack of information on this camp from my staff officers.[12]

It is clear that Clark's junior officers kept silent at first about the horrors of Ebensee because they believed, as Clark did, that the camp was still Eisenhower's responsibility, as it had been all along. It was precisely because the control and supply of these camps lay with Eisenhower that Clark wrote "I am not sure that I have the authority" to take over the rationing of the camp. He mentions no problem about finding the necessary extra space, shelter or food. All of this could have been done months before, both in this camp and 200 others in Germany.[13]

Prisoners who had been released in good condition by Clark when he was the commander in Italy were reimprisoned by officers under Eisenhower's command and sent to slave labor in France. All of the 1,000 men in the shipment of prisoners from Italy to Bavaria, which included Werner Waldemar, a corporal in a Red Cross unit, were told in Italy they were going to be released when they got to the camp in Bavaria. All of them were given discharge papers. All of them were in good health. But only 8 percent — the older, youngest and crippled — were actually released. Ninety-two percent of the prisoners were put on trains and sent to forced labor in France.[14] Once again, the Geneva Convention was betrayed, for it specifically forbade forced labor. This was done probably because Eisenhower's officers could no longer find prisoners in their own camps fit enough to fill the minimal requirements for French slave labor.

The alleged Austrian transfer is marked by a footnote to distinguish it from the rest of the numbers in the column. Far from contradicting what Colonel Lauben had originally told me, this footnote actually confirms Lauben. The few who actually were transferred are footnoted, so we know that the Army bookkeepers were distinguishing clearly between transfers and other fates under Other Losses.[15] Thus, in the Other Losses columns, all the figures not shown as transfers must have been something else. And according to the Lauben of 1987 who had not been reeducated by a Pentagon representative, that something else was death.[16]

Still another proof that Lauben was correct in his original interpretation is that deaths among the DEFs are nowhere shown, if not under Other Losses.[17] Lauben's revised version entails a new death total, which is supplied by the Army and Ambrose: 1 percent. The 1 percent estimate of deaths produces a conundrum: How could it be that deaths numbering some 50,000 to 60,000 are not shown, while transactions numbering only a couple of hundred are shown? And why is it that all other categories of losses to the system show running totals, but the Other Losses category does not?

The U.S. Army's "explanation" is incorrect, unsubstantiated and incredible. It attempts to shift guilt onto a gallant officer. It is contemptible.

One of the defenses offered by apologists for the U.S. and France is that the men at the top did not know what was happening in the camps because they were so busy setting up military government in Germany or redeploying soldiers. That this is nonsense is self-evident; it was their duty to know, and Clark himself, *who was not even responsible,* was told within a few weeks of taking charge in Austria. In any case, Eisenhower did know and did nothing. We know this through the memorandum of an interview between a U.S. Army interrogator and Dr. Konrad Adenauer, later Chancellor of Germany.[18] This document, discovered some months after the first publication of *Other Losses,* reports an interview conducted in June 1945 by the U.S. Army with Dr. Adenauer, who deplored the U.S. death camps along the Rhine in very strong terms. He said:

> Some of the German PWs are being held in camps in a manner contrary to all humanitarian principles and flagrantly contrary to the Hague [and Geneva] Convention. All along the Rhine from Remagen-Sinzig to Ludwigshafen the German prisoners have been penned up for weeks without any protection from the weather, without drinking water, without medical care and with only a few slices of bread to eat. They could not even lie down on the floor [ground]. These were many hundreds of thousands. It is said that the same is true in the interior of Germany. These people died by the thousands. They stood day and night in wet mud up to their ankles! Conditions have improved during the past few weeks. Of course the enormous number of prisoners is one of the

> causes for these conditions but it is noteworthy that to the best of my knowledge, it took a great many weeks to improve at least the worst conditions. The impression made on the Germans by the publication of facts about the concentration camps was greatly weakened by this fact. Of course there were not actual cruelties in the PW camps (*sic*) but ordinary people say "Any [person] who treats PWs this way is not much better than the Nazis." I know that in the winter of 1941–1942 the Russian prisoners were very badly treated by the Germans and we ought to be ashamed of the fact, but I feel that you ought not to do the same thing. German prisoners too in camps ate grass and picked leaves from the trees because they were hungry exactly as the Russians unfortunately did. . . . Please allow me to say frankly, in very important matters . . . the Allies have used the same methods as the Germans, unfortunately, used. It is true that in the use of these methods they do not go to the same extremes, but the methods are the same.

The extraordinary description of the men who "stood day and night in wet mud up to their ankles" as they died by the thousands is exactly like the descriptions given by the survivors and by many American witnesses, including Colonels Beasley and Mason, who wrote in almost the same words of their experience in a Rhine camp in April.[19]

The distribution list for this memorandum includes Ambassador Robert Murphy, the chief political advisor to General Eisenhower. This was precisely the sort of information Murphy was supposed to gather and pass on to Eisenhower; it is a safe bet that he did pass it on. Together with Clark's experience and the evidence provided earlier in this book, this document should end the speculation as to whether or not Eisenhower knew. Regrettably, neither Murphy in his book, *Diplomat Among Warriors*, nor Adenauer in his years in office ever made the full truth public.[20]

The General himself, a few weeks after Adenauer denounced his policies, issued a report to the Joint Chiefs of Staff summarizing the fate of the prisoners.[21] "As of July 31 the status of PW and DEF personnel in the United States Zone was as follows:

"Discharged........2,046,575.
"Transferred...........922,566.
"On Hand............1,803,696."

The General did not point out that the total thus accounted for was 4,772,837. Subtracted from the capture total of the U.S. forces of 5,224,310 in the SHAEF command, given at June 10, 1945, by his own officers, this leaves 451,473 men, women and children not accounted for. For this period in the U.S. camps, the total number of the dead estimated in this book, published a year before the discovery of this document, was 472,366.[22] Unless this "Eisenhower Gap" of almost half a million persons is accounted for by death, there is no reasonable explanation for it. Discharges and transfers have already been given. The only fate conceivable for this enormous number of missing people is death.

The most reliable capture total that we have — the 5,224,310 prisoners reported to Eisenhower on June 11, 1945 — was low by many hundreds of thousands, if we can credit a confused and suspect memorandum sent to the State Department by the War Department in two parts, dated 1946 and 1949. This memorandum, summarizing the prisoner situation, gives breakdowns showing that the U.S. captured possibly 7,200,000, or possibly 5,539,862. If either figure is correct, the prisoners Missing/Not Accounted For at various dates would be far higher than those shown in this book, which derive from the basic capture figure of 5,224,310.

The breakdown of the War Department figures as of December 15, 1946, said that 3,054,667 people had been released without documentation "as not having had a recognized military status; 2,397,588 had either been transferred to other zones to be discharged or were then on loan to other countries, 15,285 had died of wounds or other causes while pows; and 72,322 were held by the US military authorities."[23]

The death figure of 15,285 begs scrutiny. It is the only overall figure ever discovered that was issued by the Americans. Taking it as it says it is, the deaths to December 15, 1946, for all prisoners taken by the U.S. in Europe and the Mediterranean Theater, it means the death rate was .5 percent per annum, including those dead of wounds.[24] This is below the civilian death rate in Europe in 1945, and only .1 percent higher than the death rate among U.S. soldiers at base camp. This is incredible, like the statement that the Army released over 3,000,000 prisoners without documentation, contrary to its own orders. As we shall see in Appendix 11, the Army's junior officers did not disregard standing orders 3,000,000 times in 1945–46.

Although it cannot be trusted in any detail, this War Department memo silhouettes one gruesome truth: many people had been held although they had "no recognized military status." We know from other evidence that the Army herded into these camps hundreds of thousands of civilians, including women and children *who had never fought*. Many of the captives were old men of the Volkssturm, according to one U.S. officer leading his unit towards Chemnitz in the spring of 1945: "We did not encounter many German soldiers. When we were fired upon, it was often the "home guard" [Volkssturm] made up of very old men who gave up after firing a few delaying shots . . . we captured many of them . . . what happened to them we never knew. We just kept on walking."[25] In many U.S. camps, sections were devoted to women, many of them accompanied by young children. At Attichy, the so-called "baby cage" held at one time 10,000 children who had been sent there under tough conditions by truck and train. This profoundly affects our understanding of the statement by Konrad Adenauer in the Bundestag that 190,000 civilians from the western zones of occupation who had been alive at the end of the war were still missing in 1950.[26] It is very likely that a high proportion of these missing civilians had died unrecorded in the American and French camps.

A senior officer in the Army who commanded a U.S. camp in France, Lieutenant Colonel Henry W. Allard of the Corps of Military Police, wrote a report, recently discovered, of conditions among prisoners of war in U.S. camps in France from late 1944 through May 1945.[27] These men were prisoners in the time when conditions were at their best in the U.S. camps in Europe.

The only Army supplies sent to these camps were rations, according to Allard. Everything else — medicine, clothing, fuel, mess kits, cookstoves — was denied. So bad were the conditions in these camps that Allard, who was at Thorée les Pins, was horrified:

> From Oct. 1944 to June 1945, they were fighting to keep up with the day by day problem of handling PW's with an insufficient number of men and officers but also against the fact that other than limited supplies of food, there were no supplies for PW's. The standards of PW camps in the Com Z in Europe compare as only slightly better, or even, with the living conditions of the Japanese PW camps our men tell us about, and unfavorably with those of the Germans. As to work conditions and treatment, our camps made an extra special effort to treat the prisoners as human beings to the best of their ability.

The problem, as always, was shortage of supplies, a policy imposed from the top, about which the lower ranks could do nothing. After the war, of course, conditions grew a lot worse.

Martin Brech,[28] an American guard who was at Andernach during the spring of 1945, said that the 50,000 to 60,000 men in Andernach were starving, living with no shelter at all in holes in the ground, trying to nourish themselves on grass. When he smuggled a little food to them through the barbed wire, he was ordered to stop by an officer whom he recalls saying, "Don't feed them, it's our policy that these men not be fed." Later, Brech sneaked more food to them, was caught, and told by the same officer, "If you do that again, you'll be shot." For "sport" some of the guards opened the gates so the thirst-crazed prisoners would run down to the Rhine for a drink. They were machine-gunned as they ran. Brech saw bodies go out of the camp "by the truckload" but he was never told how many there were, or where they were buried, or how. Andernach was in the Advance Section zone of the Army, where the conditions were described by the Medical History of the ETO as typical of conditions throughout U.S. camps in Europe (see Appendix 11).

Memories of Andernach bothered Brech so much that, after the war, he tried to tell others at home of his experience, but no one believed him even though he was a professor of philosophy, in a small college in New York. After the newspaper columnist Patrick Buchanan described the revelations in *Other Losses*, Brech wrote a letter to the *New York Post* confirming what he had seen. He immediately received threatening phone calls, his country mail box was wrecked twice and his car was vandalized. Brech has bravely kept on speaking out ever since, but his letters to the *New York Times* on the subject have not been printed, even though he was judged credible by several television networks, which broadcast interviews with him in England, Germany and the U.S. A parallel experience was that of Merrill W. Campbell, who wrote a letter to *Time* magazine describing a mass atrocity he had witnessed in southern Germany. *Time* edited his letter down to a couple of sentences: "I witnessed cruel treatment practiced against German prisoners by the Americans in Germany in World War II. As a U.S. sergeant, I saw an American soldier kill a German officer because he did not want to give up his watch and wedding ring." They submitted this version to Campbell, who allowed them to publish it, little realizing the historical importance of the distortion they were imposing on him. Unfortunately, Campbell did not keep a copy of his original letter, but he did set down his experience for this book, as follows:

> There (were) 10,000 or more German prisoners in this open field, standing shoulder to shoulder. It was raining and sleet and some snow. This bunch of prisoners (was) there for three days or more with no food or water, no shelter. There was little concern for these people. There (were) no German civilians around. As for food and water, I personally think it could have been furnished to them. Most of the guards were very brutal. As I was not in charge of this camp, there was little I could do. On the morning the prisoners were moved out, my company had orders to leave and go to Garmisch as my company was leaving the area. I looked back where they were moving the prisoners

> out, mud was deep as far as I could see. Heads, arms and legs of the dead were sticking out of the mud. It made me sick and disgusted. Other camps I (was) at treated the prisoners fairly well.[29]

An American officer who requested anonymity, fearing reprisals, said: "The conditions you so aptly described were exactly as it was in Regensburg, Moosburg and other camps throughout lower Bavaria and Austria. Death was commonplace and savage treatment given by the Polish guards under American officers."[30] And another officer, Captain Frederick Seigfriedt, was detailed as prisoner officer in an undermanned Prisoner of War Overhead Detachment near Zimming in eastern France in December 1945, where there were about 17,000 prisoners, all presumed to be SS. According to Siegfriedt, the previous commander had been relieved of his duties because of psychiatric problems. A lifelong friend of Siegfriedt's, Captain L., was medical officer of the detachment. Writes Siegfriedt:

> Captain L. had been an extremely hard working and conscientious person all his life. It was evident that he was under extreme stress trying to cope with the conditions at CCE 27 and receiving no cooperation, no help, no understanding, was helpless, and had not even anyone to talk to. I was able to serve to fill the (last) need. He explained to me that most of the men had dysentery and were suffering from malnutrition. Some men in the cages had as many as 17 bloody stools a day, he said. He took me to one of the former French barracks that served as the hospital. It had eight hundred men lying all over, on the cold concrete floors as well as on beds. It just broke your heart to see it. . . . Almost without exception the other (U.S.) officers were reclassified because of alcoholism or psychiatric problems. . . . The operation of CCE 27 seemed typical of the entire system. When an enclosure got a bunch of prisoners they didn't know what to do with, or could not otherwise handle, they were shipped unannounced to another enclosure. . . . I have no idea how many died (or)

> where they were buried. I am sure the Americans did not bury them and we had no such thing as a bulldozer. I can only assume that a detail of German PWs would bury them. I could look out of the window of my office and tell if the body being carried by was alive or dead by whether or not there was a fifth man following with the man's personal possessions. The number could have been from five to twenty-five a day.
>
> The officers' mess was in one of the French two-storey houses. It had a staff of forty-two [prisoners] with the maitre d' of the German luxury liner *Europa* in charge. Although there were usually no more than six or eight [officers] dining at one time there were always at least that many uniformed waiters. One could not get a cigaret from his pocket to his lips without a light waiting. The facility was completely redecorated, that is repainted with murals for each special occasion, i.e. Christmas, New Year's, Valentine's Day, St. Patrick's Day. . . . For lunch there was chamber music with four to six musicians and for dinner a choir of fifteen to twenty made up of the stars of the Munich and Berlin operas. In short, the [American] staff was much more concerned with living the luxurious life than it was about the operation of the prison camps.[31]

Siegfriedt attempted to alleviate the prisoners' conditions by bribing local French guards at excess vehicle camps with cigarettes so he could use their trucks to scrounge some hay in the neighborhood "to get the PWs off the ground. When the weather warmed up the cages became ankle deep in mud. I located a pierced-plank airfield and with a convoy of trucks, brought it back to get the men out of the mud. These however were Band-Aid measures for major problems that no one seemed to be in a position to deal with, nor did anyone else seem to care."

Captain Siegfriedt concludes his letter: "Obviously we, the U.S. Army, (were) not prepared to deal with so many prisoners even when I arrived on the scene in December 1945."

Captain Ben H. Jackson said that when he approached one of the camps along the Rhine "I could smell it a mile away. It was barbaric."[32] Lieutenant Arthur W. von Fange said he had seen about twelve locked boxcars filled with men stationed on a siding near Remagen in March 1945. He heard cries from within, which gradually died down. "I don't imagine they lasted three days," he has said.[33]

Another defense of the conditions in the camps is that Germany was in such chaos at the end of the war that such suffering was inevitable. By "chaos" is implied, among other things, that the transportation system was wrecked and most of the industrial production closed down. In fact, industrial production in Germany in 1944 was 140 percent of the level it had been in the prosperous year 1938. Even during the early winter of 1945 it remained high, at probably around 105 percent of 1938.[34] The rail transportation system was "in great shape" when the Allies entered the Reich, according to Colonel Walter Dunn who was in charge of the rail network behind Patton's Third Army. "It was much better than we expected." They could move anything anywhere they wanted any time they wanted. "If anyone starved, it wasn't as a result of lack of transportation."[35] Mainly as a result of Allied policies of dismantling and reparations, industrial production did indeed fall, by about 85 percent by the autumn of 1945.

All this was the result of the furtive implementation of the Morgenthau Plan. The original proponent of the harsh treatment under this plan was General Eisenhower, according to one of the participants at a meeting at Eisenhower's headquarters in England. Fred Smith, Assistant to the Secretary of the Treasury, wrote:

> On August 7, 1944 at approximately 12.35 p.m. in a tent in southern England, the Morgenthau Plan was born. Actually, it was General Dwight D. Eisenhower who launched the project. . . . The subject first came up at lunch in General Eisenhower's mess tent. Secretary Morgenthau, Assistant to the Secretary Harry D. White and I were there. White spoke of Germany, which was now certain to be defeated. . . . White said, "What I think is that we should

give the entire German economy an opportunity to settle down before we do anything about it."

Here Eisenhower became grim, and made the statement that actually sparked the German hardship plan. [Smith notes here that "This material is taken from notes made directly after the meeting."] He said: "I am not interested in the German economy and personally would not like to bolster it if that will make it any easier for the Germans." He said he thought the Germans had punishment coming to them: "The ringleaders and the SS troops should be given the death penalty without question, but punishment should not end there."

He felt the *people* [emphasis in original] were guilty of suppporting the regime and that made *them* a party to the entire German project, and he personally would like to "see things made good and hard for them for a while." He pointed out that talk of letting Germany off easy after taking care of the top people came from those who feared Russia and wanted to strengthen Germany as a potential bulwark against any desires Russia might some day have. . . .

The General declared he saw no purpose in treating a "paranoid" gently, and the "whole German population is a synthetic paranoid. All their life the people have been taught to be paranoid in their actions and thoughts, and they have to be snapped out of it. The only way to do that is to be good and hard on them. I certainly see no point in bolstering their economy or taking any other steps to help them."

White remarked: "We may want to quote you on the problem of handling the German people."

Eisenhower replied that he could be quoted. He said, "I will tell the President myself, if necessary."[36]

Lord Keynes, the British economist, asked President Roosevelt in late November if he was planning "a complete agrarian economy" for Germany. Although the American people had been told that the Morgenthau Plan had been abandoned,

Roosevelt now told Keynes in secret that the plan would be implemented. The German economy would be reduced to a level "not quite" completely agrarian, he said. The plan went "pretty far" in de-industrializing the Ruhr and eliminating many of German's basic industries.[37] Former president Herbert Hoover, when he was in Germany in 1946, found much lying going on about conditions in Germany among U.S. officers. According to a U.S. intelligence report given to Hoover, "The figures on economic output can be believed only one-fifth — the rest is doctored to make a good impression with top levels. The lower personnel is permeated with Morgenthau people."[38]

This policy meant starvation both in the prison camps and in the civilian population generally. The Statistisches Bundesamt in Wiesbaden has conservatively estimated that 2.1 million German civilians died among the 15 million people, mainly women and children, who were expelled from East Prussia, Pomerania, Silesia, Sudetenland, Poland, Czechoslovakia, etc., after the war.[39] Many more died among the German civilians not deported. However the widespread food shortages of 1946 affected the rest of the world, it is clear that for more than a year from May 1945, Allied policies deliberately hampered the Germans in attempting to feed themselves, and in their attempts to export to pay for food imports. Nor was charity permitted at first. The governments of Sweden and Switzerland tried to ship relief food to Germany in 1945. They were both forbidden.[40] The Allies themselves, all the while complaining of shortages and excessive cost, shipped wheat to the Germans. Not nearly enough to offset the value of the dismantled factories. Not even enough to prevent widespread death by starvation. Just enough to stave off a Communist revolution.

Surely it is time for the guesswork and the lying to stop. Surely it is time to take seriously what the eyewitnesses on both sides are trying to tell us about our history. All over the Western world, savage atrocities against the Armenians, the Ukrainians and the Jews are known. Only the atrocities against the Germans are denied. Are Germans not people in our eyes?

No benefit will ever come from the mass slaughters of the 20th century until we learn to see the good in the despised.

Appendices

INTRODUCTION

It has not been possible to produce perfectly accurate figures for the deaths in either the French or the American camps. The destruction of records, the falsification at the time and later on, the genuine confusion of the times — all contribute to the inaccuracy. It would have been technically possible to reproduce death ratios to four decimal places, but that seemed pointless and even spurious, because some of the army figures that were not obviously falsified were probably approximations and therefore not accurate to the last digit shown.

The general truth in these pages depends on several basic figures which come from the most authoritative sources. They are confirmed by other figures derived from other sources. The author believes that the most important basic figure — the total On Hand figure for U.S. forces — is correct. This figure is derived from other figures beginning in June 1944, which build in a way consistent with our other knowledge of the war. The figure is inherently consistent — that is, none of the subsets is inconsistent with any other, except for deaths. The major component of the total capture figure was given by General Bradley and several others, and disputed only by SHAEF G3, as we have seen. Another basic figure is the number of captives transferred by the Americans to the French. Both armies agreed roughly as to what this figure was, despite many other reservations about what each said about the other's treatment of prisoners and other matters. Mainly correct are the numbers of people released or returned home, in figures recorded by USFET and the French Army.

Where the United States (and French) Army figures are incorrect or incomplete, it is usually on the subject of the dead, or on figures that could be used to determine the death toll. For instance, in the USFET tables, the Other Losses account is the only one for which there is never a cumulative total. For both POWs and DEFs, the Other Losses account disappears for long important periods.

The totals of prisoners Missing/Not Accounted For in American (and French) hands calculated for this book are probably out by less than five percent. Both of these Missing totals are far higher than the number of deaths that the author estimates occurred in each army's camps. Combined, they are far fewer than the number of Germans Missing/Not Accounted For in 1947. The subtotals for Other Losses in the U.S. Army are probably low. This is likely because the Army fails to account for numbers of people much larger than are indicated under Other Losses. The same is true of the French. Another reason to believe that the Army's figures are low is that the deaths reported in this book do not account for all of the 1,700,000 German soldiers, alive at the end of the war, who have never been accounted for in any way by any of the Allies. The Missing/Not Accounted For figures include and imply the dead, but define only the lower limit of the possible, for both the French and the American camps. The German Missing/Not Accounted For figures of 1947–50 define the upper limits of the possible.

In the American case, the death totals can be figured out largely through direct observations.

The following death figures are much closer to the truth than any figures so far published by the U.S. Army, or by any source that depended uncritically on French or American archival sources, without reference to common sense or to the experience of the prisoners.

The truth of these numbers lies not in their minute detail but in broad generality. Imperfectly but certainly they show that something important occurred which was hidden before. Where we had supposed there was nothing remarkable, there was a catastrophe.

Appendix 1

OTHER LOSSES IN THE AMERICAN CAMPS

Euphemism is the first step to atrocity. In the U.S. reports on the status of POWs and DEFs, starvation became emaciation, and mass deaths became Other Losses.* The Americans did not use the word death in any of their DEF reports, as if it was to be believed that no one among the millions of DEFs died in their many months of captivity. Not until the Germans started asking years later why there was no trace of millions of people did the Allied armies provide their statistics in which the euphemizing shifted from the word to the number.

Thus there are two layers of statistics: the euphemized statistics of the time and the lies told later to the Germans. This appendix is concerned only with the statistics of the time.

The statistics kept by the Americans falsify death totals or declines of prisoners on hand, and where necessary, anything revealing the likely causes of death, such as imposition of the lethal DEF status. Generally, subjects such as capture figures, transfers to other countries and discharges appear coherent, reasonable and accurate on the American side, less so on the French. However, while the basic documents were still secret, in the 1950s the U.S. Army began to publicize false capture figures, which diverted suspicion from their camps towards the Russians. For comments on the various documents in which the figures appear, see the other appendices, especially 3 and 4.

Examining the Records

In this book we examine only the statistics concerning deaths of men captured by American forces in Europe in the SHAEF area (Northwest Europe). This means they exclude captures in Italy or Sicily or the North African campaign, where a total of about 660,000 were taken. The surviving documents recording the status of POWs and DEFs** start at D-Day (June 6, 1944) and continue through victory (May 8, 1945) and on January 1, 1946. This timespan can be subdivided into six record-keeping time periods.

1. *From D-Day to about April 1 1945,* the prisoners were given reasonable care and did not die in huge numbers. Their deaths were recorded by the Theater Provost Marshal (TPM). The TPM death totals are usually so inconsistent with other reliable reports on death that the TPM totals have not been included. No captives had DEF status during this period.

2. *April 1 to May 8 (VE Day).* The TPM kept detailed records which were still not trustworthy on death totals. The DEF status was officially imposed on many prisoners on May 4.

3. *May 8 to June 2.* Many men were transferred from POW status to DEF status during this period, but the detailed DEF records start only on May 19 and only with the 12th Army Group. No other detailed DEF records are available. (The

* In the French camps, *inanition* (starvation) became *cachexie* (extreme weakness), *mort* (dead) became *perdu* (lost).

** The figures that follow are taken from documents described in Appendices 2 and 3.

HEADQUARTERS
UNITED STATES FORCES
EUROPEAN THEATER
G-1 Division

Date 21 September 1945

WEEKLY PW & DEF REPORT

AS OF 2400 HRS. 8 September 1945

	PREVIOUS ON HAND	GAINS	DISCHARGED DURING WEEK	DISCHARGED TO-DATE	TRANSFERRED DURING WEEK	TRANSFERRED TO-DATE	OTHER LOSSES	BALANCE ON HAND
EASTERN MIL. DISTRICT	263,582	18,712	13,200	1,514,207	1,619	17,201	6,532	260,943
WESTERN MIL. DISTRICT	97,752	28,825	4,564	244,248	- - - -	51,631	6,519	115,494 (1)
SCCHCB (Bremen Enclave)	2,253	18,858	927	2,095	18,066	122,590	- - -	2,118
TOTALS	363,587	66,395	18,691	1,761,350	19,685	191,[illegible]22 (4)	13,051	378,555
Prisoners of War								
TSFET	692,895	2,696	- - - -	331,[illegible]*	11,407	751,996	5,543	678,641

(1) Figures include:
Military labor service units - 22,956
Hospital cases - 41,387

* - 407,748 discharged by 12 AGp formerly included, deducted from total previo report

Distribution:

General Bevans
Col. Lauben
Col. Negrotto G-3
~~Lt Col. Petito, G-2 USFET~~ (Main)
Major Lustig, G-1 USFET (Rear)
OTCQM TSFET (REAR) APO #887

Information Control Division, USFET (Main)
SGS, Stats Section, USFET (Main)
G-3 War Room, USFET (Main)
G-4 War Room, USFET (Main)
Major ... USFET (Main)
OTCQM TSFET (MAIN) APO #757

Capt. Truelock, Army Gd Div, USGCC
Theater Provost Marshal, Hq ...,
APO 887, U.S Army
Att: Chief of PW Div.
File.

15 1106

Col. Philip S. Lauben, head of the German Affairs Branch of SHAEF, *explained the significance of the term "Other Losses" to this author in 1987. Lauben's name appears at the lower left.*

SUPREME HEADQUARTERS
ALLIED EXPEDITIONARY FORCE
G-1 Division

11 June 1945

TOTALS ON PRISONERS OF WAR TAKEN & DISARMED ENEMY FORCES ROUNDED UP

	PW	DEF	TOTAL
21 A.G.	417,063 (a)	1,322,892 (b)	1,739,955
SCOFOR		343,900	343,900
FORCE 135	26,000 (c)		26,000
U. S.	3,486,153 (d)	1,738,157 (e)	5,224,310
FRENCH	280,629 (f)		280,629
TOTAL	4,209,845	3,404,949	7,614,794

REMARKS

(a) Figure furnished verbally by 21 A. G.

(b) Excludes 456,408 transferees from 9th U. S. Army.

(c) 26,000 PW taken in Channel Islands, of which 22,500 evacuated to U.K.

(d) Figure furnished verbally by 12th A. G. (includes 7th Army).

(e) Includes 456,408 transferees to 21 A. G. Also, includes an estimated 20,000 DEF still to be taken in areas between U. S. and Russian Zones.

(f) As reported by 1st French Army, Alpine Detachment and Atlantic Detachment.

Col. Kessinger
after many attempts we have arrived at this, as probably the official PW figure for the operations.
FILE NO. 383.6/1-3.
15 1191
S May

Official total capture figure for June 11 for SHAEF applies to Allied Forces in northwest Europe, excluding the Mediterranean area and Italy. The handwritten note at the bottom reads: "Col. Kessinger After many attempts, we have arrived at this as probably the official PW figure for the operations. S. May [or Nay]."

REPORT OF STATUS OF DISARMED ENEMY FORCES

TWELFTH ARMY GROUP

-CUMULATIVE-

Date	Gains	Dschgd	Trfd	Other Losses	Balance
JUNE 1	2,118,262	431,376	430,376	96,873	1,159,637
2	2,126,545	457,985	456,822	101,053	1,110,685
3	2,135,927	488,091	456,822	115,480	1,075,534
4	2,149,597	503,585	456,822	117,877	1,073,313
5	2,169,608	524,530	456,822	118,529	1,069,727
6	2,194,657	541,468	456,822	120,417	1,075,952
7	2,205,782	564,915	456,822	123,546	1,060,499
8	2,215,854	588,414	456,822	125,895	1,044,723
9	2,231,129	613,076	456,822	127,286	1,033,945
10	2,301,170	629,505	456,822	138,136	1,076,707

15 1184

Report of Status of Disarmed Enemy Forces, 12th Army Group, Cumulative, for June 1-10, shows Other Losses totalling 138,136. The number of DEFs *on hand for the 12th Army Group went from zero at May 8 to the figure shown. Most of the discharges shown were made by Patton's 3rd Army.*

RG332
Box 50

REPORT OF STATUS OF DISARMED ENEMY FORCES
TWELFTH ARMY GROUP
CUMULATIVE

Date	Gains	Dschgd	Trfd	Other Losses	Balance
JUNE 1	2,113,960	431,976	430,976	95,543	1,156,665
2	2,122,224	457,985	456,822	99,706	1,107,711
3	2,131,574	488,091	456,822	113,603	1,073,058
4	2,145,231	501,585	456,822	115,931	1,070,893
5	2,165,232	524,530	456,822	116,571	1,067,309
6	2,190,338	541,466	456,822	118,511	1,073,539

A- GAINS Column shows all receipts from whatever source; surrender, stragglers, transfers, etc.

B- TRANSFERRED Column shows only personnel transferred to British Custody. None have been made to French or Russians to date

C- OTHER LOSSES Column shows all losses other discharge or transfer to custody of another nation; i.e., normal attritions, desertion, release without discharge of Volkssturm personnel and civilians, etc.

Document recently found in U.S. Archives reads at top REPORT OF STATUS OF DISARMED ENEMY FORCES, TWELFTH ARMY GROUP CUMULATIVE, like document on page 201. The definitions for Gains, Transferred, and Other Losses were typed in by ribbon copy <u>after</u> the statistics were entered by carbon copy on the original printed form. Box reading RG 332, etc. was written in 1991, and refers to archival source of document.

TPM did keep POW records during this period, but they are not reliable on deaths and so are not used here or in any other period covered in this book.) The records of SHAEF-USFET are deliberately distorted to hide one million prisoners, whom we have called the Missing Million.

4. *June 2 to August 4*. On June 2 SHAEF G3 division began keeping detailed records for both POWs and DEFs, including tables showing Discharges and On Hand for both POWs and DEFs, for British and American camps. This continued until July 14, when USFET replaced SHAEF and the British began to keep their own records.[1] No Transfers (including transfers to the lethal DEF status) or Other Losses are shown in either SHAEF's or USFET's records. Allowing for the Missing Million, the total Accounted For figures on the U.S. side are consistent with other U.S. Army statistics and with the death totals printed in this book. On the British side, to July 14, the Accounted For figures rise rapidly because of a rise in the On Hand numbers, apparently as a result of transfers from the U.S. side. Then these figures drop, apparently showing that camps received from the Americans did not contain as many men as the U.S. Army had said. (See Appendix 9).

5. *August 4 to September 8*. USFET, having taken over from SHAEF on July 14, began to document captives in U.S. camps only, including Transfers and Other Losses for both DEFs and POWs.

6. *September 8, 1945, to January 1, 1946*. This period is documented only with scattered records that mention no more than On Hand totals, transfers to the French and transfers back from the French.

To calculate death totals, it has been necessary to give estimates of deaths to fill in the major gaps when there were huge numbers of On Hand in frightful conditions, but no Other Losses records. These gaps occur from April 1 to June 2 for POWs, and from June 2 to August 4 for both POWs and DEFs. Finally, estimates are made for the period September 8–January 1. For deaths that occurred outside the camps but derived from conditions within the camps, a separate tabulation is given.

Our calculations of the actual number of dead have been done in one of two ways. For some periods we totalled the Other Losses, which are the body counts done by the army. These were recorded for both DEFs and POWs for certain periods. For the other periods, we computed the number of deaths by applying the death rate given in Army statistics for another period to the known number of prisoners on hand.

On Hand

On May 8, VE Day, the captives On Hand in Europe numbered 2,874,897.[2] On and after May 4, as mentioned above, many former POWs were transferred to DEF status and many new captives were brought in to DEF status. Captures had ceased by June 2, so totals of DEFs and POWs taken were static by that time. June 2 was also the date when the Theater Provost Marshal (TPM) Daily Report went weekly and when SHAEF G3 began issuing the tables of POWs and DEFs On Hand and Discharged for both British and American camps. The first SHAEF G3 tables giving the On Hand figure at June 2 incorrectly said that there were a total of 2,927,614 POWs and DEFs On Hand. A letter from General J. C. H. Lee corrects this figure to about 3,878,000.

Unexplained Gains in August-September

The USFET weekly DEF-POW tables (Period 5) show a gain of 331,016 captives in August-September, but they give no indication of the source of this gain. They did not come from the United States because the large-scale transfers back from the U.S. did not start until November.[3] Neither were there enough men in the U.S. Army camps in Italy (MTOUSA) to supply all those who were recorded as arriving in the American camps in August-September — the MTOUSA camps had only about 291,000 men in June. In any case, the projected transfers from Italy numbered only 30,000 in the first half of July, and they were all to be repatriated — that is, released.[4] Even this number were not in fact released. As for Norway, the captives there numbered only 301,729.[5] The possibility that the gain was from Norway is also reduced by the fact that some, and perhaps all of the captives in Norway, were already included in the SHAEF totals under the SCOFOR rubric, which represented the Bremen enclave (see Appendix 8). There is no other source known for these gains but the Missing Million. Because of the destruction of records, the fate of the other 600,000 or so who made up the Missing Million is not known.

Bookkeeping

Why did the Army bother with bookkeeping at all, if it was so deceptive? Not only were negotiations still going on with other governments for transfers of prisoners for labor, the Army was also using Germans as labor for its own purposes.[6] About 400,000 to 600,000 prisoners were being used in 1945 for various purposes. It was also important to know On Hand totals so transfers could be orderly. The American falsifications hid deaths in such a way that the On Hand figure remained useful. The Midnight Shift, for instance, covered the way rations were reduced and shelter denied, while leaving undisturbed the total number of prisoners on hand.

Total Capture of Germans by Allies During World War II[7]

In Northwest Europe up to June 2, 1945	
U.S.	5,224,310
French	280,629
British/Canadians	1,739,900
In Italy-Austria up to May 17, 1945	
British/Canadians	1,134,000
U.S.	291,000
In North Africa	
British/U.S. (held mainly in the U.S.)	371,000
Allied Wartime total	9,040,839

A further 100,000 to 400,000 were probably held in Canada, Norway and the United Kingdom. Because the records are not complete or detailed enough, these are eliminated here to avoid double counting.

Appendix 1

Total of U.S. captures in Northwest Europe 5,224,310
U.S. total for the whole war against Germany [8] 5,886,310

Prisoners of War Captured

The 12th Army Group captured 3,486,153 POWs between June 6, 1944 and May 8, 1945, according to General Bradley[9] of the 12th Army Group. According to the Theater Provost Marshal, the 6th Army Group (also of SHAEF) captured 684,128 as of May 8, 1945 for a total of 4,170,281. By June 2, through deaths, discharges, and transfers to other categories or countries, the total of these POWs still On Hand was only 1,816,929 and dropping rapidly. After August 4, all POWs were treated like DEFs, although — inexplicably — they continued to be recorded separately as POWs. At September 8, the last day for which we have USFET tables, the total On Hand is down to 678,641. Because no POWs retained their status after August 4, only those already discharged at that date, 372,496, had been treated all through their captivity as prisoners of war, although 4,170,281 had started their journey with that status.[10]

Disarmed Enemy Forces Rounded Up/Transferred from POW Status

The DEFs, the worst-treated of all the German captives, vary enormously in number from zero at May 4, when the first POWs were declared to be DEFs, to 2,126,545 (On Hand plus Discharged plus Transferred plus Other Losses) at June 2. The numbers oscillate through July and August, finally settling near 378,555 On Hand at September 8. Most of the DEFs were held in Germany and all the DEFs referred to in this book were held by the 12th Army Group, but it is clear that the 6th Army Group, which had taken in 684,128 POWs by May 10, must also have taken in several hundred thousand DEFs (see "The Missing Million," below). In addition, conditions in the Austrian camps were very bad in late 1945,[11] so it is reasonable to assume that many of the captives in the 6th Army Group were held in DEF status.[12] For this book, the date when the first captives were deemed to be DEF is taken as May 8 for ease of computation, although the date of the first transfer to the DEF category was actually May 4. The number of DEFs shown for May 8 to June 9 is not used to calculate the death toll for the period because the Army did a body count under Other Losses.[13]

The Missing Million

The third category is the Missing Million, which included both POWs and DEFs. These were almost certainly the 6th Army prisoners simply abolished from the records during the changeover from the TPM daily report to the weekly report on June 2.

Explanation of the Death Toll Figures

The death rate in the prisoner of war camps was closely observed[14] by United States Army Medical Corps observers in camps containing 80,583 POWs in May and early June 1945. This rate was 30 percent per year or 2.6 percent per month (see Appendix 2). The death rate observed in the camps in August-September and reported as Other Losses[15] by the Army was also 2.6 percent per month. It is assumed here that during most of the period between June 9 and

July 28, for which the Army does not report Other Losses in prisoner of war camps, the death rate continued steady at 2.6 percent per month. For the period April 1–May 8 and for the period September 8, 1945–January 1, 1946, the rate is estimated for this book to be 0.3 percent per week in order to err on the side of caution. Together with the Other Losses that were reported directly by the Army, (plus the toll April 1–May 8 of 28,585 as indicated below), this produces a total of deaths for May 8 to September 8 of 145,208 people, of whom 23,459 were counted directly by the Army.

Anecdotal evidence confirms that the death rates in the camps were high. Charles von Luttichau has said that about five to ten of the one hundred men in his section of the Kripp sub-camp died in the spring of his captivity. He believes that his cage lost fewer than normal because most of the men in it were officers between 20 and 30 years of age, who helped each other a lot. He thinks that the death rate in the rest of the POW camp was well over 10 percent during the period that he was there — that is, it was about 5.5 percent to 6.9 percent per month.

Various other witnesses have given estimates based on the number of bodies they saw go out or the number they helped to carry out. The daily observed average was then compared with the number of prisoners in the camp as recorded in the U.S. Army documents. At Bad Kreuznach, also a POW camp, the rate was 4.2 percent per month to 5.4 percent. At Heidesheim, according to Captain Julien of the French Army, who took over the camp from the Americans, it was 3 percent per month; at Remagen POW camp, between 5.5 percent and 10 percent; at Rheinberg, a POW camp, between 3 and 15 percent per month.[16]

Determining the Deaths in the POW Camps

The average holding for this period was about 1,755,198*. The Theater Provost Marshal reports deaths of 2,397 in this period, which indicates a death rate of about .13 percent per year — not a credible figure for men starved, crowded and exposed as these prisoners were. Nor is it in line with the death rates shown by Army doctors in the ETO survey starting May 1.

Figures shown in boldface in the table below are taken directly from U.S. Army documents. The others have been calculated by applying the death rate reported by the Army to the On Hand figure reported by the Army, except where otherwise noted.

April 1 to May 8 (VE Day)

For 1,755,198 prisoners held for 38 days at .3 percent per week, the death total is 28,585

May 8 to June 9

For 1,742,388 prisoners held for 32 days at .6% per week (ETO Medical History figure) the death total is 47,791

* Derived from the April 1 and April 11 figures of the Theater Provost Marshal and from the May 8 figures of 12th Army Group and SHAEF G1.

Appendix 1

June 9 to September 8

Date	On Hand	Other Losses (calculated at death rate of .6 percent)	
To June 16	**1,462,032**	8,772	
" 23	**1,399,794**	8,399	
" 30	**1,271,567**	7,629	
Subtotal			24,800
To July 7	**850,630**	5,104	
" 14	**836,117**	5,017	
" 21	**849,621**	5,098	
" 28	**892,354**	5,354	
Subtotal			20,573
August to September (Other Losses totalled direct from USFET reports)			**23,459**
TOTAL June 9 to September 8			68,832

Total deaths in prisoner of war camps from April 1 to September 8, 1945 (28,585 + 47,791 + 68,832) 145,208

Deaths in Camps for Disarmed Enemy Forces

Among the DEFs, deaths were also reported as Other Losses from May 8 to June 10 by the 12th Army Group, although these were not included in the SHAEF reports. In the 12th Army Group reports, the death rate was 2.6 percent per week. The Army began again to report Other Losses for the week July 28–August 4, when the rate was 2.9 percent per week. In August-September it averaged 2.15 percent per week. For the period June 11–July 27 when Other Losses were not recorded, the May–June Army death rate of 2.6 percent per week has been used to estimate death totals. Applied to the known totals of DEFs in the camps,[17] this means a death total from May 8 to September 8 of 310,992, of whom 192,502 were counted directly by the Army.

May 8 to September 8

(Death figures shown in boldface are from body counts done by the U.S. Army. Others are pro-rated by the author from Army death rates applied to Army counts of imprisoned DEFs. Prisoner totals shown in boldface are also taken from U.S. Army documents.) All the death rates are calculated (and rounded up) from Army rates reported during and after the period.

Date	On Hand	Other Losses/wk		Death Rate
To June 9			**127,286**	**2.6**
" 16	**849,688**	22,092		**2.6**
" 23	**709,463**	18,446		"
" 30	**609,102**	15,837		"
Subtotal			56,375	

Date	On Hand	Other Losses/wk		Death Rate
To July 7	**684,467**	17,796		**2.6**
" 14*	**601,134**	15,629		"
" 21	**568,192**	14,773		"
" 28	**535,251**	13,917		"
Subtotal			62,115	
To Aug 4	**885,951**	**26,064**		**2.9**
" 11	**754,090**	**5,129**		**.7****
" 18	**388,799**	**3,949**		**1.0****
" 25	**368,808**	**10,700**		**2.9**
Subtotal			**45,842**	**1.9*****
To Sept 1	**359,452**	**6,323**		**1.8***
" 8	**378,555**	**13,051**		**3.4***
Subtotal			**19,374**	**2.7*****
TOTAL			310,992	

Deaths among the Missing Million

The Missing Million dropped from sight when the TPM daily report gave way to the weekly report on June 2. The number who disappeared from the TPM records was 1,042,537. The number of captives in dispute between SHAEF and General Lee at June 2 was 950,923, which is the start figure used here for the Missing Million, for the period June 2 to August 4.

May 8 to June 2

It is not clear what the death rate was among the Missing Million during May 8 – June 2 so no allowance is made for them. If they were in fact treated like DEFs under the jurisdiction of the 12th Army Group, about 104,000 would have died in the four weeks. If they were treated like POWs, then about 24,000 would have died.

June 2 to August 4

Because we do not know whether the Missing Million were held in the POW or the DEF category in the period June 2–August 4 while they were missing from the records,[18] we have assumed that the same proportion of the Missing Million were DEF as among those accounted for by SHAEF-USFET, and the same proportion were treated as POWs. Therefore, we have assumed that the death rate overall for the Missing Million was the same as the death rate overall for the captives who were reported by SHAEF-USFET in the June 2–August 4 period.

* Estimates for July 7–28 have been pro-rated by the author. Taken all together, they exactly equal the difference between July 7 and July 28, as shown in Army figures.

** Apparent inaccuracies in death rate figures are due to rounding.

*** Average

August 4 to September 8

It is not clear from the USFET POW and DEF tables for this period exactly how many from the Missing Million were shown as Gains in the total number of captives who were already being reported, so we do not know how many Missing Million were still missing on September 8. Therefore, no deaths for the Missing Million are included in the figures for this period. Probable deaths being excluded here number perhaps 10,000 in August-September.

The average ratio of POWs to DEFs during this period is 60-40 — based on that same distribution in the captives who are recorded by SHAEF G3 starting June 2. After June 2, no reports exist for the POWs or the DEFs who were held by commands other than the 12th Army Group (meaning chiefly the 6th Army Group), although the 6th Army Group was under SHAEF and later USFET.[19] Therefore, it is assumed here that 60 percent of the Missing Million (about 570,554 people) died at the .6 percent per week POW rate, and the other 40 percent (about 380,369 people) at the DEF rate of 2.6 percent per week. Deaths among the Missing Million POWs at .6 percent per week for nine weeks equal 30,810. Among 380,369 DEFs at 2.6 percent per week for nine weeks, the toll is 89,006. The total toll is 119,816.

Deaths Occurring in the Camps from September 8, 1945 to January 1, 1946 and Deaths Occurring after Discharge or Transfer

From the evidence of Captain Julien and of J. P. Pradervand, we know that the death rate remained high for many weeks following release, because the effects of captivity did not disappear as soon as conditions improved. Among the survivors of the Nazi camp at Bergen-Belsen, many of whom were carefully treated in hospital by the British, between 35 percent and 40 percent died within a few weeks of release.[20] In May 1945, Number Seven Canadian Army General Hospital at Bassum, Germany, treated 556 civilians released from concentration camps, most of them suffering from extreme malnutrition. Despite everything the Canadian doctors could do, 31 of them died in 25 days. This is 5.6 percent of the number of concentration camp survivors,[21] or 6.8 percent mortality per month.

Pradervand said that one-third of the prisoners turned over to the French by the Americans at Thorée les Pins were already so sick that they could not work and were likely to die soon. The death rate was over 40.5 percent per year, or 3.4 percent per month.[22] They were so sick that Pradervand judged they would die that winter unless their living conditions improved immediately. The Americans received back from the French 52,000 such men during the autumn of 1945. Some allowance must be made for deaths among these, the sickest of the sick. It is assumed here that only half of the men predicted to die by Pradervand did die,[23] adding 26,000 more to the toll.

From several reports of starvation conditions in the U.S. camps in 1945–46, it is clear that neither the prisoners nor the DEFs received much more food in the winter than they had previously. Several reports condemn individual camps; one letter from an official of the State Department, confirmed by an official of the International Committee of the Red Cross,[24] states unequivocally in January 1946 that "conditions under which German POWs are being held in European Theater leave us open to grave charges of violation of the Geneva Convention."[25] Colonel Tom F. Whayne who visited the Continental Central enclosures, reported in January 1946 that they were "grossly overcrowded, and provide ideal conditions for epidemics." The ICRC reported from France, and the Army from Austria and Berlin, that U.S.-held prisoners were starving.[26]

In the month September 8 to October 8, the number of captives on hand continued as before,[27] and conditions in the camps remained much the same, so it is assumed here that the DEFs and POWs continued dying at the same rate as in August–September. The Other Losses total for the four weeks August 11 to September 8 was 34,023, so a similar number remains to be added for September 8–October 8. For the period October 8 to January 1, when the number of prisoners was "more than a million,"[28] it is conservatively assumed here that the monthly death rate was cut in half, to 3.2 percent. The 3.2 percent estimate produces a total of approximately 90,000 dead.

Prisoners who were discharged also died from the effects of captivity. It is assumed here that these deaths continued for one month after discharge, at 3.2 percent per month. The total for these deaths among the approximately 2,100,000 dischargees as at September 8 would therefore be approximately 67,200. This does not include deaths among more than one million captives transferred to the French, British or other Allies.

Death Totals Attributable to Treatment in U.S. Army Camps (Excluding all transfers to other U.S. Army zones or other nations)

Special Return from French	26,000
September–October in U.S. camps	34,023
October–January in U.S. camps	90,000
Among POWs discharged	67,200
TOTAL	217,223

The Final Toll

POWs (to September 1945)	145,208
DEFs (to September 1945)	310,992
Missing Million (POWs) June 2–August 4	30,810
Missing Million (DEFs) June 2–August 4	89,006
Subtotal	576,016
Deaths Attributable to Treatment in Camps (September 1945 to January 1946)	217,223
TOTAL deaths	793,239

Appendix 2

THE ETO MEDICAL HISTORY

The following notes are based on several tables found in "Medical History, European Theater of Operations," vol. 14, RG 332, Box 166, National Archives, Washington D.C., (Suitland, Maryland). The tables are based on a survey done earlier by the U.S. Army Medical Corps in the European Theater in May–June 1945. The tables are reproduced on pages 188, 189.

Number of Prisoners Covered in Table X

Table X purports to give the number of deaths by chief causes of death among the approximately 80,583 prisoners during the six weeks of the survey. The number of prisoners covered is given incorrectly in the text preceding Table IX. The text states that the survey covers 70,000 prisoners, but the ratios of absolute numbers to proportionate numbers in the table itself make it clear that the number surveyed was close to 80,583. For example, the rate per thousand for hospital admissions for injuries was 468 per year. The admissions column to the left shows that there would be 37,713 admissions per year on this basis, so there must have been roughly 80,583 prisoners in the survey. But each of the three categories, when extrapolated, produces a different number of prisoners surveyed. All are near 81,000, so 80,583 is taken. Using this as the basis later on for figuring the deaths among prisoners means that the death rate is lower, hence the deaths estimated are lower, than when using the figure of 70,000 given in the ETO Medical History text.

The number of U.S. troops surveyed is given nowhere, but it is easy to calculate it for each case by dividing the absolute numbers for any given category by the per thousand rate. Doing this, we see that the U.S. troops side of the table is either based on different surveys, ranging in size from 268,333 (deaths from disease) to 287,187 (deaths by injury), or else it is statistically unreliable. These difficulties in the Army statistics are typical and usually prevent anyone from discovering the death rate in the camps.

Table IX — Prisoner Death Rate Wrong Because it is Mathematically Impossible

These observations are based on the words at the head of Table IX ("per 1,000 per annum") that imply that the absolute totals in the table are valid for a year. For the possibility that they are valid for six weeks, see Appendix 11.

If the author of the report was giving absolute totals for one year prorated from absolute figures observed over six weeks, he must have begun with a whole number in each category. This must have been a whole number (i.e., 64, not 64.5) because he was dealing with human beings. He then divided each whole number by six, then multiplied the result by 52, to create the figures in Table IX. But it is not possible to arrive at the figures he gives by starting with a whole number as a base. For instance, the prisoners' deaths from injuries are said to project from six weeks to an annual figure of 98. But 98 divided by 52 equals 1.8846, which, multiplied by 6, comes to 11.308. Thus the nearest possible whole number that could

DECLASSFIED PER EXECUTIVE ORDER 12356, SECTION 3.3, 7/15 001

By NND NARA, Date 5/7/87.

Table IX

Comparison of Number of Admissions and Death Rates per 1000 per Annum

For Prisoners of War in ASCZ Enclosures and ETO Troops (Less UK)

During Six Week Period Ending 15 June 1945.

	Admissions				Deaths			
	P. O. W.		U.S. Troops		P. O. W.		U.S. Troops	
	Number	Rate Per 1000	Number	Rate Per 1000	Number	Rate Per 1000	Number	Rate Per 1000
Disease	345,324	4,288	155,785	551	2,754	34.2	161	.6
Injury	37,713	468	31,070	110	98	1.2	919	3.2
Battle Casualty	20, 105	250	2,204	8	16	.2	82	.3
Total	403,142	5,003	189,059	669	2,868	35.6	1,162	4.1

An average of twenty-five percent (25%) of all prisoners in ASCZ enclo sures were seen at sick call each week. Death occurred nearly nine (9) times more frequently than in U. S. troops. Table X shows the chief causes of death:

Manuscript of typed history of the Essential Technical Medical Data Section of History of European Theater of Operations found by Colonel Fisher in the U.S. National Archives in Washington

Table X

Chief Causes of Death Due to Disease in ASCZ Prisoner of War Enclosure

For Six Week Period Ending 15 June 1945

Causes	Number
Diarrhea and Dysentery	833
Cardiac Disease	811
Pneumonia	207
Exhaustion	192
Diphtheria	40
Emaciation and Dehydration	31
Typhoid Fever	30
Meningitis	25
Septicemia	25
Tuberculosis	20
Nephritis	17
Tetanus	13

includes figures based on May–June survey of POWS *in 23 U.S.* POW *camps along the Rhine. That survey is incompletely reproduced in Tables X and IX (shown here) of the* ETO *History.*

ENEMY PRISONERS OF WAR 395

TABLE 23.—*Admissions for 23 selected causes among German prisoners of war in enclosures, European Theater of Operations, U.S. Army, for 6-week period ending 15 June 1945*

[Rate expressed as number of admissions per annum per 1,000 average strength]

Cause for admission [1]	Number	Rate
Diarrhea and dysentery	159,842	349.24
Common respiratory disease	98,861	214.8
Tuberculosis	9,128	19.83
Venereal disease	7,624	16.56
Pneumonia	7,360	16.4
Vincent's angina	5,822	12.65
Scabies	4,465	9.7
Diphtheria	2,859	6.2
Malaria	2,661	5.78
Undulant fever	2,029	4.41
Infectious hepatitis	1,047	2.27
Typhoid fever	493	1.07
Paratyphoid fever	420	.91
Scarlet fever and streptococcal sore throat	294	.8
Rheumatic fever	203	.44
Tetanus	70	.15
Typhus	55	.12
Dengue	29	.1
German measles	29	.1
Measles	22	.09
Poliomyelitis	8	.0
Relapsing fever	1	.0
Trench fever	1	.0

[1] Additional significant causes for admission, as reported in various hospital records, were encephalitis, meningitis, cardiac insufficiency, nephritis, peptic ulcer, septicemia, malnutrition, emaciation and dehydration, exhaustion, and injuries.

Source: Essential Technical Medical Data, European Theater of Operations, U.S. Army, for July 1945, dated 25 Aug. 1945, inclosures 13 and 14.

Cause of death	*Number*
Diarrhea and dysentery (bacillary)	833
Cardiac disease	811
Pneumonia	267
Exhaustion	192
Diphtheria	40
Emaciation and dehydration	31
Typhoid fever	30
Meningitis	25
Septicemia	25
Tuberculosis	20
Nephritis	17
Tetanus	13
Miscellaneous	450
Total	2,754

383-612 O-71——27

The parts necessary to complete the original survey of POWs *by the medical corps in May–June 1945 are the documents on the preceding pages and the article (above) by Stanhope Bayne-Jones (in Vol. IX of the* History of Preventive Medicine in World War II, *Washington, 1969).*

be the base is 11 men dead in 6 weeks. But 11, when divided by 6, the result then being multiplied by 52, gives 95. (The base figure of 12 men dead projects out to 104.) Similarly for diseases: the nearest possible base of 318 dead in 6 weeks projects out to 2,756, but the report states 2,754. (If instead of working by the periods 6 weeks and 52 weeks, as the author says he has done, we work with single days, — that is, we divide the nearest possible starting whole number by 42, then multiply by 356 — it is still true that no whole number in existence gives the result the author says he has obtained.) Whether working to one, two or three decimal places, it is impossible to obtain the results shown in Table IX when starting with a whole number.

The death total of 2,868 is either wrong, or correct only by accident. Therefore in choosing between the death rates of Table X and Table IX, Table X is to be preferred.

Table IX — Death Rate Wrong Because Inconsistent with Table X

The second fault in Table IX is that when we apply its death rates to Table X, the results are ridiculous. If the death rate in Table IX is accurate, then it must be valid for the prisoners of Table X as well, which covers the same prisoners in the same camps during the same weeks. This means that the number of prisoners surveyed for Table X must have been 560,899, because the Table X deaths of at least 2,304 per six weeks mean an annual total of 19,968. The number of prisoners for whom the death rate of 3.56 percent per year gives a death total of 19,968, is 560,899. This means that there was a second survey of 560,899 prisoners showing causes of death not only by disease, injury and battle casualty, but also by at least twelve individual diseases, because those subtotals are given. It doesn't make sense for the ETO Surgeon to order two different surveys at the same time. It also doesn't make sense for the Surgeon, with access to such an enormous and exquisitely detailed survey, seven times the size of the other, to have used it only for an incomplete report of the relatively minor subject of the proportions among causes of deaths, while leaving out the death rate itself, and to depend upon a much smaller, less accurate survey for the all-important death rates. Nor is it likely that the Surgeon would use two different groups of radically different size for tables under the same general heading, in exactly the same camp system, at exactly the same time, without specifying such a significant change. Therefore, there was almost certainly only one survey. So the fact that we have differing results is not caused by differences between two different pools of prisoners surveyed, but rather because one table presents those results incorrectly. We already know that in Table IX, the subtotals used to make up the death rate are wrong, so lacking any new evidence to the contrary, it is now certain that the overall death rate of 3.5 percent per annum is wrong, that Table X is more accurate and that the death rate among the prisoners was at least 25 percent per annum.

It is now certain that the figure of 3.56 percent for overall deaths in Table IX is wrong, that Table X though incomplete is to be preferred as far as it goes, and that it indicates a death rate among prisoners of war of at least 25 percent per year. The author of the ETO Medical History also withheld the disease rate from Tables XI (a) and (b) (not shown here) — although it was information essential to discovering the death rate in the so-called hospitals. In the course of a very long and detailed survey for Table XI covering 10 months and many hundreds of thousands of POWs, the author of the report does not give a death rate, nor does he provide any means of discovering it. We are told the rates of occurrence of scabies and strep throat, but not the rate for the most significant occurrence of all, death. We are also not told of another highly significant rate, that of discharges, which ought to interest the Surgeon very much, because he obviously wants to know how his hospitals are doing for cures. But the discharge rate cannot be given if the death rate is to be hidden, because deaths can be approximated easily by subtracting discharges from admissions. That the death rate was important to the author of the report is evident from the fact that he provides a separate table to list the chief causes of death by twelve diseases. That he omitted the death rate from the bigger survey cannot be an oversight.

The evidence is clear that the author of this History hid the death rate by suppressing information. However, that information appears in an article by Stanhope Bayne-Jones, who used the original report upon which the ETO Medical History is based. (See Stanhope Bayne-Jones, "Enemy Prisoners of War," *Special Fields, Preventive Medicine in World War II*, vol 9. [Washington: 1969], Department of the Army, p. 341.) Bayne-Jones cites the same original survey used as the basis for the ETO Medical History, but includes the total for deaths. Apparently attempting to continue the cover-up, he does not give the total of prisoners surveyed, but since we find that total in the ETO Medical History, we can put together the fragments to make the whole.

The Table in Bayne-Jones says the death total from disease is 2,754 in six weeks, which is the same number shown for disease in the ETO History. This final piece of evidence indicates that the author of the ETO Medical History simply reproduced the POW death figures for six weeks as if they applied to a whole year. He thus apparently reduced the death rate of 29.7 percent per year for disease to 3.42 percent This is probably the reason that the author of the History did not show Table X complete. Table X's true total of 2,754 would have revealed that he had deceptively used the same number in Table IX.

When the three categories of prisoner death (disease, battle casualty, injury) are totalled using the full disease death total of 2,754 from Bayne-Jones, they come to 2,868. This makes a death rate for the 80,583 prisoners of war of .59319 percent per week, which, rounded to .6 percent, is the rate used in this book where Army body counts do not appear.

In this book, all three categories of death (disease, injury, battle casualty) are used to determine the overall death rate, because most battle casualties, though they did not occur in the camps, would in normal Geneva Convention conditions, have been easily cured. In any case, battle casualty deaths amount to only .6 percent of the total.

Because in Table IX the disease death rate has been falsified, the rates for injury and battle casualty have almost certainly been falsified downwards to reduce the death rate. However, the true figures have not been found in the documents that have survived. In any case, together they amount to less than 4 percent of the total shown. Finally, the true disease rate, when taken together with the shown injury and battle casualty rate, corresponds exactly to actual Army body counts of dead prisoners in the camps. Thus the rate of .59319 percent per week is confirmed by a second Army source, as well as by the prisoners themselves.

Appendix 3

THE PROVOST MARSHAL REPORTS

These papers are entitled PW Status Reports, issued by the headquarters of the Provost Marshal in the European Theater of Operations. They are given daily until June 2, when they become weekly. They give a breakdown of the prisoners of war (not DEFs) from D-Day (June 6, 1944) up to August 25, 1945. These are very detailed reports but they are far from accurate, especially when reporting deaths. The total of POW deaths reported here up to June 2 is 4,500, and thereafter, to August 25, a further 4,790. In the six-week period when the officers of the U.S. Medical Corps were finding 2,868 dead in POW camps of about 80,000 men, the Theater Provost Marshal reports only 4,540 for more than 1,700,000 prisoners on average. The death rate found by the surveying doctors was over 30 percent per year, but the rate reported by the Provost Marshal was as low as 0.36 percent per year for a few days in May, averaging around 2.4 percent. Later in the summer, when the USFET figures showed a death rate of 30 percent per year under Other Losses, the Theater Provost Marshal Reports were showing rates running week by week from the end of July at around 1.8 percent per year, and as low as 0.36 percent per year. Considering that the death rate for U.S. Army resting personnel in peacetime was 0.4 percent, this is not credible. Almost the same situation prevailed in March when the death rate was reported as 0.75 percent, and again in April when it was 0.67 percent per annum.

Another oddity is that transfers to the U.S. zone are shown alongside transfers to the British zone and the Russian zone. But the U.S. zone is in the ETO, so the prisoners were not being transfered at all. What can it mean? Why were they reported as a loss to the system, like the transfers out of the system? It is a fair guess that "transfers to the U.S. zone" was a euphemism for deaths, because the totals closely resemble Other Losses in the USFET reports. No death figures in this book are based on that suggestion.

The omission without remark of a million prisoners on June 2 is typical of the way in which these reports were used to give a false picture to any inspectors from Washington, while at the same time preserving information useful to the Army. In the case of the Missing Million, the Army, already oversupplied with prisoner labor, had in secret reserve a million potential workers who might come in handy but did not need to be known, like a miser's hoard.

Many other mistakes occur in these reports. General Hollar, who was a senior officer in the Office of the Provost Marshal, Ad Sec, reports during a meeting a discharge due of over 20,000 for a day in which the TPM reports show a total of under 2,000. For May 25–26, two different totals for deaths are given on different pages of the TPM reports. Both conflict with the total for that day given by General Hollar in his meeting.

The slovenliness of accounting increases as time goes on, until some of the figures are a month old when reported, and for the final two weeks, totals are not given. In general the figures are very difficult to interpret because the form and terms change often without explanation, because figures for a given week are included in totals for a different week, and because figures given as bases (i.e., not to be changed once given), are in fact retroactively changed without explanation. In figures for camps in two different reporting areas, the same number of men hospitalized is shown for different days (e.g. June 2, then again June 9, which repeats again at June 16, and again at June 30). This is hardly credible.

Making up these reports must have been a giddy business, at least in the death department, for the statisticians on duty on May 9 managed to add a subtotal of 478 from one camp area to the other dead from the rest of the theater, and get a total of 375. This ability to produce a whole smaller than one of the parts is typical of the magic that the Theater Provost Marshal office wrought for high-level officers. Nor was it caused by VE Day euphoria, for this sort of thing went on all summer.

Appendix 4

THE SHAEF-USFET PAPERS

These SHAEF-USFET documents include a series of daily reports from the 12th Army Group, accompanied by various letters from generals such as J. C. H. Lee and Omar Bradley, about POWs and DEFs. These give Other Losses for DEF in the period May 8 to June 10, then there is a gap to August 4, when Other Losses are given for both POWs and DEFs in the weekly POW-DEF reports of USFET. The June-July gap is partly filled in by SHAEF documents, found both in the Public Records Office, London, and in Abilene, Kansas, which do not give Other Losses, but do report totals On Hand, Transferred and Discharged, for both British/Canadians and the U.S.

The SHAEF reports for the British/Canadian camps, along with evidence from ex-prisoners of the camps, suggest that there were no mass deaths in those camps. This suggestion is buttressed by the fact that the SCOFOR DEFs, who were in the Bremen enclave, and ended as British responsibility, show no losses at all under the Other Losses category for the weeks in August while they were appearing on the USFET weekly POW-DEF reports.

Major May's plaintive report on the total of prisoners and DEFs dated June 11, 1945 (taken here to refer to June 2) appears in this series of documents, most of which are in the NARS, Modern Military Records at Washington. It is on these documents that the name of Colonel Lauben was found.

Appendix 5

THE JUNE 2 DISCREPANCY: SHAEF G3 AND GENERALS LEE AND LITTLEJOHN

That Lee was correct in stating on June 2 that there were 3,878,537 prisoners On Hand in U.S. camps in the SHAEF area of Europe is seen in the report of the Army Chief Historian in 1947,* which showed that at May 18 there had been 4,000,101 POWs and DEFs On Hand in the cages of the 12th Army and 6th Army Groups. More evidence that Lee got it right was provided by a different division of SHAEF, the G1 division, on June 11, 1945, when it issued the official capture figure for the operation for U.S. forces, which was 5,224,310.** When the number of men who were already dead, discharged, transferred or evacuated at June 2 — in other words, captured but no longer On Hand on June 2 — are subtracted from the total capture figure, the remainder should be the number On Hand. The men accounted for already at June 2 numbered 1,405,881. Subtracted from the 5,224,310 captured, that leaves 3,818,429 On Hand, very close to Lee's figure.

The final proof that Lee was right is in comparing the SHAEF G3 opening balance at June 2 of men On Hand with the USFET closing balance at September 8. The opening balance of 2,927,614 On Hand at June 2 was added to in August–September by a Gain of 331,016, so that the total pool of living prisoners in the camps who must be accounted for was 3,258,630. But the Army said on September 8 that it had already dealt with 3,694,513, which is 435,883 *more* than that. The only way the Army could have dealt with more men by September 8 than it said it had in June, was that indeed it had had more men on June 2 than it acknowledged, as Lee said. All of this is confirmed by the report, already quoted, of General Littlejohn, who said in August that the Army was responsible for feeding 1,500,000 more people than it had been feeding.***

---

* "Disarmament and Disbandment of the German Armed Forces," Office of the Chief Historian, Frankfurt am Main, 1947, p. 39. Xerox in author's possession, courtesy of Professor Art Smith, California State University, Los Angeles, California.

** For the week June 2–9, figures for new captures are not given by any branch of SHAEF, or the TPM, but it is clear from certain indications, not least being the passage of time, that the major captures had all been finished long before. The DEF Gains figure for the 12th Army Group rose by 104,584 during the week, but this was probably caused by POWs being turned over to DEF status.

*** Littlejohn to CG, HQ TSFET, August 27, 1945. In Quartermaster's Records, NARS, Washington.

Appendix 6

DISCREPANCY IN NUMBER OF CAPTIVES, JUNE 2 AND SEPTEMBER 8, 1945

Were the captives on hand at June 2 sufficient to account for all that the army said at September 8 was done with them?

POWs On Hand at June 2	1,816,929
DEFs	1,110,685
Total of captives On Hand	2,927,614
Gains in Period June 2–September 8	331,016
TOTAL CAPTIVES TO ACCOUNT FOR	3,258,630

Accounted for between June 2 and Sept 8

Other Losses*	125,758
On Hand September 8	1,055,078
Discharged** in Period	1,560,588
Transferred*** in Period	953,090
TOTAL ACCOUNTED FOR	3,694,513

Total to Account for	3,258,630
Total accounted for	3,694,513
Surplus of men accounted for	435,883

This means that if the Transactions figures are correct and the On Hand are correct at the end, the Army disposed of 435,883 more men than it said it had to dispose of. They must have come from somewhere. For the solution (that there were more men in the camps on June 2 than the Army showed as being present), see the Missing Million section of Chapter 5.

* These are the Other Losses accounted for by the Army, not by the author.

** Discharged equals September 8 total of 2,090,174 minus previous total of 529,586, that is, 1,560,588.

*** USFET table showing POWs at September 8 numbering 751,996, plus DEFs numbering 68,832, plus special transfer of August 4 of 132,262 to US Army in Austria, shown as loss. Total = 953,090.

Appendix 7

THE MIDNIGHT SHIFT

Under the peculiar SHAEF-USFET bookkeeping system, the closing balance for the week, produced by the transactions in the week, does not necessarily provide the opening balance for the following week.

The On Hand figures in the left-hand column are from SHAEF-USFET tables for DEFs on hand at the start of the week shown. Thus, for example, in the week June 16–23, the total On Hand at the beginning of the week, 849,688, is reduced during the week by discharges of 262,411, meaning that there should be only 587,277 On Hand at midnight Saturday. However, one second later, the number on hand must have been 709,463, if the transactions during the following week produced the result shown at the end of the week. Thus, 122,186 (the difference produced by subtracting 587,277 from 709,463) must have been added at midnight; otherwise, the discharge figure is wrong. The Army had no interest in falsifying discharge figures to show fewer discharged than was the case. In choosing between the three remaining possibilities to explain the Midnight Shift — that the discharge figures are inadvertently wrong, that men are added from the Missing Million, or that they come from elsewhere in the system, the third is preferred because of a second "Midnight Shift" — away from the prisoners of war. The shift of POWs away from their camps totals 586,003 in the period June 2–July 28. This number is so close to the Midnight arrivals in the DEF camps (588,533), that it is preferred here. In addition, the Quartermaster reports for July said that 900,000 fewer were being fed at the end of the month, who were no longer a U.S. responsibility. The report did not say that they were discharged. The clear implication is that they were still in the camps, but no longer being fed. Thus they must have been POWs who had once received food.

The Midnight Shift, June 2 to July 28

How they were inserted into the DEF *figures*

(This table is based on tables issued by SHAEF-USFET G1, showing weekly figures of DEFs)

OH Start week	Disch. in week	Result for end of wk shld be	Actual used for end week	Added in Midnight Shift	Week
1,110,685	356,934	753,751	849,688	95,937	Ju 2-16
849,688	262,411	587,277	709,463	122,186	Ju 16-23
709,463	152,153	557,310	609,102	51,792	Ju 23-30
609,102	104,383	504,719	684,467	179,748	Ju 30-Jul 7
684,467	115,605	568,862	601,134	32,272	Jul 7-14
601,134	172,481	428,653	535,241	106,598	Jul 14-28

TOTAL Present and Not Accounted For 588,533

Appendix 7

How they were taken out of the POW figures

POWs On Hand June 2, SHAEF HQ G3 Tables	1,816,929
POWs On Hand July 28	892,354
Reduction	924,575
Less Discharges shown in period	338,572
Missing and Not Accounted For (Shifted to DEF status)	586,003

Appendix 8

THE PRISONERS IN THE BREMEN ENCLAVE (SCOFOR FORCES)

These men were imprisoned in the Bremen Enclave, an area round Bremen, a port city in northern Germany, surrounded by the British zone. In the first reports from SHAEF, June and July, cited here, they were listed separately from both U.S. and British prisoner holdings. They were not included in the DEF totals used to compute deaths for this book. Because they were included in the September *overall* On Hand totals from USFET, they are therefore included here. No Other Losses were shown for them, so they do not affect the total of the dead.

Appendix 9

THE BRITISH DISCREPANCY

The 456,408 men whom the U.S.-SHAEF capture figure says were to be transferred to the British, apparently do not all turn up among the prisoners accounted for by the British in the June 16-23 period. The British figures are as follows:

June 2 Total Accounted For	1,978,521
June 9 Reports Missing	
June 16	2,447,849
June 23	2,171,343
June 30	2,187,146
July 7	2,195,985

The difference between June 2 and June 16 is a rise of 469,328, apparently due to the U.S. transfer. In May and early June, the 12th Army Group DEF figures show a drop in the prisoners Accounted For of exactly 456,408, with the note that they were transferred to the British. Thus the 12th Army Group seems to have transferred in that period all the outstanding 456,408. But the *rise* in the British Total Accounted For at June 16 is 469,328, then at June 23, only 206,304, remaining after that very close to 206,304. As we have seen, the Total Accounted For figure in principle should not vary by as much as one person. Why does it vary?

One explanation is that the figures express only the On Hand, those men for whom the British believed they were in fact accountable. This is a vital figure, more important than any other except the deaths, because of course it is the figure for rationing, as well as the figure for which they might one day be held accountable by the Red Cross, or world opinion, or a revived Germany, or their own commanders. If they found they had been mistaken and were not accountable *for men they did not receive*, they could not simply show them as discharged or transferred, because that would mean they had once had them, which was not the case. The simplest thing to do once they realized the camps did not contain as many as they thought, was, at the end of the week, to ignore the number of men *supposed* to be on hand, and enter in the opening balance for the week the correct lower figure. *This opening balance was never shown in the* SHAEF *accounting system*. Only the weekly transactions and the results appeared. So transactions up or down were easy to put in, and hard to spot. Nothing else needed to be done. The vital figure was now correct.

The U.S. figures are unreliable for deaths or anything connected with cause of deaths, whereas the British figures for Accounted For at least, stay steady near 1 percent consistency from June 23 onwards. Therefore, the total number of human beings actually transferred of the reported 456,408 is in doubt.

The British figure seems the more reliable, partly because surviving prisoners have said that the British frequently counted them, especially at Rheinberg just after the June handover. As we have seen through Herr Liebich's eyes at Rheinberg, the American camps were in dreadful condition, with men prostrate dying in holes, sick, lying on the open ground and so on. Such was the chaos that it is reasonable to assume that the British did not stop to count the men accurately on hand-over, but simply did what they could to save lives, as Herr Liebich has said. The British probably accepted the U.S. figures and used them until they did their own head counts. That was when the discrepancy, called here the British Discrepancy, appeared. This would account for the sudden drop from 2,447,849, Accounted For at June 16 to 2,171,343 at June 23 when, it is known, they did their own physical count in the camps. This drop in the Accounted For figure is the same as the unexplained drop in the On Hand figure. For the week of June 16–23, the British had, at the beginning of the week, 2,363,226. They discharged none during the week, so the start of the following week should show the same number On Hand. But the number On Hand is actually 2,033,788. This is the difference between the U.S. paper figures and what may be the British headcount figure. If the Americans did not hand over fewer than indicated on the books, we have no explanation for the sudden decline in the British figures. For all these reasons, the overall British figures are to be preferred.

What is the exact British figure for the transfer? When the last three weeks of the British figures are averaged, the total accounted for is 2,184,825. This is taken as the base from which to subtract the opening balance at June 2, of 1,978,521, meaning that the British by head count actually took in the difference, equalling 206,304.

Another question remains to be answered. If all this is so, what happened to the 250,104 men who were the difference between 456,408 and 206,304? Where were these men? Some were likely dead, and the rest probably turned up like the Missing Million, beginning August 4.

Appendix 10

ESCAPEES FROM FRENCH CAMPS

After this book was first published, new information came to light permitting a closer focus on the deaths in French camps. In his book Kurt W. Böhme says that according to General Buisson, over 80,000 prisoners escaped from French custody between 1944 and 1948. In contrast the Americans said that only about 1,191 prisoners escaped from their camps during a period of more than a year; these U.S. camps averaged nearly 2,000,000 inmates for the period. Many of these prisoners were in camps in France and Germany which were handed over to Buisson. Thus, after the French Army took over, Buisson claims that from these same camps and inmates, the proportion of escapees increased approximately 260 times. Is Buisson's statement trustworthy?

Buisson was not the only responsible French authority to report on the prisoners who had escaped. In 1946 the Labor Ministry office under M. Simon, reported on the fate of escapees.* Simon gave a breakdown of prisoners who were supposed to be at work. Under the subheading of those not available to work for the French, he gives one category named, "*les évadés repris depuis moins de 3 mois, les punis, les indésirables* ... 25,000". It is clear from the word *repris* that these men were all on hand in the camps at the end of the period reported, but had not been working during some or all of this period because they were fugitives. The report in March 1946 of M. Michel, the ICRC delegate in France, has a similar category which shows 6,102 prisoners as "Fugitives (less than three months)".** Because these temporary escapees were listed as part of the potential labor pool, we know that the Government expected to recapture all or nearly all of them.

Surely if escapes had been 80,000 as Buisson said, they would have turned up in these Labor Ministry and Red Cross reports as a separate category, but they didn't. That the Ministry and the ICRC, both depending on the Army for their figures, reported the recovery of temporarily absent prisoners but not the permanent loss of them, cannot be incidental. There is not a single entry in the ICRC reports, the detailed U.S. Army reports on French camps, or the Labor Ministry reports, for deaths or permanent escapes. All other possible permanent subtractions from the labor pool are noted, including permanently inapt for work, repatriated, medical personnel protected by the Geneva Convention, and so on. This shows that the difference between escapes and recoveries of escapees was statistically negligible. What does statistically negligible mean in this context? It means, obviously, a category so small it is not reported. Therefore, such a category must be smaller than the smallest category that is reported. In the ICRC report, this category was "Women Awaiting Repatriation", which numbered

* *L'Emploi Des Prisonniers de Guerre,* Conference Prononcee en Octobre 1946 par Monsieur Simon, Chef de Bureau. Quai d'Orsay, Paris.

** Report of ICRC Geneva, PW Section, French Delegation, in RG 332, DF 371-383.6, US National Archives, Washington. Original is in English.

44, and in the Labor Ministry report, it was "*Génie Rural*", which numbered 987.

Therefore, prisoners who not only escaped but remained fugitives for more than three months, almost certainly numbered less than 1,000 for the period reported (which was three months for both the ICRC report and for Simon's report).

Thus, both common sense and French Army reports lead us to think that the reason escapes weren't reported until 1948, was because they were so insignificant. But from 1948, this category suddenly became extremely attractive as a way of concealing deaths.

For this book, escapes are assumed to have been statistically insignificant — as they were in the French and American Army reports. This means less than 1,000 every three months, or under 4,000 per year for the two years when most of the deaths occurred.

Thus taking *Perdus Pour Raisons Diverses* (Lost for Various Reasons) as totalling deaths and escapes, it is reasonable to conclude that all but about 8,000 of the 167,000 *Perdus Pour Raisons Diverses* died. But even that total is probably very low, because a much higher number of prisoners were never accounted for by the French Army under any category. The Missing/Not Accounted For number varies according to which set of French statistics one chooses and could be as high as 250,000 *more* than the 167,000 PPRD. It is likely that most of those 250,000 died. Thus the conclusion in Chapter 9 that the range of certainties was between 167,000 and 314,241 dead, should now be revised so that the upper limit is 409,000 Germans, in French captivity, dead.

Appendix 11

OTHER GLOSSES:
How Some Critics Have Interpreted the Evidence

This Appendix, added especially for this U.S. edition of *Other Losses*, includes a summary of objections to this book raised by various U.S. government agencies. It also deals with the effect of the U.S. Army's attempt to mislead Colonel Philip S. Lauben into partially retracting his earlier statement to me that the term "Other Losses" meant mainly deaths and "very, very minor" escapes.

The first trio of objections was voiced by the Pentagon, the State Department, the U.S. Army Center for Military History and Professor Stephen Ambrose, who said that Other Losses meant variously (a) transfers within Eisenhower's command in Europe, (b) transfers to other U.S. Army commands in Europe and (c) early release of Volkssturm (Peoples' Army) without formal discharge. This Appendix also examines some explanations offered by the same people to my interpretations of two tables reproduced in Appendix 2 from the Medical History of the European Theater of Operations.

ALTERNATIVE EXPLANATIONS OF THE TERM "OTHER LOSSES"

Transfers within Eisenhower's Command in Europe

There were some very large transfers between armies within Eisenhower's command, such as those shown in the DEF documents in May 1945, in which the number of prisoners transferred from, for example, the Seventh Army were properly deducted from that Army and properly credited to, for example, the Third Army. Several such transfers were shown under Other Losses but footnoted as transfers. And of course, because the transferred prisoners were credited to another army within Eisenhower's command, the total number held by his command was unaffected. This book did not and does not include any such transfers as deaths. Only the total Other Losses figures in Eisenhower's command that were *not* denoted as transfers are used as a basis to determine deaths. Because some transfers were entered under Other Losses and footnoted as transfers, it is clear that whatever Other Losses showed, it was not transfers. Otherwise, why footnote the transfers? So this "explanation" was soon abandoned, in favor of another . . .

Transfers to Other (Non-Eisenhower) Commands in Europe

The next explanation was based on a single entry in the PW/DEF Weekly Reports for August 4, 1945. At that date, 132,262 DEFs were shown by Eisenhower's command as transferred to Austria, but as we have seen in the Epilogue, there was no separate command in Austria, and no such transfer. Therefore this explanation, too, is now being abandoned in favor of another . . .

Appendix 11

Early Release of Volkssturm without Formal Discharge

The Volkssturm* explanation is based on a report of the Military Governor of Germany, General Eisenhower, valid for August 1945, which was issued on September 20, 1945. In this report, Eisenhower partly defined Other Losses. The Manpower Annex to the report includes the statement, "An additional group of 663,576 [prisoners] are listed as 'other losses,' consisting largely of members of the Volkssturm released without formal discharge [figures valid for August 4]."[1]

This raises many questions. The most important is, What can we believe in the reports of Eisenhower and his officers bearing on deaths of prisoners of war? We have seen to be wrong the report of Eisenhower and his officers in 1945 and the report of his Army apologists in 1990 about the Austrian transfer of August 4, 1945. Because this leaves intact Lauben's statement that Other Losses largely means deaths, Eisenhower's statement that it mainly meant Volkssturm releases is largely discredited. Therefore, the people designated by Eisenhower as Other Losses in September are to be regarded as probably dead, unless the Governor's Report is confirmed by very strong evidence supported by clear documentation from someone authoritative outside Eisenhower's command. Eisenhower's statement means that we must ask, If Other Losses did not mainly mean deaths, where are prisoner deaths listed? The Army reports no deaths among Disarmed Enemy Forces. For prisoners of war, the Theater Provost Marshal reports so few deaths, and these are contradicted by so much evidence, as to be unbelievable.[2] For instance, General Eisenhower reported to General Marshall on March 18, 1945, that on March 16 at Mailly-le-Camp, 104 German prisoners had been found suffocated to death in U.S. Army boxcars. The Theater Provost Marshal recorded no deaths at all for that date. The total of prisoner deaths reported by the Theater Provost Marshal for March 9–20 was 80 prisoners.[3] Again, if the Theater Provost Marshal's 4,540 deaths recorded for the critical period May 1 to June 15 are applied to the total of captives acknowledged in the Theater Provost Marshal reports, then the death rate for these starving exposed people is only .9 percent per annum, which is unbelievably low for such conditions.[4] For all his millions of captives, the Provost Marshal reported only 10,532 deaths from June 1944 to August 25, 1945.[5]

The Theater Provost Marshal's death reports are incredible, and a zero death rate for the DEFs is incredible, yet we must believe that both of those are true if Other Losses does not, in the main, mean deaths.

The questions continue: Why put "Other Losses" and "Discharges" side by side if both mean the same thing? Why did the Joint Chiefs of Staff (JCS) suddenly, in September 1945, start getting news about Volkssturm releases that purportedly had been known from May 8 onward? Why did the JCS suddenly get their first news of the category Other Losses in September, even though the category had been in use since May?

The alert reader will have noticed that the sentence does not actually say that the Volkssturm were released, but only that they were "listed as" Other

---

* The Volkssturm consisted of civilians previously exempted from military service because of age, occupation or infirmity. They were hastily drafted in the closing months of the war for last-ditch defense.

Losses. Totals for other categories are briskly and confidently given in normal Army fashion, as for instance "POWs and DEFs discharged by the U.S. Forces as of 4 August numbered 2,083,500," whereas the news about Other Losses is presented with the weaselly words "an additional group . . . are listed as 'other losses' . . . ." This is presented not in the main body of the report but in an annex. It is as if the report writer was warning Washington not to probe closely into the figure.[6]

That supposition is supported by the very peculiar statement that these Volkssturm were released without formal discharge. This can only mean one or both of two things: that they were released without being counted, and/or that they were released, contrary to orders, without discharge papers.

If they were released without being counted from May through August, Eisenhower could not have known in September how many there were. But he said that they were the majority of the 663,576 Other Losses — he must have known, therefore, that they numbered at least 331,789. He could scarcely have known that they were more than a certain number, without knowing what number they actually were. But he does not tell Marshall, even though there is no reason to withhold this information. The evidence is irresistible that he did not know how many Volkssturm there were.

To release them without discharge papers was against Eisenhower's own orders. As had been made clear in the Eclipse orders for the disbandment of the German Armed Forces, every prisoner upon leaving captivity had to receive discharge papers. This was amplified and reinforced by Eisenhower's disbandment directive No. 1, which added to the original documentation requirements the stipulation that "the POW Registration Form will be completed by all persons prior to discharge."[7] Yet in September 1945, Eisenhower offhandedly reports to the JCS that hundreds of thousands of prisoners were released apparently without any documentation at all.

The Difficulty of Identifying Volkssturm

The Volkssturm were civilians who had not even been incorporated into the German Army. They were commanded by local civilians, usually Nazi Party Gauleiters. They had no papers showing they were Volkssturm, no identity tags, no Volkssturm uniform. Their only identification was an armband worn over civilian clothes, which could be mufti, or a uniform signifying occupation, such as policeman, railroad conductor, forester. The Americans had no way to identify Volkssturm among these people, unless they had kept their armbands, inviting imprisonment. "There was no way to sort out the Germans we encountered," Captain Frederick Siegfriedt of the U.S. Army has written. "Most claimed not to know any English and without exception the standard response to any question was 'Me no Nazi.' We had no idea what happened to the thousands of people who were moving west. I am confident that our regimental and division intelligence was not equipped to interrogate them, nor to process them."[8] Even a year later, in a U.S. camp in France in spring 1946, the Army was no more able to interrogate its prisoners than before, according to Captain Siegfriedt. "The MIS [intelligence service] had a book full of the names of Germans they were looking for. Interrogating 17,000 men was such an impossible job the MIS interrogators trained the PWs to interrogate each other."[9] Since such a laughable procedure was still being used in 1946 to hunt criminals, it is not credible that in the summer of 1945 the Army actually identified mere Volkssturm, by definition the least dangerous of all. Nor was the Army concerned about the diplomatic aspects of these para-military civilians: nothing about the Volkssturm has yet been found during a very extensive search in the State Department and diplomatic archives in Washington, even though they were a strange category demanding special recognition under the Geneva Convention.

One German Army officer who surveyed 3,000 Volkssturm for possible field service in central Germany in March 1945 says there were no weapons for them; he just told them to go home, which they did. He felt they ran no risk, because not even a German Army officer could tell that these men were deserters in German eyes, once they had taken off the armband to go home. How could the Americans tell? Anyone in the Volkssturm in danger of capture could throw away his armband, and any weapons, to become a civilian again.[10] By standing U.S. Army order, any insignia of units were immediately stripped off the prisoners as they entered the cages; any who had retained their armbands expecting prisoner of war status under the Geneva Convention were immediately rendered invisible in the crowd of other civilians. Such a person had no interest in confessing later to the Americans that he had been fighting.

In case it may be imagined that somehow, despite all, the Army managed to identify Volkssturm, it is good to listen to the prisoners themselves. Paul Kaps, a German soldier who was in the U.S. camp at Bad Kreuznach, has written an eloquent description of how identity was maintained in his cage:

> The Americans had on our arrival in the camp taken away all our passes and other personal documents. We formed circles and told each other our names, first names, army units, field post numbers and home addresses. We quizzed each other over and over to know at least in this small circle who it was who had not survived the night. This was the only chance we had left to at least inform our next of kin if the worst came to worst. . . . In our cage lay about 10,000 POW and civilians. Worst off were those who the Americans had for reasons unknown to us transported from the hospitals . . . freshly amputated soldiers with one leg and no crutches who now lay helpless in the muck or moved crawling on their stomachs, blind comrades still with their heads in turban-like bandages, who had to be led by the hand. . . . In Cage 9 there were to be found: the youngest 14, the oldest 76. What were they doing there? In one night, May 8, 1945, 48 prisoners were shot dead in Cage 9.[11]

In his September Report for August, Eisenhower pretends to know the number of Volkssturm discharged at that date, but his report in August, valid for July, does not even mention the Volkssturm, though precise numbers are given for Discharged, Transferred, On Hand, those promised to the French and so on. Yet the number of Volkssturm released must have been known in August if it was known later, in September, because the later totals depend on the earlier. If the July total was known in August, why was it not given? How could an army that literally counted captured toilet kits be so sloppy as not to know in August that well over half a million men were permanently lost to the vital labor pool? This labor pool was now the subject of many pages of analysis by Eisenhower in these same Governor's Reports, and it was causing serious international controversy in France, Switzerland and the U.S. Men even marginally capable of work were so scarce that in order to fill the quota promised to the French, Eisenhower was rounding up healthy prisoners who had already been discharged from Italy* by General Mark Clark.[12] The report that does not give in August the July total of Volkssturm does specify that 5,579,000 serviceable captured enemy toilet articles were on hand in U.S. Army warehouses.

Levels of Reporting of Prisoners

We know of five levels of reporting of prisoner statistics in 1945 and one in 1947: (1) Through 1945, reports were made in the camps. These were the basis of reports by (2) a higher command, usually 12th Army Group HQ. (3) The Theater Provost Marshal's reports were based on these as well. (4) Summaries of these were made at SHAEF–USFET HQ. And (5) Eisenhower himself reported to Washington in his Military Governor's report. In 1947, (6) another report was written by the Army Historian.

At the basic camp level, reports were filled out on printed forms that included blank spaces for deaths as a possible source of losses.[13] Volkssturm is not one of the categories included to be filled in. The different forms used at the next level up, 12th Army Group HQ, had no categories for deaths or Volkssturm; the printed categories were Date, Gains, Discharged, Transferred, Other Losses, Balance.

In the next level of reporting, in the Theater Provost Marshal's office, death is one category in the third, different, set of printed forms, but not Volkssturm.[14] In the fourth set of printed forms, used at the higher SHAEF–USFET HQ level, neither death nor Volkssturm is a category.

At the highest level, Eisenhower's Military Governor's Report, neither is mentioned in the August report for July, but suddenly, in September, Volkssturm appear *without numbers*. Death is not mentioned. Later in 1947, in the Army Chief Historian's report, through 20 pages dealing with prisoners captured, held, transferred and discharged, neither death nor Volkssturm is mentioned. The report never mentions any releases without formal discharge. Dozens of categories are mentioned, the methods of screening are given with the subcategories at camp level and "concentration" level, but there is nothing about Volkssturm or informal discharges.[15]

But one carbon copy of a set of filled-in, printed forms for the 12th Army Group Headquarters has been found. These forms report transactions for a few days ending June 6, 1945. New definitions of Transfers, Discharges and Other Losses have been typed in — not in carbon copy like the other figures, but directly by the typewriter ribbon *after* the original blanks had been filled in.[16] For Other Losses, the definition reads: "Column shows all losses other discharge or transfer to custody of another nation; i.e. normal attritions,

* Mediterranean Theater of Operations, United States Army (MTOUSA).

desertion, release without discharge of Volkssturm personnel and civilians." We know that Volkssturm were not counted at the camp level and that the other information in this report came from the camp-level reports. So we know this definition that was added later *could not be used*. And this must have been known to whoever ordered the definition to be added. The definition was unusable, it was not used, but it was typed in anyway. We will see why below.

Because Volkssturm were not recorded at the only level where counting was actually done, then all reports about them at the higher level either have no camp-level source or else are notional, if not actually invented.

To sum up: Nowhere in any of the six levels of reporting are numbers of "releases" given, nor is any number given for those released without formal discharge; the Army Chief Historian's report shows that discharge forms were mandatory as soon as discharges began; no one knew how many Volkssturm had been taken, held or released, and it was against orders to release anyone informally (without papers). Volkssturm "released without formal discharge" was an unknowable number.[17]

Other Losses and the Volkssturm

Other Losses were reported and defined to the JCS for the first time on September 20, 1945, with a chart indicating that their numbers had been recorded since long before July 30, when they totalled around 500,000.[18] Although Other Losses were an important subtraction from the labor pool that began to be recorded as of mid-May in the daily reports on the disarmed enemy forces, just like discharges and transfers, it was *only* Other Losses that were not reported to the JCS.[19] Why? The "Others Lost," who were growing fast to some 500,000 by July 31, were neglected for more than four months, although discharges of only 358,112 and transfers of only 209,084 were shown as they occurred. In the reports to Washington, only Other Losses went unreported as they occurred.

Seeing that no one knew how many Volkssturm were released, why did Eisenhower make a report about them? And why did he enter it under Other Losses? It was of absolutely no significance in Washington how many Other Losses were Volkssturm. The only subcategory covered by the new definition of Other Losses added to the 12th Army Group prisoner documents that was of any significance in Washington was transfers to the French. *But the 562,000 transferred to the French by August 30 were not reported to Washington under Other Losses in the September Report of the Military Governor*. They were reported separately, with no reference to Other Losses, whereas the insignificant Volkssturm are specifically named as originating in the Other Losses column. Yet both these losses were supposed to be reported under Other Losses according to the new definition added to the 12th Army Group documents. Knowing as we do now that this added definition could not be used when it was typed in, and was not used later, we ask, Why was it typed in at all? And why did Eisenhower pretend to Washington in September 1945 that the number of Volkssturm "released" was over a certain level, when the number was unknown? This is the point: The number of the Volkssturm was unknown. A category shapeless as a shroud was needed to camouflage the number of the dead. The Volkssturm became that shroud.

Appendix 11

The Threat of Publicity

While this August Report of the Military Governor was being prepared for distribution on September 20, a thunderstorm of terrifying publicity was building up around U.S. Army headquarters in Frankfurt. We have already seen that the International Committee of the Red Cross, the U.S. State Department and the press all knew or suspected by now that Germans were dying of exposure and starvation in U.S. camps. In August, Jean-Pierre Pradervand of the International Committee of the Red Cross had discovered to his horror that the French camps were filled with diseased, starving men in rags, dying like flies. He knew most of them were very recent transfers from U.S. camps. Thinking he might not be believed without strong evidence, he began photographing the prisoners. So ragged were these prisoners that Pradervand's delegates gave them the clothes off their backs, and drove home in their underwear.[20] While that was happening, the U.S. Army had in its warehouses in Germany 13,000,000 Red Cross prisoner-of-war food parcels. They also had clothing and personal equipment for 1,294,000 persons, plus those 5,579,000 toilet articles and 920,000 meters of cloth for making uniforms. There were more than 19,000 tons of medical equipment and supplies as well,[21] all captured German equipment. In Paris, dozens of people knew what was happening, and two big papers were getting ready to print major stories. Publication of these facts would destroy Eisenhower's reputation.

On September 14, the first lightning struck, far away in Washington. The International Committee of the Red Cross in Geneva repeated by open cable (not in code) to the State Department French accusations that the Americans were starving their prisoners, then fobbing them off on the French.[22] The International Committee of the Red Cross was "anxious" for the U.S. to feed its prisoners. Something had to be done, quickly. All of this is certain; the *conjecture* as to what happened in early September is shown by italics in the following paragraph.

Smith and Eisenhower realize the danger and consult as to how they could camouflage the dead. No dead can be added to the totals of future discharges because it has already been decided to suspend discharges for the time being. Nor can dead prisoners be retroactively inserted in the past discharge column, because those figures, too, have already been sent to Washington. The transfer figures have also been sent. Besides, they could be checked by the receiving power. The On Hand total is also known in Washington, so it can not suddenly be reduced arbitrarily. *What is needed in a hurry is another, vague category to shroud the dead.* Other Losses has already been used to cover the dead in the internal reports from the Armies in May and early August. *But everyone at Army headquarters, such as Colonel Lauben, knows it means deaths, so a new definition must be given to help explain it away, or to provide a more plausible cover story for the loyal officers who might be questioned. A typist is instructed to enter a new definition of Other Losses including the Volkssturm on the 12th Army Group records showing* DEF *transactions to June 6. He pulls out the carbon copy of the existing 12th Army records and simply types the definition in.*

Pradervand is invited to Frankfurt and reassured. His photographs disappear into Eisenhower's office, not to be seen again until they reappear as evidence of atrocities in French prisoner-of-war camps. Then they disappear forever. The Weekly PW/DEF and Theater Provost Marshal reports with their revealing details cease. The world press prints the release exonerating the U.S. Army. The prisoners go on dying.

The Fake Definition of Other Losses

However, one interesting set of the 12th Army Group DEF records is overlooked by the officers camouflaging the deaths on the set of forms dated to June 6. This other set, prepared at the 12th Army Group HQ on exactly the same kind of blank printed forms and sent on to the SHAEF–USFET HQ, gives figures up to June 10, four days later. It was typed up later than the forms with the new Volkssturm definition that end on June 6, so it provides another test of the intentions of the person who ordered the new definition of Other Losses to be typed in to the June 6 set. If the definition of Other Losses was authentic, i.e., intended to be used to convey numerical information, that definition must have appeared on all later papers dealing with prisoners at this level. *But it does not appear on this later, June 10 set.* None of the new definitions appears on this set (see p. 201). The new definition of Other Losses was unusable, was not used and did not appear on later documents where it had to be if it was authentic. The fraud is exposed.

DID EISENHOWER TELL THE TRUTH?

Perhaps this is all too much paperwork; perhaps we should set aside the details for a moment. Then we face a simple question: Can we believe that Eisenhower, fighting off ghastly accusations that would ruin his reputation, told the truth about prisoners' deaths in September? The answer lies in Eisenhower's record.

First, in the August Report issued on September 20, he does not mention deaths, even though the Theater Provost Marshal had already reported deaths of more than 10,000 prisoners of war. Because of the much higher number of DEFs, there must have been at least 15,000 additional deaths among them. But Eisenhower, the man who wrote "it is a pity we could not have killed more," now surveys the scene and sees no dead. He can see 1,694 prisoners alive and working in the Bremen enclave, he can see 7,632 hospital cases in Germany, but he sees no dead.

He said in Paris in March 1945 that the U.S. was treating its prisoners according to the Geneva Convention. This was not true.[23] In a speech before the U.S. Congress in January 1946 he said that the U.S. Army under his command had "repatriated the DPs with sympathy and high regard for the humanitarian nature of the problem." This was not true: violence had often been used by the Army in returning Russian nationals to Russia.[24] His senior officers twice misrepresented the number of prisoners with the effect that rations were reduced, causing both Generals Littlejohn and Lee to complain in writing of the inaccurate reporting of prisoners.[25] Following advice from General Hughes, he did not sign any orders reducing prisoners' rations, while at the same time telling Winston Churchill that he had reduced rations. No record of this conversation exists in the files at the Eisenhower Library in Abilene, so this would never have been known had not Churchill's staff recorded the conversation in a memo copied later to the State Department.[26] The unwritten order in Eisenhower's army that prisoners receive starvation rations was so strong that when General Lee was ordered orally to increase some rations for publicity purposes in October 1945, he asked that confirmation of the order be sent him in writing. No such order has yet been found, but the rations were briefly increased according to the prisoners themselves. What reason did Hughes have for recommending that Eisenhower not write out such orders? So as to leave no record. Why not leave a record? Because it was likely to come back to haunt him with his superiors or with the public.

Eisenhower told the JCS in his August report that shelter had been provided for the prisoners. This was not true: shelter had been forbidden by order of the Engineers' Section of the Advance Section of the Army on May 1, 1945, and by General J. C. H. Lee in April 1945.[27] All that summer, prisoners died for lack of shelter; all that summer the Army had in stock 58,000 captured German tents which, like the Red Cross food parcels and many other necessary items, were not distributed.[28] His command concealed from the Red Cross the continued existence of U.S. prison camps in France after the war, according to Jean-Pierre Pradervand.[29] Through General Bedell Smith, his chief of staff, Eisenhower told the French government, his own superiors, the State Department and the press that the hundreds of thousands of prisoners transferred to the French by September 1945 were in good condition with two weeks' rations and greatcoats and blankets. None of that was true.[30] When accused later of playing a leading role in the infamous Morgenthau Plan with Harry Dexter White, Eisenhower denied his role. That was not true.[31] He twice reported to the JCS that 132,262 prisoners had been transferred from Germany to Austria. That was not true.

This is hardly the record of a man one wishes to trust on accusations of mass deaths occurring under his command. Given the other evidence already known about the Volkssturm discharges, it is impossible to trust Eisenhower's statement in the August report.

DEATH RATES

Eisenhower's present-day defenders have said that the death rate among German prisoners in American hands was 1 percent.[32] Taking the normal medical meaning of this term as a percentage of a known population which produces a certain number of dead in a specific time, we can calculate the number that would have died at this rate for the 16 weeks of the General's report ending August 25. The Army PW/DEF Weekly Reports say that on average the camps were holding 2,117,000 prisoners for the 16 weeks ending August 25. At 1 percent per annum, this produces deaths numbering 6,514 for the 16 weeks. However, in September, the War Department in Washington reported to the State Department deaths of unidentified persons in the U.S. prisoner-of-war camps in Germany numbering 4,123 for 17 days, August 20 to September 6. In addition, the War Department had just reported[33] to State on August 20 a total of a further 5,122 deaths of unknown Germans. And these 9,245 dead people are only the *unidentified*. It is clear that because the unidentified alone outnumber the total number estimated to have died, the estimate is wrong.

When the death calculations based on the category Other Losses were first published in this book in Canada, the U.S. Army, the State Department and others rose to Eisenhower's defense with the statement that this book was not statistically sound. Now we find that the book's Other Losses figures in July (472,366) are only 4.6 percent higher than the number of prisoners (451,473) for whom Eisenhower fails to account at the end of July 1945. They are much below the Other Losses figures recorded by the General himself. For instance, Eisenhower reported to the JCS that Other Losses at August 4, 1945, were 663,576. In this book, the estimate is 513,405. He reported that as of the end of September, Other Losses amounted to 781,789. This book estimated 601,533. In each case, Eisenhower reports about 30 percent more Other Losses than are shown in this book.

If deaths were as low as the 1 percent guess of Eisenhower's present-day defenders, one wonders why the Army did *not* report them. Deaths have tremendous moral significance. They are just as important as transfers, because they reduce the labor pool, which was very significant to the Army. Deaths are also the easiest of all the categories to report. The Army and Eisenhower reports leave us not only without the true death totals for captives deemed to be prisoners of war *but without any deaths at all for the* DEFs.

The Death Survey in the ETO *Medical History*

The U.S. Army recently attacked the death figures in this book that are based on the deaths shown in a survey reported in 1945 in the Medical History of the European Theater of Operations.[34] The Army contends that Table IX in that Medical History correctly shows the death rate as 35.6 per thousand per annum (3.56 percent) as reported in a survey based on a population that the Army now says, in 1991, was 700,000 prisoners. But the Medical History survey itself stated in 1945 that the survey was based on a population of "seventy thousand (70,000)," meaning the death rate really should have been printed as 356 per thousand per annum (35.6 percent). The 3.56 percent death rate can not be true if the base population of the survey was truly 70,000 as stated in the History itself.

In deciding what is true among conflicting evidence, it is useful to compare that evidence with other related evidence known to be true and with related evidence known to be false. The death rate of 35.6 per thousand (3.56 percent) shown in Table IX can only be correct if the stated total of 70,000 base population was in fact an error for 700,000. However, the only reason to change the base population to 700,000 is that the death rate given in Table IX is 35.6 per thousand (3.56 percent) per year, which also produces a defense of the Army's case that there was no mass atrocity in the camps. To derive a base population of 700,000 from the table, one must first assume that the author of the report was wrong to state, as he does at page 88, that the survey was based on camps "with an average strength of approximately seventy thousand (70,000) persons." Right away the Army's defense theory is in trouble, because it assumes that the author twice stated incorrectly the most basic figure of the survey. The Army would have us trust a Table that they say is fundamentally flawed because of an error in the basic population figure. What confidence could we have in a survey that has to be proven wrong in order to be used? Nevertheless, let us test this assumption of the 700,000 base.

The first question is, again, If deaths were as low as 3.56 percent, why did the Army not list them along with the discharges and transfers? Many transfers, discharges and gains of only a few hundred per week were shown in the figures. To omit deaths that occurred at the rate of 3.56 percent was to omit accumulated death totals in, say, August 1945, of more than 30,000 persons. Why would the Army omit such a huge number, while reproducing, as it did, Other Losses of 274 for prisoners of war for the week ending August 11, 1945? There is no answer except to say that the Army didn't give death totals because they were much higher than 3.56 percent.

The death reports recorded between May 1 and June 15 by the U.S. Army Medical Corps in the ETO Medical History were based on the 2,868 prisoners' deaths that occurred in the prison camps in the Advance Section area of the Army, forming part of the death total recorded by the Theater Provost Marshal for the whole European Theater of Operations, which included the Advance Section. That overall European death total reported by the Theater Provost Marshal for the six weeks covered by the survey was 4,540. Subtracting the 2,868 in the Advance Section, we are left with 1,672 deaths among the rest of the prisoners in Europe reported on by the Theater Provost Marshal. Subtracting the purported 700,000 surveyed prisoners and their deaths from the totals, we see that the remaining 1,672 deaths occurred among the remaining 1,541,000 prisoners (on average) making up the holdings in the rest of the European Theater of Operations. Thus at exactly the same period when the death rate among the purported 700,000 prisoners in Advance Section camps was ostensibly 3.56 percent per annum, the death rate in the rest of the European Theater of Operations was 0.9 percent per year. But the Medical History says on page 90 that the conditions in the Advance Section were typical of the whole European Theater of Operations. It is impossible that the death rate in a section typical of the whole was four times higher than in the remaining section.[35] Something is badly amiss here. Is Table IX the cause?

Let us turn to less sensitive figures, those for hospital admissions for disease. Later in the Medical History, Tables XI (a) and (b) report a survey of a large, varying number of prisoners for nine-and-a-half months from September 1, 1944, to June 15, 1945, giving totals of admissions for 23 causes in numbers of admissions as low as none per month for certain months. It totals all these and provides the admissions rate accurately based on very large, varying base populations. It appears, therefore, to be serious and accurate. For the first seven or eight months, it reveals nothing especially shameful, because the admissions totals and rates for 1944 and early 1945 indicate no large-scale preventable diseases betraying a violation of the Geneva Convention. But in the critical six to ten weeks including May 1 to June 15, the figures enumerate a disaster. The Table shows that there were disastrously high proportions of diseases such as diarrhea and dysentery which are negligible wherever there is basic sanitation. For instance in May, the rate was 73 percent per annum. This was not only an extraordinarily high rate, it also showed that diarrhea and dysentery were by far the most prevalent diseases in the camps, having increased over the previous weeks 20 times as fast as most other diseases. That diarrhea and dysentery were the most prevalent diseases is a proof in itself of horrifyingly bad sanitation, underfeeding and lack of shelter. Table XI silhouetted a catastrophe. It was classified and kept from the public for many years. But it was still dangerous to the Army in 1969. The version of Table XI that appeared in Stanhope Bayne-Jones's report in 1969 purported to show the admissions rate for the critical period May 1 to June 15, 1945. But the rates in the table in the Bayne-Jones article were presented as if they were based on admissions for May 1 to June 15, *whereas they were actually based on the admissions for the whole nine-and-a-half months.* Because rates were much lower in the earlier months, the rates in the critical period thus appeared to be much lower than they really were. The catastrophe was camouflaged.

Thus we know that Table XI appeared to someone working for the U.S. Army 24 years later as too dangerous to reveal. The rates and totals had to be falsified downward before they could be given to the public. For our purposes, what is important about this is that it shows that Table XI was true. If it was not true, it would not have had to be falsified.

Now let us compare this Table, which we believe to be true, with Table IX. In Table IX we see that the admissions total for prisoners is far higher, 345,324, than in Table XI, although the number surveyed is much lower. Does this mean that Table IX is more to be trusted? Not really, because both Tables were classified and in any case would have revealed only to the careful observer of the hospital admissions that there was a catastrophe. Table IX further conceals that catastrophe under the falsely low death rate. The important thing is that once again Table IX is out of line with the surrounding true evidence. The admissions rate shown for Table IX is many times higher than in Table XI. But conditions were much the same throughout the European Theater of Operations, according to the Medical History. So the admissions in Table IX are inconsistent with true evidence, which, taken with the preceding evidence, means that they are almost certainly wrong. But when the admissions total of Table IX is used to determine the base population of the survey, it actually does produce a base population of 700,000. A number calculated from a number that is almost certainly wrong is almost certainly wrong. With every test we make, we realize there is less and less reason to change anything that is apparently sound to accord with Table IX, so evidently unsound.

It is known that the Theater Provost Marshal reports did not report deaths accurately. Sometimes the falsification pushed the death rate to an absurdly low level, as in examples cited before. At other times, the rate was higher, though still unbelievably low. For instance, the death rate for prisoners of war calculated from the Theater Provost Marshal figures for prisoners on hand and their deaths for the period July 7 to August 25, 1945, is about 2.1 percent per annum. This figure, from a source we know to be guilty of falsifying death figures,[36] is suspiciously close to the 3.56 percent rate of Table IX, certainly far closer than it is to the higher-than-30-percent amount shown by Table X as completed by Bayne-Jones.

Non-statistical evidence about conditions in the U.S. camps that we know is true comes from high officers such as Generals Clark and Allard, from middle-rank medical officers such as Colonels Beasley and Mason and from officers and men who worked in the camps, such as Siegfriedt and Brech. These men have described these places as being like "the Japanese camps for our men," as "deplorable . . . critical," as "heartbeaking" and as "slow killing fields." A French officer who saw them said they were like Buchenwald or Dachau; the Germans who survived them estimated death rates from 20 percent to 80 percent per annum based on experiences lasting through many weeks on burial teams or observations in big fields containing up to 1,000 persons. Knowing all this, and knowing that the civilian death rate in some towns in France at the time was about 1.5 percent to 2 percent per year, it is impossible to believe that the death rate in these slow killing fields was only a little higher than for French civilians eating every day at home. To put it another way: a death rate of 3.56 percent per annum means that if such conditions continued, more than 70 percent of these prisoners would still be alive after 10 years.[37] The reader will decide if it is believable that a large majority of starving, diseased people who are described as slithering like amphibians through the mud could live that way for more than 10 years. The life expectancy implied by the higher than 30 percent death rate, which is not much more than three years, seems too long. Thus, in sum, Table IX is certainly not sound enough to warrant changing anything else to conform with it. Therefore, there is no reason to change the original statement that "seventy thousand (70,000)" was the base population of the survey.

Table X in the ETO Medical History Survey

What of Table X? No one in the U.S. Army Medical Corps in 1945 in Germany had any interest in accusing the Army of committing an atrocity that was not occurring. Like Table XI, Table X merely by describing the causes and proportions of deaths reveals that there was a preventable disaster occurring in the camps. For instance, the highest cause of death by far were diarrhea and dysentery. Another high cause was reported to be "emaciation," obviously a euphemism for starvation. That captives originally acknowledged by the U.S. Army to have been entitled to protection as prisoners of war under the Geneva Convention were illegally stripped of that protection, and consequently began dying of diarrhea and dysentery in high proportion and large numbers, was a disaster with criminal implications. Only a few weeks before, in March 1945, the deaths of 104 prisoners in boxcars going to Mailly-le-Camp had become a big international incident involving General Eisenhower, the U.S. Army's Chief of Staff in Washington, the State Department, the Red Cross, the Swiss government and the German government. Yet now, in June 1945, no messages flash back and forth across the Atlantic expressing regret, concern or promises to prevent a recurrence. These easily preventable deaths of thousands of prisoners in peacetime are reported with indifference by the U.S. Army writer of this official Medical History.

The same Army writer complains that in the German-operated "hospitals" in the cages, "excessive convalescence was the rule, with many instances of unnecessary hospitalization. It was the impression that the German physicians were using hospitalization as a means of getting extra rations and privileges for many of these former German soldiers." He says that the German-operated "hospitals" for disarmed enemy forces fared very well for rations. "Most of them were established institutions with well planned gardens." That was how he described the camps in the Advanced Section that only a few weeks later appeared to Captain Julien of the French Army as "looking like photographs of Buchenwald or Dachau." Julien did not notice any "well planned gardens" or "well established hospitals" among the half-dead people shivering on the ground on a warm July day under tattered bits of cardboard.

The preventable deaths were catastrophically high for many weeks in the camps controlled by Eisenhower's Army, but not in these same camps once they were taken over by Captain Julien. Julien reduced the death rates in one of his Advanced Section camps, Dietersheim, from a very high level in July to zero within a couple of weeks, by taking the necessary sanitary measures and calling for help from civilian Germans nearby.

To avert most of the disaster, all the Army in Germany had to do was to reduce crowding, pipe in clean water, allow the prisoners a few primitive materials to clean up the camps and distribute tents.[38] As soon as General Clark in Austria found out about the disastrous conditions at Ebensee, he ordered them to be eliminated although he doubted he had any right to do it. Nothing was easier than to call in civilian help as Captain Julien did, and allow the Red Cross, the Quakers and others to come in and help. In Eisenhower's command, almost none of this was done, nearly all was forbidden.

The very revealing information in Table X was gathered independently of most of the other information in the report, by doctors who performed many autopsies in the field.[39] There is no doubt that autopsies were done and that the results were reported without falsification. But the doctors had no control over the use that was made of their information, specifically in Table IX. This Table was prepared months later by the writer of a U.S. Army history who certainly had an interest in the reputation of the U.S. Army. Months after the autopsies, this U.S. Army writer collated information from the Theater Provost Marshal's office with the autopsy results, to produce Table IX. It was not the doctors alone who reported the Table IX death rate, because they could not know it without knowing the camp population, which was information held only by the Theater Provost Marshal's office. In order to present the overall report, it was necessary to specify not only the causes of death including the proportions among them, but also the scale of the deaths. This figure, the most dangerous one, most easily understood by a layman, was not part of Table X. The death total was left out, and the list of causes was left incomplete. But we know that the doctors who performed the autopsies knew these figures because Brigadier-General Stanhope Bayne-Jones found them in 1969 and reproduced them. The writer of the Medical History presented a falsely low death rate in Table IX, leading the unwary observer away from the embarrassing evidence outlined in Table X. And when Table X was published much later in Bayne-Jones, the time-frame was missing, so it was impossible to figure out the death rate (see Appendix 2).

Table X appears to be authentic because it was prepared by doctors in the field, is partly confirmed by Pastor Erich Messling, accords with massive eyewitness evidence from civilians, survivors, guards, reporters, of three nationalities, and finally because it was quoted complete by Bayne-Jones. This Brigadier-General must have believed it because he reproduced it, without mentioning the base population. But Bayne-Jones's report deals specifically with mortality and death rates, so why did he eliminate the fundamental figure of base population? We can see why, on page 394, where he says that the disease death rate for PWs was "20.5 times greater than for U.S. troops." But in the lines immediately preceding, he says that the disease death rate for PWs was 34.2, and for U.S. troops, 0.6. The PW death rate he shows is actually 57 times the U.S. rate, not 20.5 times. Clumsily, he was trying to camouflage the seriousness of death the rate. Now we see why he hid the base population: once again he was trying to camouflage the death rate. Without the base population, no one can figure the death rate in Table X. And now we see that he hid the base population *because he knew the report said it was 70,000*. And he had to hide it because he knew it was true. Given that population, Table X shows the catastrophic death rate of over 30 percent per year that he was trying to hide.

If the above is not the truth, then the only explanation for all the statistical shenanigans is that Bayne-Jones's Table 23 reproduced all the figures of Table XI incorrectly only by accident; that the error in comparing army and PW death rates was a simple mistake, and that only Bayne-Jones's absurdity is significant in his statement that "little would be gained by . . . refinement of statistics to the point of numerical accuracy." Finally, we would have to believe that there was nothing sinister in the fact that all these errors obliterate deaths and death rates. Who can believe all that?

Camouflaging death rates is fundamental to Bayne-Jones's article, as is Table IX. Table IX was the source of statistics which he used to falsify deaths in the same direction, downwards. In 1969 in an official history, as in secret reports in 1945, the U.S. Army was falsifying death rates and totals. Is there reason in 1991 to think that the Army has changed its ways?

We now have even more reason to trust Table X. We are also certain that the base population was 70,000 as stated. Therefore, the death rate from disease was about 34 percent per year, which accords with the body counts euphemized as Other Losses.

To sum up: that Other Losses meant transfers to other U.S. Army commands is impossible because there were no other commands, because the transfer to Austria, on August 4, never took place and because footnotes specifically segregated transfers from the other interpretations of the term Other Losses. The notion of Volkssturm releases has been destroyed above. Lauben's original statement stands unharmed as the only credible evidence to the meaning of the term Other Losses: deaths and "very very minor" escapes.

Nothing but massive deaths euphemized as Other Losses explains most of the Missing/Not Accounted For in the Army's own figures. Nothing else fits the contemporary descriptions of the camps by objective observers. Nothing else fits the discoveries and actions of General Clark. Nowhere else could the Army have camouflaged the deaths that it nowhere reported. Nothing else completes the picture; everything else blurs it more. Nothing else fits common sense.

Notes

1

DECIDING GERMANY'S FATE

1. Teheran anecdote compiled from Winston S. Churchill, *Closing the Ring*, volume 5 of *The History of the Second World War* (Boston: Houghton Mifflin, 1951), p. 330; and from Elliott Roosevelt, *As He Saw It* (New York: Duell Sloan and Pierce, 1946), p. 190.
2. Winston Churchill, *Closing The Ring*, p. 265.
3. Bernard Law Montgomery Papers, 87–1, "Notes on the Occupation of Germany."
4. Presidential Diary, Morgenthau Papers, vol. 6, August 19, 1944, Franklin Roosevelt Library, Hyde Park, New York.
5. John Morton Blum, *Roosevelt and Morgenthau* (Boston: Houghton Mifflin, 1970), p. 591.
6. Presidential Diary, Morgenthau Papers, vol. 6, August 19, 1944, Hyde Park.
7. Presidential Diary, Morgenthau Papers, vol. 6, August 19, 1944, Hyde Park.
8. *The Memoirs of Cordell Hull* (New York: Macmillan, 1948), p. 1617.
9. Memorandum for the Secretary's files by Harry D. White, Presidential Diary, Quebec Box, September 13, 1944, Hyde Park.
10. Henry C. Morgenthau, *Germany Is Our Problem* (New York: Harper and Brothers, 1945).
11. Blum, *Roosevelt and Morgenthau*, p. 596.
12. It is reprinted in Henry L. Stimson and McGeorge Bundy, *On Active Service in Peace and War* (New York: Harper), p. 576.
13. *The Memoirs of Cordell Hull*, p. 1614.
14. "The bulk of the press strongly attacked Morgenthau." Stimson and Bundy, *On Active Service*, p. 580.
15. Both papers are from September 30, 1944, and are reproduced in the Hopkins–Sherwood Papers, Box 333, folder 1, Hyde Park.
16. Stimson and Bundy, *On Active Service*, p. 581.
17. Stimson and Bundy, *On Active Service*, p. 581.
18. Blum, *Roosevelt and Morgenthau*, p. 590.
19. Blum, *Roosevelt and Morgenthau*, p. 621.
20. Churchill to Stalin in conversation, Moscow, October 17, 1944. Reported in Martin Gilbert, *Road to Victory, Winston S. Churchill 1941–1945* (London: Heinemann, 1986), p. 1024.
21. Memorandum of Conversation, Department of State, November 15, 1944, in RG 43, World War Two Conferences, Box 3, State Department Archives, Washington.

2

WITHOUT SHELTER

1. Churchill to Clementine Churchill, from Yalta. In Martin Gilbert, *Road to Victory, Winston S. Churchill 1941–45*, p. 1167.
2. All of this paragraph is based on Minutes of the Crimea Conference, February 4, 1945. In RG 443, World War Two Conferences, Box 3, page 1. National Archives of the United States, Washington.
3. Presidential Diary, Morgenthau Papers, vol. 6, August 25, 1944, p. 1391.
4. Robert E. Sherwood, *Roosevelt and Hopkins* (New York: Harper and Row, 1948), p. 905.
5. *Report of the* ICRC *on its Activities During the Second World War* (Geneva: May 1948).
6. Dwight D. Eisenhower, *Crusade in Europe* (New York: Da Capo Press, 1983), p. 386.
7. War Department biography of Everett S. Hughes, to September 9, 1946, Library of Congress.
8. Quoted in Allied High Command Papers, 1943–45, Reel Five of David Irving Papers collected for *The War Between the Generals*. Available from Microform Academic Publishers, East Ardsley, England.
9. Eisenhower's English biographer Piers Brendon said that his method of command was "strategy by subterfuge, a generalship of nods and winks." Piers Brendon, *Ike* (New York: Harper and Row, 1986), p. 178.
10. David Eisenhower, *Eisenhower at War* (New York: Random House, 1987), p. 299.
11. Personal for General McNarney, signed "Eisenhower." ETOUSA Outgoing, February 10, 1944. NARS.
12. Eisenhower to Marshall, March 3, 1944, in Eisenhower Papers, p. 1760.
13. Richard M. Nixon, *Six Crises* (London: W. H. Allen, 1962), p. 161.

    Another example of this indirect approach is an exchange held in 1944 between Eisenhower and Hughes.

    In early August, a day or so after Henry C. Morgenthau had talked to Eisenhower about policy towards the Germans, Eisenhower made an urgent call to Hughes to urge him to move cautiously on a secret mission to the USA that Eisenhower had asked him to carry out. Hughes confirmed their conversation in a cryptic letter:

    Dear Ike:

    Your telephone warning to be careful did not fall upon deaf ears. Before I requested permission to return to the United States I had thought the problem through and had determined to be extremely careful.

    I am working for you and know that if I promote dis–harmony I shall not be doing all that should be done. You stated that you had received no complaints about my operations. I felt certain that was the case because all concerned know that I have no ax to grind and that I am doing my best to get this job over fast. Bradley, Patton and Lee appear to trust me. Lee knows that I have helped him, and am not working for myself.

So with regard to the United States you may rest easy. I appreciate the problem and promise I'll not muddy any waters.

I hope and want to see you before I leave and talk the matter over. In the event I do not succeed, this letter will express my thoughts.

Yours very sincerely,
Everett

This extraordinarily guarded letter shows how careful Eisenhower and Hughes were in their written communications. Probably Hughes is protecting his chief and himself not against the Germans, but against Americans. (From Hughes Papers, ms. collection, Library of Congress.)

14. Patton to Beatrice Patton, September 3, 1944. In Martin Blumenson, *The Patton Papers*, vol. 2 (Boston: Houghton Mifflin, 1974), p. 538.
15. D. Eisenhower, *Eisenhower at War*, p. 640.
16. Brendon, *Ike*, p. 178.
17. From Hughes Diary, Library of Congress.
18. *The Papers of Dwight David Eisenhower*, edited by Alfred D. Chandler and Stephen E. Ambrose (Baltimore: 1970, Johns Hopkins University Press, 1970), vol. 3, p. 1748. Hughes had considerable power to influence without actually going to Eisenhower, as his treatment of Bradley and Lee showed in the summer of 1944. He warned Bradley against Lee's smugness; with one brief note he ended a special War Department mission of General Henry S. Aurand, who was also a friend of the important General Smith. So powerful was Hughes that Aurand did not even protest this degrading treatment to his old friend Smith. That was the end of Aurand's mission.
19. Stephen E. Ambrose, *The Supreme Commander: The War Years of General Dwight D. Eisenhower* (Garden City: Doubleday, 1970), p. 512.
20. February 24, 1944.·*Eisenhower Papers*, vol. 3, pp. 1748, 1760.
21. This and all other Hughes Diary entries are from the transcript prepared by the author and Colonel Fisher of the original entries in the Hughes Papers, Manuscript Division in the Library of Congress, Washington. Microfilm available from (David Irving Papers at) Microfilm Academic Publishers, East Ardsley, Wakefield, WF3 2JN, West Yorkshire, England.
22. *Dear General: Eisenhower's Wartime Letters to Marshall*, edited by John Patrick Hobbs (Baltimore: The Johns Hopkins Press, 1971), p. 205.
23. This remark appears as a typed postscript in the carbon copy of the original of the letter Eisenhower sent to Marshall, May 25, 1943, Marshall Correspondence, Abilene. Also in the George C. Marshall Foundation, Lexington, Virginia. The context of the remark is the difficulty of transferring prisoners to rear bases. It has been suppressed from at least two editions of Eisenhower's letters. See Chapter 11, note 35.
24. Hughes Diary, November 4, 1944.
25. It is not clear in the diary who told whom to be careful.
26. The jottings about amusing trivia are all from the Hughes Diary at various dates in the winter of 1944–45.

27. *Eisenhower Papers*, p. 2497.

28. Author's interview with General Clarke and Colonel Fisher, Washington, 1987.

29. Col. R. J. Gill CMP to HQ Continental Advance Section, February 17, 1945. In RG 331 Box 26.

30. History of Provost Marshal Section, Ad Sec Com Z, May, 1945, signed Lt. Col. Valentine M. Barnes Jr.; in NARS, 332 Box 22, USNA, Washington.

31. Eisenhower to Marshall, March 18, 1945. In RG 383.6/10, 31.6, NARS, Washington.

32. Maj. Gen. Milton A. Reckord, Theater Provost Marshal, U.S. Army, to G1, ETO, March 20, 1945. In RG 331 Box 26, NARS, Washington.

33. According to the last wartime German cenus, there were in 1941 within the boundaries of prewar Germany 63,343 **Rathauser* (town halls), meaning at least that many mayors. The Gestapo numbered tens of thousands.

34. Captain Harry C. Butcher, *My Three Years With Eisenhower* (New York: Simon and Schuster, 1946), p. 610.

35. Personal letter of Eisenhower to Marshall, April 27, 1945. In Eisenhower Library, Abilene.

36. Reported by Stephen E. Ambrose, in conversation with Dr. Ernest F. Fisher, Washington, December 1987.

37. Brigadier General T. J. Davis to SHAEF, February 1, 1945. In RG 331 Box 26, NARS, Washington.

38. Over 93 percent of French railway trackage was operating in the spring of 1945. Minutes of Meetings of Rosenman Report, Box 30, Hyde Park. Also printed by U.S. Government for use of House Committee on Foreign Affairs.

    The supplies going through northeast France next to Germany in May 1945 required only 70 percent of the U.S. Army transport capacity which had been in use there in February. In other words, as army consumption dropped with peace, enormous unused transport capacity lay behind the army. Daily Tonnage Reports, HQ of Ad Sec Com Z May 13, 1945. In RG 332 Box 25, NARS, Washington. Also Bykofsky and Larson, *The Technical Services; The Transportation Corps Operations Overseas.* In the series, *The United States Army in World War II* (Washington: Department of the Army, 1957).

    On the oceans, far more merchant ships existed in the world in 1945 than had ever existed before. The Allied shipbuilders, mainly American, produced more ships in fifteen months 1942–43, than were sunk in the whole war by the Germans. Lloyds Registry 1939–1940–1941, 1945–1946; and Samuel Eliot Morison, *The Battle of the Atlantic* (Boston: Atlantic Little Brown, 1961).

39. Rosenman Report to the President of the USA, April 26, 1945, Hyde Park.

40. "The common belief among nutritionists is that about 1,800 calories per day are necessary to maintain life in a normal male adult aged 20–30 years, weighing about 70 kilos. Influences on this level include ambient temperature, activity, exposure, clothing, general health." Dr. A. B. Miller, Depart-

ment of Preventive Medicine and Biostatistics, University of Toronto, in conversation with the author.

41. Hughes Diary, April 11, 1945.

42. The combined population of the British, French and U.S. Zones at January 1, 1946, was 40,311,000, compared to 39,351,000 in 1939. About 2,493,000 had arrived after May 8, 1945, as refugees. Thus the population in May 1945 was about 37,818,000, or some 1,533,000 (4 percent) less than in 1939. Malcolm J. Proudfoot, *European Refugees 1939–52* (London: Faber and Faber, 1957), table 40.

43. The increase in production of wheat in 1945 over 1939 in the combined area noted was 12,100,000 tons. This increase was almost three times the total one–year shortage in Germany in 1945. Surpluses cited were recorded after all other West Europeans had been fed. For corn (maize), the overall increase was 7,400,000 tons. The total French–German shortfall (1939 less 1945) in potatoes in 1945 of about 17,000,000 tons was partly offset by a North American–U.K. rise of 7,000,000 tons. Figures for production are from B. R. Mitchell, International Historical Statistics: The Americans and Australasia (London: Macmillan, 1983); and from Mitchell, European Historical Statistics, 1750–1975 (Macmillan). Figures for wheat surpluses are from the International Wheat Council, Haymarket House, Haymarket, London, 1955.

44. General McSherry, SHAEF, to Judge Rosenman, March 15, 1945. In Rosenman Papers, Hyde Park. The Belgian wheat crop for 1944 was normal.

45. Churchill to Roosevelt, C911, March 16, 1945. *In Churchill and Roosevelt, The Complete Correspondence* (Princeton University Press, 1984), vol. 3, p. 570.

46. World food figures are from John C. Campbell, *The United States in World Affairs 1945–1947 (New York: Harper and Brothers, 1947), p. 323.*

47. Eisenhower to Combined Chiefs of Staff, March 10, 1945. In RG 331, NARS, Washington, also SHAEF Cable Log, Abilene. This message appeared in the SHAEF Cable Log initialled DE.

3

NO PUBLIC DECLARATION

1. SHAEF Cable Log (In) April 26, 1945. In Abilene, initialed DE.

2. At this date, the British and Canadians, who comprised about 29 percent of the strike force of SHAEF, had about 19 percent of the prisoners. In the final roundup of prisoners on June 11, the British and Canadians held about 29 percent, the Americans about 68 percent and the French the rest. The British and Canadians were also faced with large captures at the end of the war. In a day and a half at the beginning of May, they took in approximately 500,000 prisoners.

3. Eisenhower to Marshall, April 21, 1945. In RG 331, SHAEF, G4, Exec. Sec. 383.6 POW vol. 4, NARS, Washington.

4. The army had surplus tents plus a 100–day surplus of food. See note 20 in this chapter.
5. CCS to Eisenhower, April 25, 1945. In RG 331 387–4, NARS Washington. Also in Cable Log (In), Abilene, initialled DE, received April 26.
6. Captain Harry C. Butcher, *My Three Years with Eisenhower*, p. 789.
7. Secretary of State (at this date Acting Secretary) Dean Acheson told the ICRC that even the DEFs were treated as POWs according to the Geneva Convention. "It is the policy of this government that such detainees [DEF and SEP] be given the same status as prisoners of war . . . . Appropriate steps are being taken to insure for all enemy military personnel . . . treatment provided for in the Geneva Convention." Acheson to E. Gloor, ICRC, Geneva, March 17, 1947. In 740.00114 EW/2–1447, State.
8. Treaty Series No. 846, *Prisoners of War, Convention Between the United States of America and Other Powers*. Signed at Geneva, July 27, 1929. United States Government Printing Office, Washington, 1932.
9. See, *Morgenthau Diary* (China), vol. 2 (New York: Da Capo Press reprint, 1974). Reprint of the original edition from the U.S. Government Printing Office, under the authority of the Committee on the Judiciary, United States Senate. Also Chapter 6.
10. Clay succeeded Eisenhower in November 1945.
11. Lucius D. Clay, *Decision in Germany* (Doubleday, 1950), p. 19.
12. Trivers Papers, Box 1, Truman Library, Independence, Missouri. A graduate of Harvard and former student at Heidelberg, Trivers joined the State Department in 1941. He worked on JCS 1067 with White et al. Parts of JCS 1067 were taken to Potsdam by Truman to use as the basis for American policy proposals.

    Trivers was not the only one who thought that White was a communist. Anthony Kubek, Chairman of the History Department of the University of Dallas, in the foreword to *The Morgenthau Diaries* (Washington: Committee on the Judiciary, U.S. Senate, U.S. Government Printing Office, 1965), said "Ultimately, Mr. White was revealed as a communist agent."

    Professor Stephen Ambrose has written of White, in connection with White's subversion of U.S. China policy: "There is no doubt that he was a communist. But I would never accept . . . that he caused the collapse of Nationalist China . . . That he wanted it to happen, no doubt; that he did what he could to bring it about, no doubt; that what he did had an impact, no doubt; that White brought down Chiang all by himself is ridiculous . . . ." Letter to the author, October 1988.
13. *The Morgenthau Diaries*, vol. 1, foreword by Anthony Kubek, p. iv.
14. Presidential Diary, April 11, 1945, Image 1503, Hyde Park.
15. Priorities in Construction of PWTE, May 1, 1945, HQ of Ad Sec Com Z, Engineer Section, U.S. Army. In RG 332 Box 12, NARS, Washington.
16. Amid orders for much barbed wire, Priority Six stipulates, "No housing will be provided in PWTE [Prisoner of War Temporary Enclosure]." HQ, Ad Sec Com Z, Engineer Section: Orders entitled Priorities in Construction of PWTE, May 1, 1945. Both Eisenhower and General J. C. H. Lee at other

times specified that "cover is not essential" for the Germans. At midsummer, a Provost Marshal report said that "less than 20% of the prisoners were under cover."

17. Hughes Diary, March 21, 1945.
18. *Eisenhower Papers*, p. 2485.
19. Butcher, *My Three Years with Eisenhower*, p. 639.
20. "By VE–Day . . . tentage was required for only 50% of the continental troops, and supplies were ample." William Ross and Charles Romanus, *The Quartermaster Corps: Operations in the War Against Germany*. In the series, *The United States Army in World War II* (Washington: The United States Army, 1965).

    Over 6,000,000 yards of water–resistant cotton duck were produced new in Europe for the U.S. Army, and 40,000 new tents were delivered to the army from May 8 to August 1945. In Progress Reports, *TSFET*, August 1945. In Abilene.
21. The rations were nearly all standard U.S. Army A rations. Half of the total was in the form of rations already made up in balanced menus giving proper proportions of protein, legumes, grain, and the other half in the same commodities not yet sorted into balanced menus. Quartermaster Reports, Status of Rations on Continent as of April 22, 1945. At page 70, Section One, Progress Reports, April 1945. The same 100–day surplus is noted in the Quartermaster Reports for June and July. DDE Papers, NARS, Abilene, Kansas.
22. Walter Bedell Smith *Eisenhower's Six Great Decisions* (New York: Longmans Green and Co., 1956), p. 172.
23. The ETO Medical History, NARS, Washington. See Appendix 1.
24. Ross and Romanus, *The Quartermaster Corps*, p. 537.
25. General J. C. H. Lee said on April 7, 1945, in a general order covering the camps, that for the German POW, "cover is not essential." In RG 331, 383.6 Box 156, NARS, Washington.
26. Heinz Janssen, *Memories of a Time of Horror* (Rheinberg: Town of Rheinberg, Germany, 1988).
27. History of the Provost Marshal, May 18, 1945, p. 4. In RG 332 Box 22, NARS, Washington.
28. Provost Marshal Report, undated. In RG 332 Box 22, NARS, Washington.
29. This message told Marshall that the SHAEF estimate of the total catch to come by May 30 was 1,150,000, which would make a total of about 2,500,000, although the Theater Provost Marshal had predicted on April 9 that there would be 3,500,000 in U.S. custody at May 30 "if troops in front of the Russian Army elect to surrender to U.S. Forces." This of course they were already doing in such numbers that the Russians later suspected a plot among the Allies to turn the Germans against them.
30. Col. R. J. Gill, Office of the Theater Provost Marshal, G1, to Eisenhower, April 10, 1945. In RG 331 383.6 Box 26, NARS, Washington.
31. Daily PW Report, TPM (Theater Provost Marshal), April 30.

32. The U.S. Army was dealing on June 2 with far fewer captives deemed to be prisoners of war than the range of 3,000,000 to 3,500,000 POWs predicted early in April. The SHAEF officers had told Eisenhower in April that there would be between 3,000,000 and 3,500,000 prisoners in total to deal with at the end of May, depending on the size of the flight to the west. In the SHAEF zone of Europe, which did not include Italy, the total of prisoners of war (excluding the DEFs) on hand at May 30 was 2,879,874. Weekly PW and DEF Reports, SHAEF G3 and TPM, NARS, Washington.
33. "Report of a visit to a U.S. Army prison camp for German prisoners of war," by Col. James B. Mason, MC–USA (Ret.) and Col. Charles H. Beasley, MC–USA (Ret.) in "Medical Arrangements for Prisoners of War en Masse," originally published in *The Medical Surgeon*, vol. 107, no. 6 (December 1950), p. 437.
34. Heinz Janssen, *Kriegsgefangenen in Rheinberg* (Town of Rheinberg, Germany, unpaged, 1988).

4

THE CRUELTY OF THE VICTOR

1. Interviews of the author 1987–88, with von Luttichau of Washington, D.C.
2. The statement by Charles von Luttichau of Washington, made to the author in May 1988, is confirmed by many other prisoners. The rainy spring is confirmed by a Canadian Army war diary including weather reports for north Germany for the period. The rapid onset of death is confirmed by the study in the U.S. Army Medical History of the ETO for May–June (Appendix 1). The space allotment is confirmed by several U.S. Army reports of overcrowding in the Rhine cages in the spring of 1945. The implication of common graves is confirmed by evidence from postwar discoveries. See note 16.
3. Gertrude Maria Schuster, *Die Kriegsgefangenenlager Galgenberg und Bretzenheim* (Stadt Bad Kreuznach, 1985), pp. 40–41.
4. Gertrude Maria Schuster, *op. cit.*
5. Author's interview with Heinz T., together with Mavis Gallant, Paris, June 1986.
6. "All non-record camp documents were destroyed in the 1950s," said Eddy Reese, Senior Archivist, NARS, Washington. Interview with the author, 1986.
7. Report by Captain Julien of the Troisième Régiment des Tirailleurs Algériens. See Chapter 7.
8. History of Provost Marshal Section, Advance Section Com Z, by Valentine Barnes. In NARS, Washington.
9. Author's interview with George Weiss of Toronto, 1988.
10. Barnes, p. 4.
11. See ETO Medical Survey, Appendix 1.

12. Interview with the author, 1987.

13. Heinz Janssen, *Memories of a Time of Horror.*

14. There were ten or eleven cages containing around 10,000 people each, according to Thelen. Interview, November 1987.

15. From an interview with Iff, November 1987. Also from Janssen, p. 468.

16. Source: author's conversation in Rheinberg with Town Archivist Heinz Janssen. Also with the Groundskeeper in the town cemetery. Also, letter to the author from WASt, Berlin, enclosing photocopy of the letter of January 7, 1966, from the town clerk of Rheinberg, informing WASt that three sets of human bones in an unmarked shallow grave one meter deep, spaced a few centimeters apart, without coffin or grave marker, had been uncovered on the site of the former PWTE at Rheinberg.

17. Francis Biddle Papers, Notes on Conference, International Military Tribunal Papers, George Arents Research Library, Syracuse, New York, at October 2, 1945 entry. The date shows that the dead Germans could not have been recent battle casualties. In any case, the deaths in the French and American camps were at this date eight to ten times as high as all Wehrmacht casualties on the western front for the previous four years of war. See Chap. 5, note 52.

18. Author's interview with Thelen, Rheinberg, November, 1987.

19. Daily PWTE Situation Report, April 30, Col. C. H. Beasley, U.S. Army Medical Corps. RG 332 Box 17, NARS, Washington.

20. Beasley and others in their situation reports refer several times to dusting the POWs with DDT. See also the Medical History of the ETO: "Prevention of disease in the PW enclosures was directed primarily toward DDT dusting of prisoners." Source reference in Appendix 1.

21. Doctor Siegfried Enke of Wuppertal has described to the author his experiences in both French and American camp hospitals in France, where he attended the sick. In the French and the American hospitals it was the same: in over a year of captivity, working with very sick men, he never saw a dead body. The reason was that the dying were taken away from the real hospital to a "hospital." He never saw them again. He was never asked to do an autopsy or to sign a death certificate.

    The Linfort "hospital" information is from Heinz Janssen, *Memories.*

22. See Appendix 2.

23. Draft PWTE Situation Report, April 30, Beasley, NARS, Washington.

24. They project out to 0.3 percent per year for the two camps, which is less than the 0.4 percent death rate observed for U.S. troops from May 1 to June 15, 1945. This sample is of course far too small to make an annual projection: it is cited here only as a rate so low that it might be expected to cause a remark from Beasley, which it does not do. Nor is it an isolated example: several other reports indicate death rates that were impossibly low given the conditions that the reports themselves acknowledge.

25. Beasley, April 30.

26. Beasley, *loc. cit.*

5

SUMMER OF STARVATION

1. Minute of Meeting of Churchill, Eisenhower and Field Marshal Sir Alan Brooke, CIGS, May 15, 1945. In RG 59 740.00119, Control Germany 161445, Box 3666, State Department Archives, Washington. Quotation marks are used to indicate direct quotations from the Minute. The Minute, prepared by Prime Minister Churchill's staff, paraphrases the words of the participants.

   Field Marshal Brooke commented that in view of the "overall shortage of food, it would be wrong to feed German prisoners of war on the same scale as British and American troops. If widespread starvation was to be avoided, it was essential that the rations of the enemy troops and civilians should be reduced to the bare minimum," which, he implied, was 1,550 calories, the same ration that civilians got. This neglects the fact that the official ration of 1,550, just below subsistence level of 1,800–plus, was for civilians, who were at least free to try to supplement it through friends in the countryside, black market, garbage or family hoards. Prisoners and DEFs of course had no such options. In the U.S. zone, the official civilian ration later in 1945 was only 1,350 calories.

   It is clear from the policy towards the DEFs that Eisenhower was not including them in the ration scale indicated here.

2. See ETO History, Appendix 2.

   The U.S. Army Medical Corps believed that the absolute minimum to sustain life for a normal adult in good health with good clothing and heated shelter, doing no work but self–care, was 2,000 calories per day. Investigation of Treatment of PWs by the U.S. Forces, January 7, 1946, RG 332 383.6/10 NARS, Washington.

3. Quartermaster Reports, July 1945, Abilene.

4. The average issue of rations to POWs in the enclosures of the U.S. Army on June 2 was to only 54 percent of the number of men reported to be in the cages, which actually contained far more than the reported number. History of the Quartermaster Corps in the ETO, p. 335, NARS, Suitland, Md.

   By the middle of June, the army was feeding about 2,900,000 U.S. military, plus about 650,000 in a mixed bag of civilians, French Moslems and Russians. The prisoner strength on the ration list at that point was shown as only 1,421,559, although the SHAEF G3 report showed over 2,300,000 "on hand" in addition to another million left unreported (see Chapter 5). Thus the 2,000 calories per day ration which Eisenhower told Churchill that the POWs were getting was, if spread over the whole 3,300,000 on hand, about 840 calories per day. Then it was reduced.

5. Brig. General R. B. Lovett, "By Command of General Eisenhower," May 20. 383.6–2. Also, Bradley to SHAEF Forward, May 16. 383.6–4. NARS, Washington.

6. Cable 12th Army Group to all concerned, May 13, in 383.6–4, NARS.

7. From SHAEF Main signed "Eisenhower," to 6th Army Group, in 6th Army Group Records, NARS. According to Martin Blumenson, "it is reasonable

to assume" that Patton, well aware of the situation in the cages, discharged many prisoners against the wishes of officers at SHAEF, in order to save their lives. Author's interview with Blumenson, 1988.

8. On May 19 SHAEF said, "There are 2,880,000 prisoners in Theater, and 1,000,000 disarmed German forces." The next figure from SHAEF, dated May 29, states 2,090,000 prisoners of war and 1,208,000 disarmed German forces on hand. Lee to SHAEF; see note 9.

9. Lee to SHAEF Fwd June 2, 1945. In RG 331, SHAEF G1 Admin Sec, 383.6 1/2, NARS, Washington.

10. The Quartermaster Reports for June (issued in July) show the effects of SHAEF G3's reduction in POW numbers. Rations issued dropped by 900,000. QM Reports, July 1945, Abilene.

    Further proof that Lee was right is seen in the total of the Theater Provost Marshal Weekly total of 2,870,400 POWs for June 2, which, added to the 12th Army Group holding of 1,110,685 DEFs on June 2, comes to 3,981,085, very close to Lee's 3,878,537. Also, the Office of the Army Chief Historian in Frankfurt am Main said in 1947 that there had been approximately 4,000,101 captures on hand in Europe on May 18, 1945.

11. William F. Ross and Charles F. Romanus, *The Quartermaster Corps: Operations in the War Against Germany* p. 634.

12. Smithers to Littlejohn, April 27, 1945. History of QM Ad Sec, pp. 36–37. Quoted in Ross and Romanus.

13. "By VE Day . . . tentage was required for only 50% of the continental troops, and supplies were ample." Ross and Romanus, p. 634.

14. Littlejohn to Crawford at SHAEF, May 23, 1945. In NARS, Washington.

15. Major General R. W. Barker to Smith, May 30. In NARS, Washington.

16. The French first asked for 1,750,000 Germans. This was finally scaled down to about 750,000. At no time did the Germans used by the Allies for unpaid reconstruction work total more than about 1,900,000.

17. Eisenhower to Marshall, copied to AGWAR, May 31, 1945. In RG 333, = Box 30.

18. Eisenhower to CCS, June 4, 1945. SHAEF Cable Log, Abilene.

19. See Appendix 1.

20. Nigel Hamilton, *Monty* (London: Hamish Hamilton, 1986 Sceptre Edition), p. 462. The paraphrase is Hamilton's.

21. Omar N. Bradley, *A General's Life* (New York: Simon and Schuster, 1983), p. 423.

22. George S. Patton Jr., *War As I Knew It* (New York: Bantam Books, 1980), p. 314.

23. Eisenhower to CCS, May 4, 1945. In SHAEF Cable Out Log, Abilene.

24. Eisenhower to CCS, CCS, May 16, 1945. In SHAEF Cable Out Log, Abilene.

25. Eisenhower to Marshall, May 31, 1945. In RG 333 Box 30, NARS, Washington.

26. Quartermaster Reports, April, Abilene.

27. Grasett to Smith, June 8, 1945. Grasett further notes that prewar Germany was 85 percent self-sufficient in food, and that the zones now making up West Germany were approximately 60–70 percent self-sufficient. As the prewar German diet was about 3,000 calories per person per day, this would mean that with the same population (it was slightly lower in May 1945), western Germany could just support itself at between 1,800 and 2,000 calories per person per day, once production was back to normal. About 97 percent of the land normally planted was actually planted that spring in western Germany. If the British experience in 1945 with Operation Barleycorn was valid for all three western zones, then western Germany in the summer of 1945 was producing at around 70 percent of normal, or about 1,260 to 1,400 calories per day. As little as 700 to 1,190 calories per day was the *official* ration in many cities of over 50,000 population. "Even these scales can not always be met," Grasett adds. In Smith Collection, World War II, Box 37, Abilene.
28. See Quartermaster Progress Reports, April, Abilene.
29. Interview with the author, October 1987.
30. Quartermaster Progress Reports, April, May, June, July 1945. Every month shows a vast surplus amounting to more than 100 days on hand for the whole army. All reports in Abilene.
31. Quartermaster Reports, June 30, Abilene, p. 81.
32. Record of meeting G5 of SHAEF, in Paris, June 13, 1945, with various Red Cross representatives. In NARS, Washington.
33. Littlejohn to Eisenhower, October 10. In RG 92, Office of the QMG, General Correspondence, Subject File 1936–1945, Box 587, NARS, Washington.
34. Littlejohn to Eisenhower, *loc. cit.*
35. "In consequence of the general food shortage caused by the occupation army's normal requisitions and the dislocation of transport, these Germans were unable to allot even a minimum ration to the Balts, Bulgarians, Hungarians, Italians, Rumanians and apatrides [stateless people] on German territory." Max Huber to State Department, August 30, 1945. (Received September 27.) In 800.142/9–2745, State, NARS, Washington.
36. Guillano to Bacque, September 7, 1945. In 11 P60, (possibly 11 P165) Vincennes.
37. War Department to SHAEF Forward, June 9. In SHAEF Cable Log, June 9, 1945, Abilene.
38. Series Y Internationale 1944–49, Y 59–2, vol. 363, November 45–May 46, p. 169, (October). Quai d'Orsay, Paris.
39. Littlejohn to CG, HQ TSFET, August 27, 1945. In QM records, NARS, Washington.
40. QM Reports, ETO, June, July 1945, Abilene.
41. RG 332 file 333.5/20, NARS, Washington.
42. Eisenhower's friend General Everett S. Hughes said in his diary on March 28, 1945, apropos certain officers who were resisting reductions in POW rations, "I suppose that all afraid of Geneva Convention." Hughes Diary, Manuscript Division, LC, Washington.

43. Ernest F. Fisher to the author, May 1988. This was also told to the author by Germans in Rheinberg. It was partly confirmed by Professor Peter Hoffmann of McGill University, who lived near a U.S. camp near Ulm in 1945. He saw the U.S. Army deliberately burning surplus food from their mess tables just outside a prisoner cage. "It was well–known among the Germans that the Red Cross could do nothing for the prisoners," he has said. He never saw Germans take food to the camp.

44. See Chapter 7.

45. Described by E. W. Meyer, ICRC Delegate in Washington, letter to Edwin Plitt, State Department, July 26, 1945. In 711.62114 MAiL/7–2645, State. See Chapter 6.

46. Vinson to Secretary of State, November 28, 1945. In 740.62114/11–2845, State.

47. Dunning of Amcross to SHAEF G1, May 29. In 383.6/6 Box 27, NARS, Washington. Also see Huber to State, *loc. cit.*

48. Memo to Littlejohn, July 20, 1945, describing actual situation in the camps, from officer with initials R.F.C. citing study by Col. W. Griffith, Office of the Chief Surgeon, and Capt. C. R. VerMurlen. RG 332, ETO Historical Division, Files USFET, QM Section, Ops Reports, Boxes 586–599, NARS, Washington.

49. F. S. V. Donnison, *Civil Affairs and Military Government North–West Europe 1944–1946* (London: H. M. Stationery Office, 1961), p. 338. Germany's production figures are taken from Morgenthau, *Germany Is Our Problem.*

50. Eisenhower to CGs of both Eastern and Western Military Districts, August 4, 1945. In RG 332 U.S. Theaters of War, World War II, SGS 370.01 NARS, Washington.

51. Weekly PW and DEF report, USFET, G1. Although the food for the POWs newly termed DEFs was reduced, as ordered, and as the death rate shows, for some reason not visible in the USFET documents the former POWs continue to be classified in the records as POWs, separately from the former DEFs. See also Chapter 11.

52. Charles von Luttichau informed the author that 80,719 Germans died in all the fighting on the western front from June 22, 1941, through March 31, 1945, when the German records stop. Source: Percy E. Schramm, ed., *Die *Kriegstagbuche des Oberkommandos der Wehrmacht* [*OKW* War Diaries] vol. 8, p. 1515.

53. See Appendix 2.

54. See Appendix 2.

55. ETO Medical History, p. 91.

56. Empty beds totaled 1,062 in the 9th, 12th, 28th, 50th, 61st, 62nd, 78th Field Hospitals, and 77th Evacuation Hospital; plus a further 391 empty (40 percent vacancy rate) at the 180th General Hospital at Frankfurt in June. In so–called "hospitals supporting PWTE," 16,229 beds were unoccupied in June. Daily Ad Sec Report, June 18, 1945. RG 332 Box 15, NARS, Washington.

57. See testimony of Dr. Enke of Wuppertal, Chapter 4, note 21.

58. See Appendix 2.

59. From the Medical History of the ETO, fully described in Appendix 2. It must be remembered that as the appendix demonstrates, this report was designed to cover up most of the worst features of the camps, including the high rate of starvation, so it is not fully reliable. For instance, starvation is euphemized under "emaciation and dehydration," or "exhaustion." Lack of shelter appears as "exposure to intense sunlight." But because there is nothing especially damaging in the proportions of causes of deaths, provided the death rate itself is kept low, the report serves in that respect as a useful guide — the proportions were most likely not falsified.

60. "Prevention of disease in POW enclosures was directed primarily toward DDT dusting of prisoners." The DDT was to prevent typhus, which they knew would spread to their own men. Vol. 14, Medical History of the ETO, NARS, Washington. Also cited in Stanhope–Bayne Jones, *Special Fields*, vol. 9 of Colonel Robert S. Anderson, ed., *Preventive Medicine in World War II* (Washington: Department of the Army, 1969).

61. Notes on Conference re PWTE, May 28, among Hollar et al. RG 332 Box 22, NARS, Washington.

62. Daily PW Report, TPM.

63. Several Germans report common graves. See Chapter 4, note 16.

64. The report, dated May 10, 1945, is headed "Daily Activities Report of the HQ Ad Sec Com Z, Office of the Surgeon." In NARS, Washington.

65. Interview with the author, 1988. Zobrist is now Director of the Harry S. Truman Library, Independence, Mo.

66. Quoted in Philip Knightley, *The First Casualty* (New York and London: Harcourt Brace Jovanovich), p. 315.

67. Quoted in Knightley, p. 333. Repeated in conversation with the author, February 1988.

6

KEEPING HELP AWAY

1. RG 59 State Decimal File 1945-49 740.581112a/1-146 and 740.62114/6-445 Box 59. Also 740.62114/3-2045.

2. State to Amembassy, Paris,May 12, 1945. In 740.62114/5-445. State.
   See also memorandum of Brigadier General R. W. Berry to Deputy Chief of Staff,War Department,May 9, 1945. RG 383.6 NARS, but found in photocopy, Reel 370, Item 5369, in Lexington. Barry's memo summarizes a previous informal advice from Herrick, Special War Problems of State.

3. Marshall to Eisenhower, cable, received May 17, 1945, NARS, Washington.

4. See note 2.

5. Under the Convention, the visiting ICRC delegate would talk privately with

a representative of the prisoners, then write a report on camp conditions to the ICRC, which would then submit it to the Protecting Power (the government of the prisoners' country) and to the Capturing Power, the government of the army holding the prisoners. No one else saw the reports. In 1988 the ICRC was still refusing to release these reports to private researchers.

6. See note 22.

7. FO File 916 1219. In Public Records Office, Kew, London.

8. Mr. McNeil, Reply to a question, November 5, 1945, *Hansard*. Quoted in Achilles to State, November 7, 1945. In 740.62144/11-745. State.

9. Chief among many examples is the assurance given by Secretary of State James F. Byrnes to President Max Huber of the ICRC on October 4, 1945, to which Huber replied, "We note with gratification that your government's policy is . . . complete conformity with the letter and spirit of the Geneva Convention." Huber to Byrnes, Geneva, January 9, 1946. State. (See also RG 59 Box 3971, NARS, Washington.) Among others, Secretary of State Dean Achesop affirmed that the U.S. abided by the Geneva Convention.

10. Chief among many private protests ignored by the Americans was Huber's long letter to State, August 30, 1945. In 800.142/9-2745, State. (See also RG 332 Box 7, NARS, Washington.)

11. R.A. Haccius, ICRC, Geneva, to Major T.R. Crawford, War Office, London, February 15, 1946. In FO 371/55738.

12. Fairman to General Betts, May 28, 1945. In 383.6/3-4 image 16 0979, NARS.

13. Exact citation missing, but probably in or near RG 112 Box 167, NARS, Washington. Paper is headed "Packaging Centers," dealing with American Red Cross work. Copies were sent to State, 1945. See also report of U.S. Army Captain Burdick (in or near RG 112 Box 167), saying his life was saved by British, Canadian and USA food parcels while he was in German captivity.

14. This was the percentage reported by the War Department (in 1948, they said the death rate was 1.26 percent. At RG 407 AG055, August 26, 1948) and by the Red Cross. In SHAEF Papers, NARS, Washington. See also, article by Maurice Pate of Prisoner of War Relief, American Red Cross, included in letter by Gilbert Redfern of Amcross, May 9, 1945, to Kuppinger at State.

15. "The U.S. Army made it difficult for relief." The Friends were not allowed into Germany until the spring of 1946. Interview of the author with Stephen Cary, European Commissioner of the AFSC, 1986.

16. Letter of Tracy Strong to Major H.G. Hyde, July 3, 1945, and cable of Paul Anderson to Strong, June 30, 1945 and letter of D.A. Davis of YMCA to State Department, July, all in State Department Archives.

17. The reason given was that relief shipments might tend to negate the policy of restricting the German standard of living to the average of the surrounding European nations. Earl F. Ziemke, *The U.S. Army in Occupation of Germany* (Washington: Center of Military History, 1975), p. 410.

18. Described by E.W. Meyer, ICRC Delegate in Washington, letter to Edwin Plitt, State Department, July 26, 1945. In 711.62114 MAiL/7-2645, State.

19. E.W. Meyer ICRC, to Edwin Plitt, State; see note 18.

20. FO 939 Items 448 and 469 PRO London.

21. Huber to State, August 30, 1945. See note 10.

22. "The food was very satisfactory, up to about May 1945, when regulations were issued to all Camp Commanders to cut the rations." Report on the Activities of the ICRC in the USA. In Red Cross Archives, State Department, NARS, Washington.

23. Huber to State, August 30, 1945.

24. Huber to State, August 30, 1945.

25. Eisenhower to Marshall, November 2, 1945. RG 332 Box 7, NARS.

26. In Statement of Policy Regarding Disposition of Red Cross Supplies dated June 15, 1945, between SHAEF on the one hand and the American Red Cross and the British Red Cross Societies on the other, Red Cross food parcels may "in emergency be distributed to recipients" other than Displaced Persons, a category which in itself included displaced Germans. This is the only agreement between the army and the two Red Crosses found in the archives. It fits in general and in detail the description given in the response signed "Eisenhower," except for the falsifications noted. Original seen in American Red Cross Archives, Washington, RG 200 Box 1017. Available in photocopy RG 200, Records of the ARC, 619.2/01 from NARS.

27. "As of 31 July, the following seven voluntary relief agencies had approved agreements with UNRRA, The International Red Cross [and six others]." Malcolm J. Proudfoot, *European Refugees, 1939–52*, p. 187.

28. Proudfoot, *European Refugees*, p. 187.

29. From Memorandum Regarding Disposition of Surplus Prisoner of War Supplies, June 15, 1945, among BRC, ARC and SHAEF, distributed (restricted) to ARC, BRC and 13 SHAEF officers. In RG 200, Records of the American Red Cross, NARS, Washington.

30. Minutes of informal meeting of delegates of three Red Crosses, Geneva, January 14-15, 1946, in RG 200 Box 1016, NARS, Washington.

31. Huber to State, August 30, 1945.

32. "Rolling stock exclusively employed in transporting ICRC goods now consists of 211 trucks of French and 56 of Belgian origin, both sections being engaged for the coming months in a shuttle service Geneva-Paris and Geneva-Brussels to convey back to the respective owners relief goods not belonging to the pool." Allowing one week per round trip for two months, this comes to 2,136 train-car loads. Huber to State, August 30, 1945.

33. Eisenhower to War Department, November 2, 1945, RG 332 Box 7.

34. The correspondence, beginning July 13, continues between Pickett, Eisenhower and Marshall until mid-September. For those who doubt Eisenhower's personal involvement in decisions they imagine may have been taken by his staff, one of the copies in the NARS files is signed by Eisenhower himself. All in NARS, Washington.

35. Minutes of the Informal Meeting of Delegates of American, French and

British Red Cross Societies, Geneva, January 14, 1946. Speech by Mr. Dayton of American Red Cross.

36. Many sources confirm this official diet of which the Report of Paul R. Porter may be the most objective. "In the Essen district, coal miners were issued only 900 calories per day." In Papers of Paul R. Porter, Independence, Mo.

37. Joint Chiefs of Staff to Eisenhower, September 3, 1945. In RG 332 Box 37 (SGS-USFET File No. 312), NARS, Washington.

38. Eisenhower to Pickett, September 19, 1945. Exact citation missing but probably with other correspondence cited on this subject in RG 332 Box 37, in NARS, Washington.

39. In RG 332 Box 19, NARS, Washington.

40. Strong to Major G.H. Hyde, U.S. Army, Special Services Division, July 3, 1945. In 740.00114 EW/7-945, State.

41. Davis to State, July 9, 1945, 740.00114 EW/ 7-945, NARS, Washington.

42. General Lucius Clay to War Department, October 30, 1945. In RG 332 Box 37. Reference 383.7/11, NARS, Washington.

43. Interview of the author with Stephen Cary, November 1986.

44. Lucius D. Clay, *Decision in Germany* (New York: Doubleday, 1950), pp. 18–19.

45. *Morgenthau Diary* (China) vol. 2, p. 1529 ff. All the quotations from Somervell, Morgenthau and others in this passage are from the *Morgenthau Diary*.

46. Hilldring to State, RG 59, 3726A, NARS, Washington.

47. This and subsequent quotes from Gollancz, including the reference to Belsen, are all from the pamphlet by Victor Gollancz, *Leaving Them to Their Fate: The Ethics of Starvation* (London: Victor Gollancz, 1946). All statistics about German rations and death in this chapter are from Gollancz.

48. Donnison, *Civil Affairs and Military Government*, p. 338.

49. JCS Memo 1662 to the President, April 27, 1946. In RG 260 Box 16, Clay Papers, NARS, Washington.

50. Reparations from Current Production and Present Economic Policy, RG 332 Box 22, NARS, Washington.

51. Gollancz, *Leaving Them to Their Fate.*

52. Gollancz, *Leaving Them to Their Fate.*

53. FO 1050, in Public Records Office, Kew, London.

54. The North American surplus at the end of 1945 was 173 million bushels, about 5,140,000 tons *after* all European needs had been met. International Wheat Council, Haymarket House, Haymarket, London, 1955.

    To maintain a near-starvation ration, the shortfall in Germany estimated by the British in 1945 (shortfall being the same as the need to import), was about 4,440,000 tons for the year September 1945 to September 1946. This was about 87 percent of the North American surplus. R. Mitchell, *International Historical Statistics* (London: Macmillan, 1983.)

7

THE SLOW DEATH CAMPS

1. Report of Captain Julien of the Troisième Régiment de Tirailleurs Algériens, Box 11 P 60, Vincennes. In this chapter, all the material by Julien is from this report, or from Box 11 P 65, Vincennes.
2. Box 11 P 65 Vincennes.
3. Report of Lt Colonel De La Bosse, Troisième Régiment de Tirailleurs Algériens, to his CO, II Corps, September 15. In Box 11 P 60, Vincennes. Also Juin to Lewis copied in Despatch no. 3470, October 15, 1945, Caffery to State, NARS, Washington.
4. Report of Lt. Colonel Sury of the Troisième Régiment de Tirailleurs Algériens, December 31, 1945. Box 11 P 60, Vincennes.
5. Memorandum to General Paul, July 7, from Lauben. NARS, Washington.
6. All these reports of weakness caused by American mistreatment are from various officers to Juin etc, in Box 11 P 165, 7 P 40 and 11 P 60, Vincennes. Translations by the author.

   Juin's complaint to General John T. Lewis, USFET Mission to France, dated October 11, is in the State Department Archives, letter 3470, Caffery to State, NARS, Washington.
7. Despite Thrasher's order, the notes were taken, according to the statement attested by Haight and Major William G. Downey. In RG 332.6/1 Box 50, NARS, Washington.
8. In RG 332 383.6/1 Box 50, NARS.
9. Report of Lt. Colonel Gobillard to the Military Governor at Coblence [Koblenz], August 27, 1945. In Box 11 P 60 Vincennes.
10. Letter of Lieutenant Himmeur to Captain commanding Troisième Régiment de Tirailleurs Algériens, September 1945. In Box 11 P 60 Vincennes.
11. Letter of Lieutenant Soubeiray, Troisième Régiment de Tirailleurs Algériens, September 3, 1945. In Box 11 P 60, Vincennes.
12. At August 30, 1945, Billotte to the Deuxième Bureau, Paris. Attribution unclear, but either Box 11 P 60 or 11 P 165, Vincennes.
13. Compte Rendu of Maurice, August 14, 1945. Translation by the author. Vincennes.
14. Jean-Pierre Pradervand was the head of the ICRC delegation in North Africa in August 1944, when Paris was liberated. He was appointed to head the ICRC delegation in France, a position he took up in January 1945. He remained in France as chief delegate until January 1946. At this time it was the largest national delegation connected with World War II problems, numbering 112 by 1947. The report on Thorée is contained in a letter of Pradervand to de Gaulle, September 26, in Box 7 P 40, Vincennes.
15. André Durand, *From Sarajevo to Hiroshima, History of the International Committee of the Red Cross* (Geneva: Henry Dunant Institute, 1984), p. 593.

16. Durand, *From Sarajevo to Hiroshima*, p. 593.
17. This cable and the related documents used in this passage are all from the State Department Archives, NARS, Washington.
18. Dunning to State, September 5, 1945. Exact citation missing. In State Department Archives, Washington.
19. Caffery to State, September 25, 1945. In 740.62114/9-2545 CS/LE. State.

8

LIMING THE CORPSE

1. *Le Figaro* September 22 and 29, 1945.
2. Pradervand to de Gaulle, September 26, 1945. In Box 7 P 40, Vincennes.
3. That it was not de Gaulle's hand was attested by Professor M. R. D. Foot of London, who read a photocopy of the letter in the author's possession.
4. Lee to USFET Main, November 10, 1945. RG383.6/1 NARS, Washington.
5. Minutes of Conference, USFET Mission, Paris, between French Army and U.S. Army on Interzone Transfers of German Prisoners of War, September 22, 1945. In Box 7 P 40, Vincennes. All references to Lauben et al are based on the minutes of this conference.
6. At the meeting he "handed General Smith photographs which he had taken at a number of PW camps. General Smith took these photographs in to General Eisenhower." Minutes of Conference, Chief of Staff, G1, September 28, 1945. Copied in Caffery to State, 740.62114/10-545, State. The Red Cross archives have no such pictures. The Committee of the International Red Cross in Geneva have no copies. No such pictures accompanied the dossiers in the French army archives in Vincennes, the U.S. Army archives in Washington, or the Eisenhower Library, Abilene. M. Pradervand confirmed this to the author in June 1989.
7. Pradervand to Smith, October 23, Paris. In 383.6/1, NARS, Washington.
8. Pradervand to Smith, October 23.
9. Memo to Major General A. W. Kenner, Chief Surgeon, U.S. Army, TSFET HQ, October 4, 1945. In 383.6/1, NARS, Washington.
10. Littlejohn to Eisenhower, October 10. In RG 92, Office of QM General, General Correspondence, Subject File 1936—45. Box 587, NARS, Washington.
11. *Le Monde*, September 30—October 1, 1945. Bibliothèque Nationale, Paris.
12. Caffery to State, about October 7. NARS.
13. Caffery to State, October 5, 1945. In 740.62114/10—55, State.
14. From several sources, chiefly Charles de Gaulle, *The Complete War Memoirs, 1940–1946* (New York: Simon and Schuster, 1955).
15. Caffery to State, October 13, 195. In 70.6211/10-1345. State Department Archives, NARS, Washington.
16. Caffery to State, October 13, 1945.

17. Eisenhower to AGWAR October 1945 (date not clear). Found in Bundesarchiv, Koblenz.
18. Interview with the author, 1987.
19. Colonel Lauben to the author, November 1987.
20. Caffery to State, October 13, 1945.
21. Series Y *Internationale* 1944–9, vol. 604, p. P000062, Quai d'Orsay.
22. Series Y *Internationale* 1944–9, vol. 604, p. P000020, Quai d'Orsay.
23. Marshall to Eisenhower, November 2, 1945. Marshall Library, Lexington.
24. Lee to USFET Main. In 383.6/1, NARS, Washington.
25. General Buisson, *Historique du Service des Prisonniers de Guerre de l'Axe, 1943–48* (Paris: Ministère de la Défense Nationale, 1948).
26. ICRC Delegate in France Quoted in Memo to General McNarney, November 12, 1946, RG 332 DF 383.6, NARS, Washington. Also Secret Report, Office of the Chief of Staff, File No. 383.6/1 vol. 1, from January 1, 1946. In RG 332 Box 120.
27. K. Royall, Acting Secretary of War, to President Truman, December 31, 1945. In White House Central File, Independence, Mo.
28. See Appendix 1.
29. The food mentioned was 1,212 tons. Smith to Pradervand, October 19, 1945. In RG 383.6/1, NARS, Washington.
30. Lee to USFET Main, November 10, 1945. In 383.6/1, NARS, Washington
31. Lauben in conversation with the author, 1987.
32. Lewis to Eisenhower, October 13, 1945. In 383.6/1 of SHAEF Papers, NARS, Washington.

    The ICRC later said that "The American Command" had made available over 3,000 tons of food, without specifying the date. The extra must have been existing Red Cross stocks seized by SHAEF, then turned over to the prisoners. André Durand, *From Sarajevo to Hiroshima*, p. 645.
33. ETO USFET Adjutant Section, Decimal Files, 1945, Boxes 430-442. November 17, 1945. NARS, Washington. Earlier, a SHAEF officer had reported 13,000,000 parcels. The extra 500,000 probably were returned to stock after the returning Allied military personnel, for whom they had been intended, had not needed them.
34. The *New York Times*, October 11, 13, 14, 20, 1945. In the New York Public Library.
35. Middleton's stories, datelined Frankfurt, were printed in the *Times*, as noted above in October 1945.
36. Interview with Middleton, New York, June 1988.

9

INSIDE THE GREENHOUSE

1. Series Z, *Europe-Allemagne* 1944–49, *Prisonniers de Guerre*, vol. 22, p. 3, September 18, 1945. In *Archives de la Ministère des Affaires Etrangères*, Quai

d'Orsay, Paris. Also ICRC report cited in Memorandum to Colonel Whitted, United States Army, 765041, Koblenz. Also Report of General Lewis, Paris, October, 1946. In RG 332 DF 383-6, NARS, Washington.

2. ICRC General Report of German POW, Paris, October 31, 1946. In RG 332 DF 383-6, NARS, Washington.
3. Memorandum of U.S. Army Colonel Whitted of meeting of Länderrat Main Committee on Prisoners of War, Stuttgart, November 28, 1947, quoting ICRC report by Mr. Meyer of the ICRC. In Bundesarchiv, Koblenz, West Germany. This document, photocopied, like many others in the Bundesarchiv furnished by the U.S. government (or army), reports serious criticism of French camps. The author found among the documents sent by the U.S. to Germany nothing critical of U.S. camps, although such criticism is plentiful in the French army archives in Vincennes.
4. Series Y *Internationale*, 1945–49, P000149, Quai d'Orsay, Paris.
5. See note 1. General John T. Lewis to Commanding General U.S. Forces, European Theater.
6. "By 1946, approximately 60 percent of the Legion's 20,000 men were Germans. Arthur L. Smith Jr., *Warrior Without Honor: Germany's War Veterans 1945–49*. From Chapter Two in the English manuscript, at page 70. Published in German as *Heimkehr aus dem Zweiter Weltkrieg* (Stuttgart: Deutsche Verlags-Anstalt, 1985).
7. Huber to State, January 9, 1946. In RG 59 Box 3971, NARS, Washington.
8. All the letters cited among Pradervand, Kuppinger, Byrnes et al are in the State Department Archives, NARS, Washington. In the 740 File under dates shown.
9. Henri Amouroux, *La Vie des Français sous l'Occupation* (Paris: Fayard, 1961), p. 139.
10. General McSherry of SHAEF to Judge Samuel Rosenman, March 15, 1945. In "Rosenman Report to President of United States, April 1945", *Rosenman Papers*, (Box 30, Hyde Park).
11. Amouroux, *La Vie des Français sous l'Occupation*, p. 139.
12. Consumption of meat from Amouroux, *La Vie des Français sous l'Occupation*, p. 139; production from Jean-Pierre Rioux, *La Francc de la Ivème République: L'Ardeur et la Nécessité 1944–1952*, (Paris: Editions du Seuil, 1980), p. 250.
13. Secretary General of German Austrian Affairs, August 2, 1945, in Series *Y Internationale* 1944–49, vol. 282, p. 120, Quai d'Orsay.
14. Report of French diplomat M. Layeillon to Government of France, in Series *Y Internationale*, 1944–49, Y 59–2, p. 169.
15. Many sources confirm this, including eye-witness reports of German civilians, and Paul R. Porter who discovered that German miners were getting only 900 calories per day (*Papers of Paul R. Porter*, Independence). This is also confirmed by Max Huber's letter to the U.S. State Department referring to failure of allies to provide even a "minimum ration" to Displaced Persons, who came ahead of the Germans in the queue for rations. See Note 24, Chapter 6.

16. "Direction Générale des Étude et Recherches, Note pour De Gaulle", in Series *Y Internationale,* Y51–1, November/December 1945, vol. 283, p. 241.
17. Raoul Laporterie to General de Gaulle, June 1946. In the private archives of Raoul Laporterie, Grenade sur l'Adour, Landes, France.
18. Acheson to Wallace, May 1, 1946. In 740.62114/4-2346, State.
19. Acheson to Byrnes, April 23, 1946. In 740.62114/4, State.
20. Roger C. Wilson, *Quaker Relief* (London: George Allen and Unwin), p. 156.
21. *Notes Documentaires et Études,* No. 270, March 26, 1946, p. 7. In Quai d'Orsay, Paris.

    At the end of 1945, there were still about 1,000,000 prisoners in U.S. hands in Europe, plus another 400,000 in the USA or en route to Europe. Of these, about 400,000 were actually working for the U.S. Army in Europe as laborers, drivers, stevedores, carpenters, technicians, freeing American personnel to go home. (Most of the 400,000 in the USA were at work in fields, forests and mines.) If the half million German prisoner-workers in British hands are included, there were around 1,900,000 German men repairing some of the damage caused by the war, or replacing some of the goods stolen by the Germans when they were in power in France.
22. et seq. Told to the author by prisoner Hans Goertz of Bonn in March 1986.
23. Author's interviews in 1986 with various prison guards M. Cazaux, Raphael Conquère, Messieurs Labat and Marc, in Labouheyre, Buglose and surrounding areas.
24. Interview with Raphael Conqueré, of Buglose, 1986.
25. Interview with Heinz T. conducted by Mavis Gallant and the author.
26. From interviews with Werner Steckelings in Straelen, West Germany, 1986 and 1988, by the author.
27. Buisson, *Historique,* pp. 37–41. Buisson's figures roughly confirm U.S. Army figures on the number of transfers in 1945. By October 9, about 724,000 had been transferred according to the U.S. Army. Allowing for the French discharges of 30,000 women, children, dying and old men in the camps round Dietersheim in July, plus the 70,000 sick Buisson claimed the French returned to the U.S. camps, plus the 638,000 remaining in November according to Buisson, the number taken in by the French must have been about 738,000. However, Buisson's claim to have returned over 70,000 sick men is refuted by Royall's statement to Truman (note 24) that returns totaled about 52,000. In this instance, the lowest figure — leading to the lowest number of deaths — has been used.
28. Tappen's judgment proved him right. He was put into a labor battalion in Cherbourg where he was well treated by the Americans until his release four days before Christmas 1945. Author's interview with Alfred Tappen of Toronto, 1988.
29. Inspection report of Lt. Colonel Sarda de Caumont, November 10, 1945, to Minister of War. Vincennes.
30. The list is in the Town Archives of Thorée les Pins. The proportion of the

camp covered by the list is not given, but the list cannot cover the whole camp, because it shows no day in August or September when more than twelve people died, whereas Pradervand said that on the day he was there, 20 died.

31. Interview with the author, Thorée les Pins, 1986.
32. Acting Secretary for War Kenneth C. Royall to President Truman, December 1945. In White House Central, Independence.
33. The story of Stock as told here comes from several printed sources, chiefly Erich Kock, *l'Abbé Franz Stock*, (Paris: Casterman, 1966).
34. Buisson, *Historique du Service des Prisonniers de Guerre de l'Axe 1943-1948* (Paris: Ministère de la Défense Nationale, Paris, 1948 privately circulated).
35. Juin to Lewis, October 27, 1945, cited in Buisson, op. cit., p. 47.
36. ETO Medical History, vol. 14, NARS, Washington. See Appendix 2.
37. This is a series of books under the general editorship of Dr. Erich Maschke, issued in Germany in the 1960s and 1970s, in which the authors tried to trace the history and fate of German prisoners of war in the two world wars. Series title was *Zur Geschichte der deutschen Kriegsgefangenen des Zweiten Weltkrieges*. (Bielefeld: Verlag Ernst and Werner Gieseking).
38. Smith, October 9; USFET tables and Juin, October 27, all previously cited.
39. *Notes Documentaires et Études*, March 26, 1946, Secrétariat d'Etat, Paris. In Archives de la Ministère des Affaires Étrangères, Quai d'Orsay, Paris.
40. Buisson, *Historiques*, p. 48, and Kenneth C. Royall to Truman, December 31, 1945. In White House Central Files, Confidential File, Harry S. Truman Library, Independence.
41. *Notes Documentaires*, p. 8.
42. Buisson, *Historique*, p. 240. See also general heading for all statistical tables in the appendices.
43. After this table was first published, new information came to light making a little clearer the death rate in French camps between 1945 and 1946. Ex-prisoner Joachim Theys, who was in St. Medard-en-Jalles, Gironde, for five to six months after May 15 1945, witnessed an epidemic of typhus there which killed 500 to 800 prisoners in two to three months. Theys said that apart from the epidemic, about five people died per day, but he was not sure how many men were in his camp. The ICRC reported that on a visit to St. Medard during the period Theys was there, thirty percent of the 9,500 prisoners were not fit to work. Given the low French standards of the time, this means that some 2,850 men were so weak that they could not work at all, which goes some way to confirming Theys' observations. The deaths estimated by Theys run between 20 and 29 percent per year when applied to the whole camp as observed by the ICRC. Applying the deaths noticed by Theys only to his section of about 3,000 men, the death rate varies between the minimum of 53 percent and maximum of 100 percent per annum. For purposes of this book, the death rate at St. Medard-en-Jalles is assumed to be 30 percent. Theys' observations are old and limited, but the contemporary ICRC figure of 30 percent of prisoners being unable to work after only four months of

captivity, corresponds closely to the prediction of mortality by Pradervand, and is reliable. Also, 30 percent per annum is very close to the death rates noticed by prisoners and agencies in other camps at different periods during the year October 1945 to 1946.

44. Series B *Amérique*, 1944-52, *Etats-Unis*. Vol. 79, pp. 78-9. Quai d'Orsay, Paris.

45. Roger C. Wilson, *Quaker Relief*, p. 154.

46. For Thorée les Pins, witness Langlais said that between 18 (per day) x 180 (days) and 12 (per day) x 150 (days) died, or 3,240 down to 1,800. The difference between the Red Cross figure of 17,000 to 20,000 complement for the camp and 12,000, which is the French army figure for the camp, is probably caused by the deaths among the prisoners predicted by Pradervand. It may also have been caused by transfers out of the camp.

    Rivesaltes: Witness Werner Steckelings of Issum, West Germany, said 3-5 died per day per barracks of 80 men. He also said that on many days, 20 died. Figure shown is 15 per day for the whole camp times 90 days equals 1,350.

    Marseille: Witness Hubert Heyer of Dusseldorf said 3-6 died per day while he was there. Rate here is based on five per day.

    Information for Labouheyre and Daugnague/Pissos and Buglose was gathered by the author from guards, local records, grave lists and one survivor.

    Saint Paul d'Égiaux. The report in *Le Monde* appeared September 30–October 1, 1945. (End of reel two, *Le Monde* microfilm at Bibliotheque Nationale, Paris.)

10

THE BRITISH AND CANADIANS

1. In conversation with the author, Toronto, 1987.
2. Letter of H. F. McCullough of West Hill, Ontario, to the author, March 1988.
3. Interview of Werner Heyne with the author, April 1988.
4. In Nigel Hamilton, *Monty*, vol. 3, p. 523.
5. Montgomery to Commander, 1st Canadian Army, 2nd Canadian Army, March 22, 1945. In RG24, vol. 10 651, 215.C, NAC, Ottawa.
6. All the experiences of Corporal Liebich are taken from an interview with the author in Rheinberg in November 1987.
7. See Appendix 1. According to one survivor, it was much higher than 30 percent per year.
8. Interview with Herr Liebich conducted by the author and his research assistant, November, 1987, in Rheinberg, West Germany.
9. Interview of the author with Heinz Janssen, town archivist of Rheinberg, together with the town clerk, Herr W. Hucklekemke, and Assistant Anja Kiechle, November 1987.
10. Letter of Françoise Perret, ICRC, to the author, June 12, 1987. The ICRC has refused to allow the author to see this report. The U.S. State Department archives have no copy of the report. Such reports were always sent to the

Protecting Power under the Geneva Convention.

11. See Appendix 9, The British Discrepancy.
12. USFET Weekly PW and DEF Report, in RG 331 Box 26, 383.6/1-3, NARS, Washington.
13. This story of mass deaths in a British or Canadian camp is the only one encountered by the author in two years of research, including interviews with over a hundred men — guards, survivors, a priest and a camp commander — who were in American, French, British or Canadian camps in Europe.
14. Alfred Nutt, a private in the Wehrmacht, who was in a camp in Kreis Stade near Hamburg, wrote to his mother in July. She received the letter in August. Several weeks later, he was released "in good condition." Interview with Nutt's brother Hans, Edmonton, Alberta, December 1988.
15. FO 916/1433 PRO, London.
16. "Senior British officers bore the ultimate blame for conditions in the Belgian camps. As a result, the camps were not supplied as they should have been. The consequences [were] described later by a representative of the War Office as an inexcusable failure in [British] obligations toward the Geneva Convention." Quoted from Fax of Colonel Henry Faulk to the author April 4, 1989. See also *Hansard* 2. 7. 1946.
17. ICRC Report to Foreign Office, London, January 1946. In FO 916, Piece 1433. PRO, London.
18. ICRC Letter to Under Secretary of State, April 17, 1946. In FO 916 Piece 1433. PRO, London.
19. Mitscherlich, Haas and Seemann, *Bericht über eine Befragung heimkehrender deutscher Kriegsgefangener*. (IYMCA). Quoted in Henry Faulk, *Group Captives* (London: Chatto and Windus, 1977). Faulk does not believe that the views of the prisoners applied to British camps.
20. Von Baden does not mention his source, which must have been either a discharged prisoner or one within the camp. Because omitting the source might tend to discredit his letter to the *Times*, it is obvious that von Baden had a strong reason to cover the source. The likeliest reason to hide the source was that it was a letter from a prisoner still in the camp who may have feared reprisal.
21. On June 2, 1945, Patton's 3rd Army, part of the 12th Army Group, discharged 406,926 (89 percent) of the 457,985 DEFs discharged by the 12th AG. In SHAEF G1 DEF Reports, RG 331 Box 26, 383.6/3-17, NARS, Washington.
22. FO 371/55742. In PRO, London. In the spring of 1946, the British had around 400,000 prisoners of war at work in the British Isles.
23. Minutes of Potsdam Conference, in RG 43 Box BA, NARS, Washington.
24. Interview with Heinz T. See Chapter 4. Colonel Lauben, representing SHAEF, went to Norway to arrange the transfer of these men.
25. The Geneva Convention Article 11 covering food was stated in an official British policy review "to apply with the exception of quantity of food. PW and SEP are on the same scales authorized by the War Office." The excep-

tion was made because the British did not have enough food to maintain the Geneva Convention scale, which was far higher than necessary to maintain life. As is clear from the good health of the POWs, their ration was also good enough to maintain the SEPs in good health, despite the inferior accommodation. Appendix A to GHQ CMF Letter July 6, 1946. In FO 371/55742, PRO, London.

26. In conversation with the author, April 1988.
27. Bernard Law Montgomery Papers (BLM Papers) 127/54, Imperial War Museum, London.
28. Hilldring to State, September 4, 1945. In RG 59, 3726A, NARS, Washington.
29. Series Y *Internationale* Y51-1, November—December 1945, vol. 283, p. 241. Direction Générale des Etudes et Recherches, Ministère des Affaires Etrangères, Quai d'Orsay, Paris.
30. F. S. V. Donnison, *Civil Affairs and Military Government, North West Europe 1944-46*, p. 465.

11

MYTH, LIES AND HISTORY

1. Martin Blumenson, *The Patton Papers.*
2. According to the ETO Medical History. See Appendix 1.
3. The variation is caused by uncertainties in how the bookkeeping was distorted by Canadian generosity. H. Duncan Hall, *North American Supply* (London: H.M. Stationery Office, 1955).
4. Paul Kennedy, *The Rise and Fall of the Great Powers* (New York: Random House, 1988); pp. 461 and 475 in the Fontana Edition.
5. Hall, *North American Supply*.
6. Weekly PW and DEF Report, USFET, September 8, 1945. In RG 331 Box 26, 383.6/1-3. NARS, Washington. To the 5,224,310 noted in the SHAEF total capture figure of June 11 must be added a further approximately 400,000 held in the USA but captured in the Mediterranean Theater, plus the 291,000 captured and held in Italy. The U.S. in Europe still had over 1,000,000 prisoners in January 1946, the same as in September 1945, so the number released must have been the same as then, when it was 36 percent of the total catch. Any prisoners returned to Europe from the USA by January (few were) were more than offset by the several hundred thousand captives first held in Italy who had been shipped to U.S. camps in Austria and Germany starting in July 1945. These captives are nowhere included in overall death totals in this book.
7. In RG 332, 383.6.10 Box 51, NARS, Washington.
8. *The Stars and Stripes*, November 20, 1945, RG 332, NARS.
9. Lt. Colonel H. N. Kirkman, Director, Enemy Prisoner of War Information Bureau, to State, August 20, 1945. In 711.62114/8-2045, State, Washington. None of the 5,122 reports of burial survived in the State Department archives.

10. Blumenson, *Patton Papers* p. 784.
11. Blumenson, *Patton Papers* p. 702. The quotation beginning at "he outlined a form of organization," up to "supporting it in general" is from the diary itself, May 10, 1945.
12. Blumenson, *Patton Papers*, p. 732.
13. Blumenson, *Patton Papers*, Chapter 40.
14. Buisson, *Historique*.
15. Robert Murphy, *Diplomat Among Warriors* (New York: Doubleday, 1964), p. 294.
16. Cited in F. S. V. Donnison, *Civil Affairs and Military Government*, p. 240.
17. Smith, *Warriors Without Honor*, Chapter 3.
18. Smith, *Warriors Without Honor*.
19. Charles B. Macdonald, *The Last Offensive* (Washington: United States Army, Office of the Chief of Military History, 1973). Also Forrest C. Pogue, *The Supreme Command*, (Washington: Department of the Army, Office of the Chief of Military History, 1984), pp. 472-3 ff. Also, Major L. F. Ellis, *Victory in the West*, vol. 2, (London: H.M. Stationery Office, 1968), p. 339.
20. See Appendix 1.
21. SHAEF PW and DEF capture figure, already cited. See also Böhme, *Die deutschen Kriegsgefangenen in amerikanischer Hand* vol. 15 of E. Maschke, ed., *Zur Geschichte der deutschen Kriegsgefangenen des Zweiten Weltkrieges*, p. 196, where the Soviet Union, at January 1947, has 1,019,155 prisoners on hand. See note 22.
22. In late May, 1945, Stalin told Roosevelt's representative Harry Hopkins that the Russians had about 2,500,000 prisoners, of whom around 1,700,000 were Germans and the rest Rumanians, Italians, Hungarians, etc. Sherwood, *op cit*, p. 904.
23. *Yearbook of the United Nations*, 1950, p. 565, and *Communist Treatment of Prisoners of War*, USGPO, 1972.
24. Congressional Record — Senate, p. 1675 (1947).
25. Lt. Colonel A. D. Poinier, GSC, U.S. Army, Germany, to Dr. G. Hoffmann, ICRC, Berlin, March 19, 1948. 765041, Koblenz.
26. Quoted in Helmut M. Fehling, *One Great Prison* (Boston: The Beacon Press, 1951), p. 138.
27. Smith, *Warriors Without Honor*, Chapter 3.
28. *Communist Treatment of Prisoners of War, A Historical Survey (Washington: U.S. Government Printing Office, 1972)*.
29. Stalin told Hopkins in Moscow in the summer of 1945 that the Russians had about 2,000,000 prisoners, who were working. Stalin had no need at that time to reduce the true figure, for each side was trying to claim the largest possible share of the credit for defeating Hitler. However, a report

cited by several American writers attributed only to Tass without date or printed source, was said to have given a total Russian take of 3,000,000 Germans. If that were true, then using the figure of 837,828 discharges accepted as true by the Allies in 1947, the Russians would have "failed to account for" which, in the parlance of the Cold War, meant killed off, about 73 percent of their useful prisoners in peacetime.

30. Böhme, *Die deutschen Kriegsgefangenen*, pp. 33 ff.

31. Böhme, *Die deutschen Kriegsgefangenen*. Böhme's source was the U.S. Army Archives in Washington in the 1960s; the earlier higher figure quoted for Rheinberg was given by the local U.S. Army Command in the area in 1947.

32. In the present book, the death rate for camp Rheinberg is quoted because it is known how long the camp was under American administration, 61 days to June 15, 1945.

33. Buisson, *Historique*.

34. *Notes Documentaires*.

35. One of the assistant editors of *The Papers of Dwight David Eisenhower*, Joseph Hobbs, suggested the possible origin of the suppression to the author in an interview in August 1988. (The original of the letter is in the George C. Marshall Research Library, Lexington, Virginia. *Dear General*, by Joseph Patrick Hobbs, was published by The Johns Hopkins Press in 1971.)

36. David Eisenhower, *Eisenhower at War*, p. 810.

37. Minute of Churchill to Eisenhower, May 15, 1945. See Chapter 12.

38. Smith, *Warriors Without Honor*, p. 22.

39. Smith, *Warriors Without Honor.*, p. 1.

40. Interview with the author, 1987. The name of the German is omitted as the author does not want to criticize the man, but the attitude.

41. Mitscherlich et al. See Chapter 10.

42. This happened to the author and his assistant during their visit to Koblenz. As we pursued the investigation into the atrocity in the French camps, we did not believe that the Americans had done such things. There were just enough hints of the American death camps that we decided to go from Toronto the relatively short distance to Washington — where we found the documents bearing the words "Other Losses."

43. Lewis Lapham, *Money and Class in America* (New York: Weidenfeld and Nicolson, 1988).

44. Elias Canetti, *The Conscience of Words*, translated by Joachim Neugroschel (London: Andre Deutsch, 1986), pp. 21—22.

12

BY WINKS AND NODS

1. Priorities in Construction of PWTE, May 1, 1945. In RG 332 Box 12, Washington.

2. "No non-German voluntary welfare agencies are permitted to operate in

the American occupied zone for the benefit of German nationals." From OMGUS, signed Clay, to WARCAD October 30, 1945. Clay makes it clear in the paragraph beginning, "Only commitment made by General Eisenhower" that he is explaining an overall policy already set by Eisenhower. In RG 332, NARS, Washington.

3. Marshall to Roosevelt, quoted in Ambrose, *The Supreme Commander*, p. 424.

4. *The Eisenhower Papers*, edited by Alfred D. Chandler and Stephen E. Ambrose, p. 1750.

5. *Eisenhower Papers*, p. 2529.

6. Ambrose, *The Supreme Commander*, p. 592. Also, Pogue, *The Supreme Command*, p. 63: "Many items of correspondence prepared for the Supreme Commander's signature were issued by the chief of staff for his chief without being passed on to him. To make certain that General Eisenhower was kept informed of all action, the secretary of the general staff (Smith) prepared a special log of incoming and outgoing messages which was shown to him each day."

7. Weekly PW and DEF Report, G1 USFET, September 8, 1945. In RG 331 Box 26 383.6/1-3, NARS, Washington. The text (above) refers to Germans captured in all theaters and held both in the U.S. and Europe. Of the 5,900,000 total, about 2,200,000 had been discharged as of the beginning of October. Because the total on hand in Europe was the same in January 1946, and virtually none from the U.S. had been discharged (Smith), it is highly likely that only 36 percent had actually been discharged as of January. All but a few criminals had been discharged by January 1947.

8. Colonel Ernest F. Fisher, *Cassino to the Alps*, (Washington: Center For Military History, Department of the Army.)

9. Report of Lt. Colonel Herbert Pollack, MC to HQ TSFET, Chief Surgeon, August 31, p. 348 of QM History. In NARS, Suitland, Md.

10. Gollancz, *Leaving Them to Their Fate.*

11. *Eisenhower Papers*, p. 2208.

12. CCS to Eisenhower, June 6. In *SHAEF* Cable In Log, June 6, Abilene.

13. Eisenhower to Truman, October 1945, quoted in *Eisenhower Papers*, vol. 6, p. 416.

14. "By VE Day . . . tentage was required for only 50% of the continental troops, and supplies were ample." Ross and Romanus, *The Quartermaster Corps*, p. 634.

15. Littlejohn to Eisenhower, October 10, 1945. RG 92, Office of the QM General, General Correspondence, Subject File 1935-45, Box 587, NARS, Washington.

16. Dwight D. Eisenhower, *Crusade in Europe*, p. 386.

17. Minute of Meeting among Churchill, Eisenhower and Brooke, May 15, 1945, from PM to Eisenhower. In RG 59, 740.00119, Box 3666, State.

18. Lt. Colonel B. W. Grover, 1st Canadian Infantry Division, May 13. In 142.11009 (D2), Canadian Army HQ, Ottawa.

19. Major B. J. Guimond, 2/7 Canadian Infantry Brigade, in 142.11009 (D2), Canadian Army HQ, Ottawa.
20. How much Eisenhower valued Hughes's services was expressed by the general himself on February 25, 1948. He wrote "Dear Everett

    This is no letter of farewell. I know that our friendship will last as long as we live, and I know also that if ever I need wise counsel or a tough job done, I could do no better than to call for your help. I want to express my lasting appreciation for your devoted and invaluable service. Throughout the campaigns from North Africa to Germany, I was extremely fortunate to have, as my trouble-shooter and personal representative in the field, a man of your professional ability, judgement and character. I can never thank you enough for the load you took from my shoulders during those trying years. I wish you health and happiness in the future and success in all you undertake. You deserve the best of everything." (From Hughes Papers, LC, Washington.)
21. Diary of George S. Patton, August 18, 1945.
22. The ICRC delegate in France said he visited "about" 60 camps a total of 70 times in 1945, plus three hospitals. Six internment camps for Nazi civilians were visited. In 1946, there were 100 visits to 80 camps. Letter of Françoise Perret, ICRC, to the author, January 1987.

EPILOGUE

1. Both books are published by the University of Nebraska Press.
2. Medical Department, U.S. Army, Volume IX, Special Fields, Office of the Surgeon General, Washington, 1969, pp. 341–95. Article by Stanhope Bayne-Jones.
3. Ambrose to interviewer, BBC "Timewatch" television program, telecast September 1990. Available on video-cassette from the BBC, London.
4. See Appendix 11 in this book.
5. See Appendix 11.
6. As we have seen, Clark was not in charge of the camps when this alleged transfer occurred, but he was responsible for border control, and thus had to know and report on the number of crossings of the U.S. boundary by various persons. Report of the United States Commissioner, Military Government Austria, November 1945. The Citadel, Charleston. Courtesy of Jane Yates, Archivist.
7. Because the Missing Million were located in and near Austria, the dead among them may have been accounted for by the "transfer" of August 4. The dead among the Missing Million estimated in this book for the period to August 4 are 119,816. The transferees of August 4 never received by Clark numbered 114,309. Clark also noted in his Report that "the American authorities have disposed of about 360,000 DEFs . . ." since May 8. This disposal was chiefly through discharge, labor service, repatriation and "a small number of deaths and escapes." He was very careful to dissociate himself from the figures in this summary, which were not his responsibil-

ity. He was simply quoting what he had been told by Eisenhower. He reminded the JCS that the camps had been commanded, and therefore the statistics provided, by USFET under Eisenhower. For instance, he refers to "the American authorities," who had done this, and not to anyone in his command. The number of prisoners in the Austrian camps was always small: when Clark first noticed the disaster at Ebensee, there were only 107,561 prisoners on hand in all the U.S. zone in Austria. This was about 6 percent of the overall U.S. holding. Clark also points out that a new program of registration of prisoners in the camps had begun during November "as directed by USFET," which was of course controlled by Eisenhower. All the statistics, and therefore the remark about "deaths and escapes," are the responsibility of Eisenhower.

8. "As commanding general of U.S. forces, European Theater, [Eisenhower] will *command and supply* all U.S. forces assigned or attached thereto and will delegate to the commander in chief of the U.S. forces of occupation in Austria such operational control of U.S. forces in Austria as General Eisenhower may decide." Clark was ordered to be responsible for political matters pertaining to Austria and for the administration of military government there, for purposes of occupation and administration only. Joint Chiefs of Staff to Eisenhower, June 28, 1945. USNA.

9. The Army's Chief Historian wrote a report in 1947 summarizing the U.S. prisoner holdings as of October 1945 under subsections according to geographical area. Austria is frequently mentioned as part of the total area under consideration, but the prisoners held there are not shown separately, because they are included in the overall statistics for the ETO (p. 46). Thus the prisoners held by the U.S. in Austria were in the opinion of the Army's Chief Historian supposed to be covered by the reports issued by USFET under Eisenhower's command. Office of the Chief Historian, Frankfurt/Main, 1947.

10. The problem of incorrect totals first noticed by Lee was still present, for the figure noted by Colonel Pollack, of 80,000 prisoners, was double that noted by Brigadier General Edgar Erskine Hume, who reported to General Clark on the same day in September 1945 that there were only 41,000 prisoners left in Austria. Hume is more likely to be correct, because he was arranging transport home for these people, whereas Pollack was simply taking the camp commanders' words for the number in each camp, which by then had been seriously depleted by death. Hume, thinking of transportation for the prisoners, had both a strong reason and the means to get the number right, while Pollack, as a medical officer, did not. This 41,000 represents only about 3 percent of the total of Germans then held by the U.S. or about 4 percent of the total held in Europe.

11. Clark technically assumed command in Austria in July, but spent only a few days there before flying to Brazil for a visit, whence he returned only in August.

12. Memo dictated by General Clark for files, August 30, 1945. Courtesy of Jane Yates, Archivist, Citadel Archives.

13. Clark may have continued on the sly to provision camps that were under Eisenhower's control. The political prisoners released by the Americans

from a camp at Bezirk Grieskirchen, Austria, in January 1946 were all well-fed and "unbroken," according to Colonel C.C. Sloane who reported to Clark on January 14, 1946. Citadel Archives, courtesy of Archivist Jane Yates.

14. Experience of Werner Waldemar of Toronto. Interview December 1990.

15. This did not occur only once in the records, but also earlier, in May, when the same heading, Other Losses, appears in DEF daily total summaries. In these documents (shown in Appendix 1) the distinction is made by a footnote, showing that in the minds of the Army record keepers, whatever they were recording under Other Losses was quite distinct from footnoted "transfers within the U.S. army." In May the transfer from one army to another was properly shown as a loss to one army and a gain for the other, thus leaving the total within Eisenhower's command unaffected. It is the totals under Eisenhower's command that have supplied the death figures in this book. It has been alleged by Ambrose that I included these as dead. The reader may get a general idea of the accuracy of Ambrose's criticism by inspecting the total for Other Losses shown for any week (Appendix 1) to see if it includes the Austrian "transfer" of 132,262 shown for August 4.

16. See note 13.

17. A few deaths among prisoners deemed to have PW status were recorded by the Theater Provost Marshal. These deaths are far below the truth. The TPM figures show only 7,534 dead for three months ending in August 1945, whereas in the State Department files in Washington are reports of the burials of almost 10,000 unknown German personnel. The second report of some 4,500 burials, of unknown German personnel, was made only two weeks after the first.

18. Report No T 264, Views of Konrad Adenauer, 22 June 1945. RG 226 (OSS) OSS R&A, XL 12708, USNA, Washington. Courtesy of Professor Peter Hoffmann, McGill University, Montreal.

19. See pp. 35–36.

20. See note 17 above. See also Murphy's description of the camps in *Diplomat Among Warriors,* above, pp. 149–50. Murphy also touched on the subject of treatment of the Germans in his foreword to Alfred De Zayas' authoritative *Nemesis at Potsdam*.

21. War Department, Bureau of Public Relations, press release, September 1945, National Archives of Canada, Ottawa.

22. Totals as of July 28: PWs, 121,749; DEFs, 245,776; and Missing Million, 104, 841. See Appendix 1.

23. 711.62114/9-1246, Archives, State Department.

24. The U.S. held on average the equivalent of about 3 million persons for one year in Europe, Africa and North America. Even if the death figure is spread over only the U.S. holdings in Europe itself 1944–46, the death rate is less than 1 percent.

25. Letter of Captain Frederick Seigfriedt to the author, July 1990.

26. See pp. 154-55.

27. Memorandum, "Handling of Prisoners of War in the Communications Zone," by Lieutenant Colonel H. W. Allard, June 1946, Archives, Fort Leavenworth, Kansas. Allard, wounded twice in service with the Second Armored Division, commanded a U.S. prison camp in France during the war.
28. No address is given for Brech or any other ex-guard, because of the danger of harassment. Interested scholars may write to the guards by name, in care of the publisher or the author.
29. Campbell to the author, March 1990. The letter to *Time* was in October 1989. The international edition of *Time* ran a comprehensive one-page article about *Other Losses*, which was fair and balanced, except for one egregious error. The U.S. edition reduced this article greatly, and altered the tone so that the book appeared less reliable.
30. Interviews with the author, 1990.
31. Letter of Captain Siegfriedt to the author, June 1990. The death figures estimated by Siegfriedt of 5 to 25 per day range from a death rate of 53.5 percent per year down to 10.7 percent per year, or an average of 32 percent, approximately the rate noted in the Rhine camps by the U.S. Army Medical Corps report in June 1945.
32. Conversation with the author, 1989.
33. Conversation with the author, May 1990.
34. Michael Balfour, *Four-Power Control in Germany and Austria 1945–1946*, London, Oxford University Press, 1956; and Gustav Stolper, *German Realities*, New York, Reynal and Hitchcock, 1948.
35. Conversation with the author, 1990.
36. Fred Smith, *United Nations World*, March 1947. Available from the UN Library, New York. Smith had previously been one of the editors of the magazine. In 1947 he was appointed by President Truman to be chief of public relations for the national Labor Management Conference.
37. Memorandum of conversation, Lord Keynes, November 26, 1944. NARA.
38. Conversation with A.H. Graubart, Captain, U.S. Navy Intelligence, Berlin, Lochner Reports, Herbert Hoover Famine Emergency Com., Herbert Hoover Library.
39. Alfred De Zayas, *Nemesis at Potsdam*, Lincoln and London, University of Nebraska Press, 1989.
40. De Zayas, *op cit.*

Appendix 1

1. The PRO does not have these records.
2. TPM, RG 112, Box 316, NARS, Washington.
3. Arthur L. Smith, Heimkehr.
4. Field Marshal Alexander to SHAEF Fwd, 9 June. 383.7/4. NARS, Washington.
5. SHAEF G1, Daily DEF Report for 26 May WO 291/1451, PRO, London.

6. SHAEF-USFET papers July-September, as cited.

7. Sources: *NW Europe*: SHAEF G1, June 2, loc cit; *Italy-South Austria*: Field Marshall Alexander to SHAEF; in In-Log, May 8 and May 17, 1945, Abilene. *Germans in the US*: Daniel Costelle, *Les Prisonniers* (Paris: Flammarion, 1975), p. 208.

8. All the figures in this section are taken from sources previously cited — that is, Provost Marshal Reports, SHAEF G1 and G3 reports, SHAEF-USFET Weekly DEF-PW Reports, and ETO Medical History. The total capture of 5,224,310 according to the official SHAEF figure in the final capture report is dated June 11, 1945.

   In this book, this figure is taken as applying to June 2, because it is clear that no significant captures were made between June 2 and June 11. It does not include — because SHAEF did not include — prisoners taken in Italy or North Africa.

   The total captures in the SHAEF area were probably higher than 5,224,310. General Bradley, 12th Army Group, reported that as of May 8, he had taken in 3,486,154 prisoners of war. To this by May 25, he added 834,057 DEFs for certain, plus an estimated 231,350 then being rounded up. The 6th Army Group under Devers had taken 684,128 POWs at May 8. All together these total 5,235,689, confirming the official SHAEF figure. Devers probably took in several hundred thousand DEFs as well, but none is included here. In addition. The XVIII Airborne Corps took in about 400,000 who were US responsibility, says a handwritten note on Bradley's message of May 25 to SHAEF HQ. They are not included here because some or all of them may have been included in the prisoners reported under the heading SCOFOR-Bremen Enclave.

9. In RG 331 383.6/1-2, NARS, Washington.

10. All the statistics in the preceding paragraph are taken from SHAEF papers, G1, RG 331, Box 26, 383.6/1-3, NARS and from SHAEF HQ G3 papers, Abilene, and from the Office of the Provost Marshal Reports for the period, RG112, Box 316, entry 383.6, NARS.

11. Lt. Col. Pollack reported "advanced starvation" in U.S. camps in Austria, September 26, 1945. In RG 112, 54B, and 36, NARS; Major W.F. Ashe reported starvation in Berlin on November 24, 1945 in RG 112, Box 615, NARS; and the ICRC reported "alarming conditions" in two U.S. camps in France in 1946. In 740.00114 EW 1-146-3047, Box 3624, State.

12. For sources for this paragraph, see note 11.

13. The holdings of DEFs from June 9 on are given in documents from SHAEF G1, Abilene, and USFET, NARS, Washington.

14. Medical History of the ETO, NARS, Washington. For an explanation of the statistics in this report, see Appendix 2.

15. The term Other Losses means deaths and escapes. This was stated by Colonel Lauben in March 1987, in an interview with the author, when Lauben and the author studied the xeroxes of documents cited immediately below. Lauben, who read the originals of the reports every week in 1945, was familiar with the figures, some of the subtotals of which he helped to prepare. A transcript of this interview signed by Colonel Lauben

is with the author. A tape recording of the conversation is also with the author. Colonel Lauben has also repeated his statement in an interview with Colonel Fisher. The documents in which the heading Other Losses appears are the weekly DEF and POW reports of USFET July 28–September 8, 1945, in NARS, Washington. The term was also used in the DEF reports of 12th Army Group in May–June 1945.

Escapes from prison camps for the United States Forces in Europe for June 6, 1944, to January 17, 1945 were 1,191. Total losses by escapes in the whole U.S. Army camp system in Europe were 141 men for April and May 1945, according to the Provost Marshal. It is clear that as Colonel Lauben said, escapes were "very very minor." I have treated them as statistically negligible. Escape figures are from Provost Marshal Progress Reports (May 1945) NARS, Abilene, Kansas, p. 205.

16. Author's interview with George Weiss of Toronto, who said that at Bad Kreuznach, during a period of three days in May when the prisoners had no water at all, they "died like flies." In that period, about 10 percent of the people in his section died.

The Heidesheim source is Captain Julien, Report, 11 P60, Vincennes.

At Remagen, Charles von Luttichau of Washington observed the deaths in his own section for three months.

At Rheinberg, Wolfgang Iff of Frankfurt observed the deaths in sub-cages measuring 300 meters square containing 900 to 1,500 people depending on the week. Between 30 and 50 per day died. The variation is between 3 percent and 15 percent per month; the mean is 9 percent.

17. The totals for POWs and DEFs through this period are given in various places, notably the SHAEF papers at Washington, in the Provost Marshal's Reports, Abilene, in the G3 reports of SHAEF, Abilene, Kansas; and in the G1 PW and DEF Weekly Reports of USFET, NARS Washington. For the table of totals, see Appendix 6.

18. Senior Archivist Edward Reese at the National Archives in Washington told the author in September 1986, that most of the camp records were destroyed in the 1950s. Many cover documents listing contents of files display the mark "Non-record material destroyed 1947." The file titles show that many of these destroyed documents contained statistics about the fate of German prisoners. All the pertinent records of the MP units that guarded POWs and DEFs are missing from the files.

19. Oliver J. Frederiksen, *The American Military Occupation of Germany, 1945–1953* (Historical Division, HQ, U.S. Army, Europe, 1953), p. 29.

20. Michael Marrus, *The Holocaust in History* (Toronto: Lester and Orpen Dennys, 1987); and F.S.V. Donnison, *Civil Affairs and Military Government in North-West Europe 1944-6*, (London: Her Majesty's Stationer's Office, 1961).

21. W. R. Feasby, ed., *Official History of the Canadian Medical Services 1939-45*, vol. 1, (Ottawa: Queen's Printer, 1956).

22. The death rate of Thorée les Pins of 40.5 percent per year is projected from the single day's observation made by Pradervand, when 20 people died. Normally a one-day sample is far too small to be statistically significant,

but it is given here because it is confirmed by other observations (e.g., those in Chapter Nine reporting French camps). It is also confirmed by the parallel observations in U.S. camps.

23. The death rate assumed for the French camps among the 148,000 left over from Pradervand's 200,000, is 100 percent. This is because the French camps, although they provided roofs, offered little or no food for long periods. The 52,000 prisoners returned to the Americans began leaving French camps many weeks after Pradervand made his prediction. Given the death rate at Thorée les Pins for the period between the prediction and the actual start of returns, it is quite likely that as many as 20-3- percent of the 148,000 leftovers were already dead in French hands by the time returns started. In all calculations of the French deaths, it must be remembered that many of the deaths were caused solely by American neglect.

24. Marc Peter of the ICRC to Bailey, SPD, State, January 14, 1946. In RG 59, Box 3971, NARS, Washington.

25. B. Gufler, Special War Problems Division, State Department, letter of January 11, 1946. In RG 59, Box 3457, NARS, Washington. See also Report to USFET HQ January 8, 1946 by Col. Tom F. Whayne, in RG 332, 383.6 Box 51.

26. See note 11.

27. Memo of Major General Evans, October 4, 1945. He says "This Headquarters is currently holding 1,000,024 Prisoners of War and Disarmed Enemy Forces in the United States Zone in Germany and in France." In Box 32, 3 176–2/10 to 2/13, Bundesarchiv, Koblenz.

28. George W. Garand, United States Army Medical Department, "Medical Care For Prisoners of War," manuscript in preparation, 1986, pp. xv–84.

Appendix 11

1. Recently revealed and commented upon by Stephen Ambrose at a meeting of the American Historical Association, New York, December 1990. In Eisenhower Library, Abilene.

2. Theater Provost Marshal Reports, 1944–45, NARS, Washington. Previously cited.

3. HQ ETO, TPM Reports, March 1945. RG 112. 383.6 Box 316, Suitland.

4. For the period May 1 to June 15, 1945, the death rate derived from the 4,540 deaths actually reported by the TPM for prisoners of war is about 1.7 percent per year. The TPM death reports may have been intended to cover only prisoners of war, but the overall figure for captives (including DEFs) actually held appears in these reports as well. In any event, there are no separate reports of deaths among DEFs, unless one includes the Other Losses columns in the Weekly PW/DEF reports.

   For the same period in the same conditions in a sub-category of the same area for which the TPM was reporting, the ETO Medical History reported a death rate of 3.56 percent. This was falsely low, but even at this level it is more than twice as high as the worst TPM rate.

5. See note 3.
6. This is also suggested by the fact that the total of Other Losses reported to Eisenhower by the Weekly PW/DEF reports at August 4 was only 138,136, whereas the total Eisenhower reported to the JCS for the same day was 663,576.
7. Message to JCS and British Chiefs of Staff signed by Eisenhower, June 3, 1945. RG 331, 383.6/ 1-1 to 383.6/3-17, Box 26.
8. Letter of Captain Frederick Siegfriedt to the author, July 1990.
9. Captain Siegfriedt, correspondence with author. See also the Epilogue in this book for more about Siegfriedt.
10. Author's interview with Wolf von Richthofen, Toronto, 1990.
11. Paul Kaps, ". . . und taglich sang Zarah Leander," *Die Rheinpfalz*, July 27, 1985.
12. Experience of Werner Waldemar of Toronto. Interview in December 1990.
13. Extracts from Military Police Reports, July 1950, NARS.
14. The Theater Provost Marshal reported all through the summer of 1945 seven different categories (for example women, over 50, coal miners) without mentioning Volkssturm. Navy, Army, Air Force, SS, Waffen SS, Nazi Party Motor Corps and other such military and para-military categories are named and counted, but not Volkssturm.
15. U.S. Army, European Command, "Disarmament and Disbandment of the German Armed Forces," Frankfurt am Main, Office of the Chief Historian, 1947. Courtesy of Professor Arthur Smith.
16. 12th Army Group Records, RG 331 Box 26, folder 3, file number 383.6/1-3, NARS, Washington.
17. Any Volkssturm released before the end of July 1945 must have included many released in the period May 8 to June 10, when more than 600,000 were allegedly discharged. Eisenhower says that Other Losses (mainly Volkssturm) at the end of July numbered 500,000. But it was in precisely this period that Germans of all kinds — women, children, patients sick in hospitals, old men, cripples and amputees — were being rounded up to be put *into* the camps. Seen this way, the Eisenhower interpretation means that many thousands of Volkssturm were rounded up and then *released without any proof that they had been released*. Thus they were in the same legal condition after release as they had been before, and were therefore likely to be rounded up again. Was the Army so eager to do the same job twice? "I was visibly pregnant when the Americans came to Bad Harzburg and had to have a special permit to be able to go out for medical assistance any time of day or night, "Gisela von Richthofen told me in 1991. No one could get food without ration cards authorized by the U.S. Army, and those cards could only be obtained by producing papers that showed that one did not belong in a prison camp. How then could Volkssturm or anyone be discharged without any papers?
18. Through six months of avid hunting for PW records in many archives, the author never saw these July figures reported *in July*.

19. The Other Losses category was created for the DEFs in mid-May (p. 201).
20. Pradervand to the author in conversation, Switzerland, October 4, 1989.
21. Inventory of serviceable enemy war materiel. Report of the Military Governor, August 1945, Abilene.
22. See pp. 94–95.
23. See p. 29 above.
24. Mark R. Elliott, *Pawns of Yalta*, University of Illinois Press, pp. 93 and 107.
25. See pp. 55 and 166 above.
26. See p. 50 above. When I informed Ambrose of this statement of Eisenhower's as reported in Churchill's staff minutes, his comment was, "That's pretty damning."
27. See notes 15 and 25, Chapter 3.
28. See p. 32 above. Many surviving prisoners have said that they continued without shelter all summer, i.e. well past the date when Eisenhower said this. Tentage figures from Inventory of Serviceable Enemy War Materiel in August 1945 Report of the Military Governor, Abilene.
29. In conversation with the author, Switzerland, October 4, 1989.
30. See Chapter 4.
31. Fred Smith, "The Rise and Fall of the Morgenthau Plan," *United Nations World*, March 1947.
32. Professor Stephen Ambrose, speaking to a seminar of the American Historical Association, New York, December 1990. He was quoting Dr. Albert E. Cowdrey of the United States Army Center for Military History, Washington.
33. H.N. Kirkman of Provost Marshal General's Office, War Department, to Special War Problems, State, September 6 and August 20, 1945. State.
34. See Appendix 2.
35. It is also impossible that the death rate for camps in the condition reported by Colonels Beasley and Mason could have been as low as .9 percent. It is impossible to resolve this contradiction without the help of reliable outside sources (see below).
36. See above, pp. 218–19 and 231.
37. This is a statistical rate of attrition, which in the short term roughly approximates life expectancy. Life expectancy is influenced by several factors (not included here) such as aging and gender distribution in the population, introduction of new disease, etc. The figure is given only so the lay reader can compare in a readily understandable form the implications and credibility of the various mortality rates. With thanks to Robert Rosenblat of Toronto.
38. See p. 251, note 20, and note 28 above.
39. The German Protestant pastor Erich Messling witnessed the burial at Ahrtal near Sinzig of autopsied cadavers from Sinzig Remagen in May 1945. Letter to the author, 1990. Messling also wrote about this to the newspaper *Die Zeit* on February 23, 1990.

Archives Visited with Their Short Forms

Abilene. The Dwight Eisenhower Library, Abilene, Kansas. The Cable Log (In) and (Out) refers to incoming and outgoing messages in a special log prepared for Eisenhower by his staff.

Buglose. Archives of Town of Buglose, in St. Paul les Dax, France.

The Citadel. (The Papers of General Mark Clark) Charleston, South Carolina.

Hyde Park. The Roosevelt Library, Hyde Park, New York.

Independence. The Harry Truman Library, Independence, Missouri.

IWM. The Imperial War Museum, London.

Koblenz. The Bundesarchiv, Koblenz. (West German National Archives.)

Labouheyre. Archives of Town of Labouheyre, France.

Laporterie. Archives of Raoul Laporterie, Grenade sur l'Adour, France.

LC. The Library of Congress, Washington.

Lexington. The George C. Marshall Library, Lexington, Virginia.

NARS. National Archives and Records Service. (Usually Washington, sometimes Suitland, Maryland.)

Ottawa. National Archives of Canada.

PRO. Public Records Office, London. (British National Archives.)

Quai d'Orsay. Archives de Ministère des Affaires Étrangères (Department of External Affairs), Paris.

State. Archives of the State Department, Washington.

Syracuse. The George Arents Library, Syracuse, New York.

Thorée les Pins. Archives of Town of Thorée les Pins, France.

Vincennes. Archives de l'Armée de la Terre (French Military Archives), Paris.

Not all the references to documents in archives are perfectly complete. In some, only the author of a paper and the date and the destination are given, along with the archive in which it was found. It was not always possible to give the exact location in an archive by box number, etc., because in a few cases I did not make notes at the time of finding, or the note was lost afterwards. This is an inconvenience to future researchers for which I apologize. However, even the papers without box numbers should be retrievable in the archive named through the use of the information given. It was not always possible to discover the first names of some of the people mentioned, because in many army reports, rank but not first name is given.

Selected Bibliography

Ambrose, Stephen E. *The Supreme Commander*. New York: Doubleday, 1970.

Anderson, Robert S., ed. *Medical Supply in World War Two*. Washington: Department of the Army, 1968.

Blum, John Morton. *Years of War: From the Morgenthau Diaries*. Boston: Houghton Mifflin, 1967.

Blumenson, Martin. *The Patton Papers 1940-1945*. Boston: Houghton Mifflin.

Böhme, Kurt W. *Die deutschen Kriegsgefangenen in amerikanischer Hand*. In Maschke, Erich, ed. *Zur Geschichte der deutschen Kriegsgefangenen des Zweiten Weltkrieges*. Bielfeld and Munich: Verlag Ernst und Werner Gieseking.

Böhme, Kurt W. *Die deutschen Kriegsgefangenen in französischer Hand*. In Maschke, *op. cit*.

Bradley, Omar N. *A General's Life*. New York: Simon and Schuster.

Brendon, Piers. *Ike*, New York: Harper and Row, 1986.

Buisson, Major General. *Historique du Service des Prisonniers de Guerre de l'Axe (1943-1948)*. Paris: Ministère de la Défense Nationale, 1948.

Butcher, Harry C. *My Three Years With Eisenhower*, New York: Simon and Schuster, 1946.

Byrnes, James F. *Speaking Frankly*. New York: Harper and Brothers, 1947.

Campbell, John C. *The United States in World Affairs*. New York: Harper and Brothers, 1947.

Chandler, Alfred D. and Stephen E. Ambrose, ed. *The Papers of Dwight D. Eisenhower. Baltimore: The Johns Hopkins Press, 1970*.

Churchill, Winston S. *Closing the Ring*. Boston: Houghton Mifflin, 1951.

Clay, Lucius D. *Decision in Germany*. New York: Doubleday, 1950. Committee on the Judiciary, U.S. Senate. *The Morgenthau Diaries*. Washington: U.S. Government Printing Office, 1965.

Costelle, Daniel. *Les Prisonniers*. Paris: Flammarion, 1975.

De Gaulle, Charles. *The Complete War Memoirs*. New York: Da Capo Press, 1984.

Donnison, F. S. V. *Civil Affairs and Military Government, North West Europe 1944–46*. London: H. M. Stationery Office, 1966.

Durand, André. *From Sarajevo to Hiroshima: History of the ICRC*. Geneva: Henry Dunant Institute, 1984.

Eisenhower, David. *Eisenhower at War 1943-1945*. New York: Random House, 1986.

Eisenhower, Dwight D. *Crusade in Europe*. New York: Da Capo Press, 1983.

Faulk, Henry. *Group Captives*. London: Chatto and Windus, 1977.

Fisher, Ernest F. Jr. *Monte Cassino to the Alps*. Washington: Center for Military History, Department of the Army.

Gilbert, Martin. *Winston S. Churchill: Road to Victory, 1941-1945*. London: Heinemann, 1986.

Gollancz, Victor. *Leaving Them to Their Fate*. London: Gollancz, 1946.

Hall, H. Duncan. *North American Supply*. London: HMSO, 1955.

Hamilton, Nigel. *Monty, The Field Marshal, 1944-1976*. London: Hamish Hamilton, 1986.

Hull, Cordell. *Memoirs*. New York: Macmillan, 1948.

The International Wheat Council. "World Wheat Statistics." London: Haymarket House, April 1955.

Irving, David. *The War Between the Generals*. London: Allen Lane, Penguin Books, 1981.

Janssen, Heinz. *Kriegsgefangenen in Rheinberg*. Rheinberg: Stadt Rheinberg, 1988.

Kimball, Warren F., ed. *Churchill and Roosevelt: The Complete Correspondence*. Princeton: Princeton University Press.

Knightley, Philip. *The First Casualty*. New York: Harcourt Brace Jovanovich.

Kock, Erich. *L'Abbé Franz Stock*. Paris: Casterman, 1966.

Maschke, Erich, ed. *Zur Geschichte der deutschen Kriegsgefangenen des Zweiten Weltkrieges (several volumes)*. Bielefeld and Munich: Verlag Ernst und Werner Gieseking.

Mitchell, R. *International Historical Statistics*. London: Macmillan, 1983.

Mitchell, R. *European Historical Statistics*. London: Macmillan.

Morgenthau, Henry C. *Germany Is Our Problem*. New York: Harper and Brothers, 1945.

Morgenthau, Henry C. *Morgenthau Diary*. New York: Da Capo Press, 1974.

Murphy, Robert. *Diplomat Among Warriors*. New York: Doubleday, 1964.

Nixon, Richard M. *Six Crises*. London: W. H. Allen, 1962.

Patton, George S. *War As I Knew It*. New York: Bantam Books, 1980.

Pogue, Forrest C. *The Supreme Command*. Washington: Department of the Army, 1954.

Proudfoot, Malcolm J. *European Refugees 1939-1952*. London: Faber and Faber, 1957.

Roosevelt, Elliott. *As He Saw It*. New York: Duell Sloan and Pierce, 1946.

Ross, William and Charles Romanus, *The Quartermaster Corps, Operations in the War Against Germany*. Washington: The U.S. Army 1965.

Schuster, Gertrude Maria. *Die Kriegsgefangenenlager Galgenberg und Bretzenheim*. Bad Kreuznach: Stadt Bad Kreuznach, 1985.

Sherwood, Robert E. *Roosevelt and Hopkins*. New York: Harper and Row, 1948.

Smith, Arthur L., Jr. *Churchill's German Army*. Beverley Hills: Sage Publications.

Smith, Arthur L. *Heimkehr aus dem Zweiten Weltkrieg*. Stuttgart: Deutsche Verlags-Anstalt, 1985. (The book's English version is entitled *Warriors Without Honor: Germany's War Veterans 1945-49*.)

Smith, Jean Edwards. *The Papers of General Lucius D. Clay*. vol. 1. Bloomington: Indiana University Press.

Smith, Walter Bedell. *Eisenhower's Six Great Decisions*. London: Longman's, 1956.

Ziemke, Earl F. *The U.S. Army in the Occupation of Germany 1944-1946*. Washington: Center of Military History, 1975.

Acknowledgments

Many are the friends, and friends of friends, in Grenade who helped us, chiefly Raoul Laporterie and his wife Laure, as well as his daughter Irene, and son-in-law Roger. Dominique and Nicole Houdy were good friends through some wonderful times there. Jack McClelland of Toronto offered me a contract and a sizable advance when things looked very bleak. To Charles von Luttichau, as well as Martin Blumenson and Ed Cowan in Washington, my deep thanks. To my friends John F. M. Hunter and Michael Marrus and my cousin Alan G. Watson in Toronto, thanks for important advice. My gratitude to the Honorable Douglas MacArthur II in Washington for instructive opposition. Many thanks as well to the staff of the National Archives at Washington, and at the French Army Archives at Vincennes and at the wonderful Public Records Office in London. Thanks as well to Lisa Dillon and Dr. Norman Hillmer of the historical section of the Canadian Army for finding documents in Ottawa, and for help in attempting to find documents in Switzerland and London. Thanks to Naomi Roberts of Ottawa who loaned me precious books. And to Charles Israel of Toronto, for his special knowledge of Germany in 1946, as well as for expert reading. To Tom Summerville, Noreen and Charles Taylor, thanks for the patient counsel for so many years. To Joanne Collie, M. R. D. Foot and Brian Griffith of London, my gratitude for much good talk, hospitality and help. To Colonel Henry Faulk of Glasgow, and to Roy and Ria McMurtry of London and Toronto, who helped in innumerable ways, my thanks. To Professor Arthur L. Smith of Los Angeles, I owe a special debt for his helpfulness and honest advice, which he generously tendered to me even though he knew that my thesis contradicts his own writing. And warm thanks to Gisela and Wolf von Richthofen of Toronto, who have assisted my wife and me with their expert knowledge of Germany during and after the war, especially of the camps.

To Professor Peter Hoffmann of Montreal, I owe many thanks for expert help and strict academic guidance. He also encouraged me and believed in the book when it was not easy to do so.

To Hans Goertz, who inadvertently started us on our first long trek in Europe, *Danke schön*. And also to Petra Post and Martina Rassmann in Frankfurt, Dr. and Mrs. Siegfried Enke of Wuppertal, and Werner Steckelings, Klaus Birkenhauer and Anja Kiechle, in and near Rheinberg, and to the many German prisoners and Canadian guards who gave me their time in interviews. My gratitude to my German agent, Corry Theegarten-Schlotterer, and to my dear friend, Ruth Liepman of Zurich, who helped, although it was not easy. To Lori Thicke and Mavis Gallant in Paris, *Mille fois merci*. Thanks as well to Ben Zobrist and Jane McClain of Independence, and to Marlene Campbell of Abilene. I received much good advice from the helpful people at Stoddart Publishing in Toronto and at Ullstein in Berlin. Special thanks to Doctors Anthony and Rick Miller, and Christy and Ben Bacque for valuable editing help.

And for this new 1991 edition, thanks go as well to John Fraser and Robert Rosenblat of Toronto, Jane Yates of Charleston, Henry Baessler and Willi Pohl of Montreal, and the late Hamilton Fish of Cold Spring,

New York. Because of the danger of harassment, some people can be identified by name or nickname only, without address. They are "Chip," Martin Brech, Fred Siegfriedt, Walter Dunn, Johnny Foster.

So many guards and ex-prisoners have written to me that I cannot thank you all, but I am grateful for your encouragement and knowledge.

And warm thanks to my stalwart friends at Prima Publishing.

Index